■ ■ ■ On Edge

WESLEYAN UNIVERSITY PRESS

ON EDGE

PERFORMANCE

AT THE END

OF THE

TWENTIETH CENTURY

■ ■ ■ C. CARR

Published by University Press of New England   Hanover and London

Wesleyan University Press
Published by University Press of New England, Hanover, NH 03755
© 1993 by Cynthia Carr
All rights reserved
Printed in the United States of America
5 4 3 2 1
CIP data appear at the end of the book

"This Is Only a Test" and "Trying Times" first appeared in *ARTFORUM*
(© *ARTFORUM*, September 1989; © *ARTFORUM*, September 1990).
"With Mapplethorpe in Cincinnati" appeared in the *L.A. Weekly.* The
remaining essays first appeared in *The Village Voice.*

This book is dedicated to the artists in it.

And all their showes but shadowes . . .
—*The Faerie Queene*

■ ■ ■ Contents

Contents   ix

■ ■ ■ Acknowledgments

Special thanks for editing my words and encouraging these adventures: Vince Aletti, Karen Durbin, David Frankel, Richard Goldstein, Lisa Kennedy, Erika Munk, Kit Rachlis, Amy Virshup, and Ellen Willis.

I'd also like to thank the following for their help and advice in preparing this book: Stacey D'Erasmo, Karen Durbin, Su Friedrich, Tom McGovern, Kate Thompson, Lynne Tillman, and especially Ira Silverberg, who first thought it possible.

■ ■ ■ Introduction

Leaving Terra Firma

I came to New York to live on the art frontier, and I remember the moment when I had to face the fact of its evaporation. A week after getting caught up in the 1988 Tompkins Square riot, which was basically a turf war over gentrification, I went back to the park to report on the all-day lovefest that was supposed to heal the wounds. After hours of talking to homeless people, skinheads, old yippies, and other twains that weren't going to meet, I felt that this war was already lost, that whatever the East Village had ever meant to me was over. The wretched park just symbolized the tension in the air.

More than a year later, I stopped in at Gargoyle Mechanique on Avenue B one night for "Amongst the Rubble," a benefit for the rubble-bound in Tompkins Square and the squats. Here was an event run by utopians. I didn't see any money changing hands; no price tags on the art; no entrepreneurs trying to deal it. On a tiny color monitor and two black-and-white sets in the corner of the front room ran the cheerless videos of the uncompromisable: a Butoh performance, Einsturzende Neubauten, jackhammers hitting concrete.

In Peter Missing's back-room installation, the uncorporate logo of his band, Missing Foundation, spewed over every inch of wall and the hole in the ceiling. The upside-down cocktail glass ("the party's over") covered street signs and a jacket and pictures cut from newspapers. He'd chiseled it into marble, etched it onto glass, bent one out of pipe. Votive flames wavered along the floor. A film of surf crashing on rocks played against a scrim. But the words emerging from among the hieroglyphics were what I noticed most: "There's No Making Peace with the Planet." "Sucked into Reality." Yes, a certain fatalism prevailed. On a flyer, Missing had written: "The demise of mankind has been a preoccupation of every generation, but now the signs are all there and the vision is clear . . . we need to ride this decline because we can't get off the wheel. . . ."

This is the pathos which has prevailed down the whole long history of anti-art. I felt the old tingle of stretched nerves I associate with a leap into the void. Here was the energizing quiver of unsettled ground. It made me realize that I hardly ever sensed that anymore. And that's what I'd come to New York to find. And that's what was over.

This book tells the story of a unique period in cultural history, a period of sea-change in the cultural margin.

When I began writing for *The Village Voice* in 1984, while employed there part-time as an assistant art director, I was ambivalent about a journalism career. But I had no doubts at all about who and what I wanted to cover: artists who worked in that precarious area just a little off terra firma. No one knew what to call that territory. Some said it wasn't even art. Others called it "performance art" because that category is still relatively uncodified. These were the artists I wanted to track. As they entered new territory, I would follow, trying to draw the map.

So in the fall of '84, while passing through Amsterdam, I decided to call Marina Abramovic and Ulay, whose work both fascinated and alarmed me. At one performance done in Naples before she met Ulay, Marina had announced to an audience that she would remain a completely passive object for six hours and they could do whatever they wanted to her. Someone eventually responded by putting a gun in her hand and trying to work her finger around the trigger. A fight broke out in the audience. But she completed the six hours. Marina and Ulay shared this need to confront their limitations, their egos, their identities—sometimes at great physical risk. They shared the same birthday, and felt they were karmic twins. Together, they'd completed a series of classic Body Art pieces. In one, Ulay sewed his mouth shut with needle and thread while Marina answered questions directed to him, ending the piece when she felt she'd spoken as herself. Permanent movement had been such an ideal that for years they lived in their car. During the mid-eighties, they traveled the globe performing *Nightsea Crossing*, a piece in which they sat motionless for seven hours facing each other at opposite ends of a long table.

I did not expect to find them home. But, by chance, they had a week layover between trips. And though they had no idea who I was, they invited me over. I had published all of three articles at that point. Yet there I sat, in Ulay and Marina's sparsely furnished loft, telling them that if they ever performed in New York I would like to write about them. They told me they were planning a performance in which they would walk the length of the Great Wall of China, starting from opposite ends, meeting in the middle. And, said Ulay, "We will need someone in New York to write about it. Maybe you."

Four years later, as we were walking the Great Wall together, Marina gave me her prescription for the ideal journey: when nothing is fixed. In this way, you find your destiny.

The artists in the first section, "In Extremis," exemplify for me the artistic impulse at its purest—as the search to transcend one's own limitations, the search for something more. These artists sculpt the intangible. Often this work was done for no audience, for no money, and at great physical peril. It's work that isn't fashionable anymore. "Body" or "ordeal" art was a seventies phenomenon, yet two of the most important pieces in the history of the genre took place in the eighties: when Ulay and Marina walked across the Great Wall of China; when Linda Montano and Tehching Hsieh spent a year tied together with an eight-foot rope.

But the performance continuum shifted away from such anti-tainments, toward entertainment—or at least, the proscenium—as boundaries between mainstream and margin began to dissolve. The culture had cracked open in the late 1970s behind the headbanging force of punk, when anti-art made the charts. When negation erupted into pop through the Sex Pistols. These one-chord wonders in bondage clothing rode old definitions to a quick crash-and-burn. What was music now? What was art? Or fashion? Anything went. And anyone could do it.

"Schizo-culture" emerged from the alternating currents of postmodern theory and nightclub energy: no linearity, no harmony, no syntax, no future. Those were the days, but mostly nights, of pointed hair and fashionable heroin, Theoretical Girls playing off the Dead Boys, and Super-8 blockbusters shot on Avenue D. Outsiders were in, and bad was good. But only, of course, in the anti-spaces—from Fashion Moda in the South Bronx to the Mudd Club downtown. "We are prospectors of slum vintage. Who renamed the city after our own names," wrote Edit DeAk, art critic and denizen of the nightclub generation in

1981. "We have taken your garbage all our lives and are selling it back at an inconceivable mark-up."

In 1978, in the not-yet-global East Village, young refugees from suburbia opened Club 57 in the basement of a Polish church on St. Mark's Place. In this burnt-out rec room of a space, they screened favorite B-movies and high-kitsch television shows, ridiculing them and reenacting the roles. A similar love/hate attitude governed the many theme parties (a Trucker's Ball or homage to Lawrence Welk, for example). Club 57's manager was a performance artist named Ann Magnuson.

The playful trash-and-vaudeville ambience spread to other neighborhood nightspots as soon as they opened: the Pyramid Cocktail Lounge (1981), wow Cafe (1982), Limbo Lounge (1982), 8BC (1983), Darinka (1984), and Club Chandalier (1984). Chandalier was a second-floor railroad flat on Avenue C. Darinka was a garden apartment, while Limbo and wow were both storefronts about as wide as an airplane. At 8BC, located in a one-hundred-plus-year-old Loisaida farmhouse, the owners removed the entire first level except for that piece of it serving as the stage; audiences (in the early days) stood on an uneven dirt floor in what used to be the basement, craning heads backwards to catch the show. (Eventually, the club's success made a real and somewhat higher floor possible.)

The East Village clubs created a milieu that was unique in performance art history. They began naively and precariously, run by artists for artists. They began for the fun of it—for incandescent evenings of incongruous acts—and since the clubs were a short walk apart, audiences and performers alike sometimes migrated from space to space. If you started at wow Cafe, that "home for wayward girls" featuring (mostly) work by lesbians, you might see the resident Split Britches company doing *Upwardly Mobile Homes* on a stage just wide enough for the three of them. Or maybe there'd be a theme party like "I Dreamed I Paid the Rent in my Maidenform Bra" with a comedienne directing audience members in love scenes from *Cat on a Hot Tin Roof*, while a woman in a Maidenform longline played the accordion. Perhaps the reigning Miss Loisaida, Carmelita Tropicana, would make a brief regal appearance before moving on to her own show at Club Chandalier. You might follow her over there and still have time to make it to the 2 A.M. performance at the Pyramid. It was all very fluid and playful and little seemed at stake. Few critics went to see shows that kept them out till four in the morning. Playing to crowds of friends, other artists, and drunks, performers experimented, even dared to fail, and worked for the joy of it. But above all—they worked. While performance artists can expect to get one New York gig a year in art world venues, some performers worked almost every week in the clubs.

In 1985, as a fledgling columnist for *The Voice*, I went "backstage" one night at 8BC to talk to Ethyl Eichelberger, who'd just finished a performance of *Leer*, his very first solo out of drag. He explained that the huge gold fly pinned to Leer's suitjacket was also part of his Nefertiti costume. The gold fly was what Egyptian soldiers won for valor, he claimed, and the very brave had whole chains of them around their necks. It was just the sort of arcana Ethyl would know. At forty, he was a much-respected elder on the scene. But as we sat down in his dressing room—a back corner of the stage cordoned off with a curtain—he told me not to worry about quoting him accurately. He would be grateful for anything. Ethyl still supported himself by dancing in drag on the bar at the Pyramid Club. And he could be grateful for anything because he'd come to expect nothing.

As it turned out, the East Village performance clubs peaked in 1985—and most of them died that same year. Hype generated by the neighborhood's storefront gallery scene drew tourists by the busload on weekends. Thanks to the next-big-thingism which so afflicted the galleries, a whole new audience began showing up to Make The Scene at the clubs. City agencies took notice of the overflow crowds, and most of these dives were not up to code. Then, for the first time, performance artists began to "cross over" into Hollywood and record deals and slick magazine spreads—not in massive numbers, of course. But as soon as a few had climbed the ladder, thus establishing that there *was* a ladder, it changed the perspective of those at the bottom rung. The axiom "money changes everything" had never been illustrated more graphically than it was in the East Village. The fun (for which the neighborhood's first gallery had been named) degenerated into ambition and cynicism, and a few years later, into violence. The section of this book called "Underground" describes that particular story arc, whose turning point came with the Tompkins Square riot.

The club scene left an impressive legacy, however: the artists who emerged from it. Artists who otherwise might have emerged with much greater difficulty. Among the most groundbreaking were transgressive women performers who worked straight from the id to address issues of power and control, who made themselves monstrous onstage, acting out every definition of "filthy" and "mad." I had no category and knew no precedent for the aggression-a-go-go of Dancenoise, or the scabrous trance-rap of Karen Finley, or the confrontational sexual rage of Lydia Lunch. But the work validated feelings in me I could barely acknowledge, and I followed these performers to every hellhole and hotspot. Somehow these women had burst simultaneously and outrageously onto the scene, and they weren't alone. Soon I had also encountered the wild bloody rites of Johanna Went, the primal scream songbook of Diamanda Galas, the dyke noir theater of Holly Hughes. None of these women intellectualized about their acts. They were working in emotional territory where discourse had never gone, where the "critique of representation" bursts right from the gut.

Here at the end of the twentieth century, few things are truly subversive, truly unprocessed and unlabeled, or more than just fashionably shocking. But what can still push an audience to either catharsis or panic is graphic, angry, impolite talk from the Other. Most of the artists in the section called "Regenerate Art" fall into that category. Or so I've noticed in retrospect; I had never analyzed it that way as I decided what to cover. These were simply the artists who interested me because they rubbed up against something—the dominant culture—and they rubbed it the wrong way, thus pushing everybody's limits.

Throughout modernism, the historical avant-garde sought to destroy the existing order—that is, the existing art tradition. "Flood the museums!" cried the First Futurist Manifesto (1909). "Oh, the joy of seeing the glorious old canvases bobbing adrift on those waters, discoloured and shredded." In the postmodern era, the traditions to be challenged exist in the world beyond art. Performance dealing with sex, sexism, and sexual identity had blossomed in the clubs, where what worked best on an often-tiny stage before an often-drunk audience was something short, sharp, and raunchy. Later a few of these performers gained a special notoriety when they were targeted by the Religious Right during the censorship crisis described in Section Five, "War on Art."

But I think the real taboo topic in the nineties is race. Not that it's unusual for a performer to bear witness about racism. (Unless the performer is white.) What's much more rare and frightening is, for example, the dialogue between black and white—about race—that Robbie McCauley specializes in. She created *Sally's Rape* for herself and a white performer, Jeannie Hutchins. I saw the piece in a number of different venues, and the revelation for me was how much white spectators wanted Hutchins to disappear. Her presence kept them from identifying with McCauley, kept them from escaping the implications of her story about her great-great-grandmother, Sally, a slave.

As the buzzword of choice shifted during the eighties from "postmodernism" to "multiculturalism," the Others not only became visible but began to shape the discourse about Otherness. Guillermo Gómez-Peña, who always seemed to be at the center of these debates, is another artist interested in dialogue. His early performances and manifestoes described life in that fissure between two worlds: the border at Tijuana/San Diego. "All we want is to go back, but there's no place to go back to," he wrote. Born in Mexico but now living in the States, Gómez-Peña feels that he is neither Mexican nor Chicano but a "border citizen." He believes in hybrids, in the cross-fertilization of cultures. And he has a vantage point from which to act as translator between these worlds. Gómez-Peña is a bridgebuilder, and the border artist an emblematic figure in a world where alienation is a given.

As in "Underground," the pieces in "Regenerate Art" move in chronological order, from Karen Finley to Shu Lea Cheang. Cheang is a filmmaker, and as the piece on her begins, she is directing a scene exactly one block east of the former 8BC. The old buzz around vanguard work can now be felt on the low-budget filmmaking scene, where—even if Super-8 still existed—few on the margin would be satisfied anymore with a form so marginal. I used to see the films of Scott B and Beth B or Vivienne Dick in nightclubs. Dick would show up, for example, with her one print of *Beauty Becomes the Beast*, and run the projector herself. In comparison, artists like Cheang and the "queer cinema" directors now reach a relatively mass audience with films that play the multiplexes and the international festival circuit.

I've given work inspired by media its own section, "Unplugged." While traveling the club circuit, I saw countless pieces of anti-television —parodies or vulgarizations of beloved or dreaded old shows. Much of it was worse than anything I'd seen on the tube, and not worth reviewing, but the fact of its existence still meant something. Artists who came of age in the seventies and beyond can't disown the television parent. They treat media as primary experience, and the best of them go well beyond manipulating its imagery. John Jesurun, for example, uses the stage to address issues central to the media age—issues of authenticity, illusion, identity. Ann Magnuson's character pieces are critiques of pop-culture images, as well as the audience that believes in them. She's also the only artist here who wants to "cross over." And has.

"Crossover" used to be synonymous with "sellout," but the equation has become more complicated than that. The paradox of the avant-garde project was its hope to transform all of society coupled with an inability to reach beyond its audience of like minds. I recall dropping by a tiny music store called Generator on East Third Street in the fall of '89 to hear the Haters. Or unhear them, since this was a nonperformance by an anti-band. Gen Ken, the store's proprietor, sprinkled some dirt onto a Haters LP, then rubbed a live mike over the vinyl. I looked at the sleeve of the record he was mutilating: *This Record Is Played by Rubbing Dirt on It*. The amplified crunch was . . . hateful. And for me, the appeal was in its willful obscurity, its transgression of the way things oughta be. But was it a challenge to received ideas? Or was it elitism?

Perhaps both.

There was simply no escape from the suffering that multiplied during the Reagan-Bush years. By the end of the eighties, the same East Village streets where the clubgoers once made their rounds exhibited raw evidence of the crises in homelessness and the AIDS epidemic. The old punk nihilism looked like a luxury in the face of *real* nothingness. The old ironic tone proved worthless in the cultural emergency room. The war waged on the marginal devastated the art fringe, and that's the subject of the last three sections of this book.

When reactionaries launched a censorship attack on the arts in 1989, they didn't go after mainstream stars like David Salle or Eric Fischl. Instead, they attacked the obscure and the powerless—many of them performance artists—and imputed to them great power. According to Pat Robertson's "700 Club," these artists were engaged in no less than "a hellish plot to destroy this nation"; while right-wingers in Washington decried "tax-funded filth." But the war on art (Section 5) was really an attack on difference, a reaction to the fact that the Other was becoming visible, and doing it on government grants. When museum director Dennis Barrie was indicted in Cincinnati for showing the photographs of Robert Mapplethorpe, no public monies were involved. The reality is that nearly every artist targeted, from Mapplethorpe to Annie Sprinkle to David Wojnarowicz, had challenged the sexual hierarchy.

On that glittery globe called the art world, performance is an impoverished country, generally unsupported by prestigious museums or rich collectors. And it has long been easy to ridicule. Perhaps John Frohnmayer, chairman of the National Endowment for the Arts, thought he could pluck his scapegoat offerings to the Far Right with ease from such a context. In the summer of 1989, Frohnmayer overruled a panel of theater experts and defunded four performance artists—Karen Finley, John Fleck, Holly Hughes, and Tim Miller. That same summer, an investigator from the General Accounting Office, acting at the behest of Senator Jesse Helms, requested information from both Franklin Furnace and the Kitchen on performances done there by Finley and three other artists: Cheri Gaulke, Frank Moore, and Johanna Went. All address sexual themes or use sexual imagery, while Gaulke, Fleck, Hughes, and Miller are gay. Never before had performance art attracted this much scrutiny. Of course, the right-wing scrutinized without seeing the work. And they seemed on the verge of reconstituting an "avant-garde" simply by attacking it—long after the concept had lost its meaning in the art world.

The art community never managed to mobilize around censorship. But was there even such a community anymore? I began to think about the corruption and disintegration of the artists' milieu, and the implications of this have been developed in what is now the book's epilogue, "The Bohemian Diaspora." Certainly, the most important aspect of that place called bohemia had always been something intangible—its spirit—even in the East Village in the eighties, before assimilation. Critic Craig Owens had labeled it "faux bohemia." True enough. But it suited faux times. And for a while there, its community was real and infused with a sense of possibility. Then, the many losses to AIDS began to contribute immeasurably to a growing sense of despair. Whatever community remains today is a community in mourning. Sometimes when I look through pictures of this recent past, I can't help but run

a tally in my head: Oh, he's dead. He's dead. She's dead. He's dead.
. . . I mean John Sex, Ethyl Eichelberger, Cookie Mueller, Jack Smith,
and so many many others. Like Craig Owens.

What if the torch can't be passed?

The section called "Portrait in Life and Death" is devoted to one
exemplary artist, David Wojnarowicz. David was an openly gay man,
a former runaway and street hustler who worked constantly to transform his personal history, his political convictions, his sense of loss and
cataclysm into art. He painted and photographed and wrote and performed and made films and videos and installations. Perhaps because
he had no training in art past high school, he'd never learned that he
wasn't supposed to do it all. Early in the eighties, his work found an
audience in the East Village, where the door had opened for a moment
to the disenfranchised. He had discovered that in art he could conduct
the search for something more. As he began to document the ravages
of the AIDS epidemic, he helped his dead friends become history, become art. He was a witness against their vanishing. When he lost his
beloved friend and mentor, Peter Hujar, to AIDS in 1987, for example,
he incorporated the image of Peter—just dead—into his angriest political painting. It's only appropriate that David's life too became part
of someone else's art, a film called *Postcards from America*, after David
died of AIDS in 1992. This process of recuperation, reinvention—art's
lifeforce—is the subtext to "Portraits." But the exploitation of the art
margin by those outside it and the death of so many who populated it
explains why so much of this introduction is about loss.

New York City
April 1993

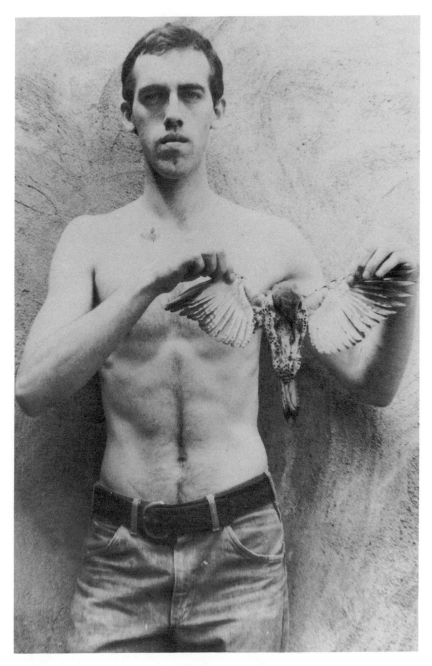

David Wojnarowicz. (Estate of David Wojnarowicz.)

■ ■ ■ In Extremis

▪ ▪ ▪ Roped

A Saga of Art in Everyday Life

Even as they came to the window to throw me a key, it was Art. Linda Montano and Tehching Hsieh have engaged in living every moment as Art since last July 4 when they were tied together at the waist with an eight-foot rope, declaring then that they would neither take the rope off nor touch each other for one year. When one of them had to get something, they both went to that something. When one went to the bathroom, they both were in the bathroom. When I saw Tehching at the window, I knew that Linda had to be there too. They both answered the door, the rope catching most of my attention. It was grayish, freakish, with a padlock at each waist. This July 4, 1984, at 6 P.M. in a ceremony suitably undramatic, the witnesses who hammered those locks onto the ropes last year will testify that they haven't been tampered with. Then Montano and Hsieh will each cut the rope at their waists to end *Art/Life One Year Performance 1983–84*.

It's a piece no one's watched but in bits, with the performers often hiding from their audience, since they never set out to be spectacles of themselves. They have worked to keep their lives noneventful, avoiding those colorful interactions that would interest a reporter, confining their activities on most days to Chinatown and their Tribeca neighborhood where people are used to seeing them. Daily life is as simple as Hsieh's Hudson Street loft where they've been living—two captain's beds at one end near the windows, two work tables down at the other.

They go out on jobs together. They must. They aren't funded. Often they work for other artists or art groups—to hang a show, put up a wall, do a mailing list, clean a loft, give a lecture. They split the money. Boredom, yes, it's just part of the piece. On a day without a job they may get up late, Montano often rising before Hsieh and exercising be-

Linda Montano and Tehching Hsieh at home. (Photograph by Sylvia Plachy © 1993.)

tween the beds till he wakes. They take out the dog, they may run, they have tea, watch a lot of TV, spend hours at the work tables sitting back to back. For pleasure, they see movies and ride their bikes around, one following behind the other. It's like Life, only harder. "We can't ask too much of each other," says Montano.

They rehearsed the piece for a week to determine the length and size of rope, how to tie it, how to make it comfortable at night, etc. Once during that week they had to cut themselves out of the rope when it began to shrink around them in a Chinese restaurant; they had showered before dinner. They would need a preshrunk rope. Then, last July 4, they both shaved their heads and began the piece. Hair length would measure the passage of time.

They have had difficulty seeing old friends and keeping old habits. Both must agree to do something before they can do it. On jobs, they found they had totally different work styles. Committed together to this arduous performance, they found they didn't agree on what it meant to be doing it.

I told them that when I pictured myself in the ropes, it felt like strangling in total dependency and lack of privacy.

Tehching said my reaction was just personal. Just emotional. Here, we were talking about Art.

Linda said Tehching thought the performance was subsumed by the Art. But she was interested in issues like claustrophobia, and ego and power relationships—Life issues. They were as important as Art.

No, Tehching said, that was too personal. The piece was not about him with Linda. It was about all people.

See, Linda said, this is the way the man traditionally talks about his work. Most women traditionally talk about their personal feelings while the man says, "I am everybody."

Tehching said he hadn't finished. He wanted to say the piece was about individuals, all human beings. He had wanted to do the piece with a woman because he liked to spend time with women. But it didn't matter if it was two men or two women or a man and woman tied together. Didn't matter if they were husband/wife or total strangers before it started, or if they planned to ever see each other once it ended. These things were personal and not important.

Linda said the piece was more than just a visible work of Art. It was a chance for the mind to practice paying attention, a way to stay in the moment. If they didn't do that, they had accidents. One would get into an elevator, the other wouldn't, and the door would close.

One or the other wears a Walkman at all times to record whatever they say. She sees this as a way to be conscious that she's talking. He says it symbolizes communication, that they're conceptual art tapes. (Indeed, they will never be listened to.)

Montano thinks of art as ascetic training. Hsieh thinks his art is often misunderstood to be ascetic training.

This is his fourth year-long performance. In 1978–79 he lived in an eight-by-nine-by-twelve foot cage in his loft, without speaking, reading, watching TV, etc. In 1980–81, he punched a time clock every hour on the hour every day, every night. In 1981–82, he lived on the street, never entering a building, subway, tent, or other shelter. Hsieh communicates in English with a limited but direct vocabulary about what motivates him. Though he painted in Taiwan, he says he's working now from his experience of this country and what he does is "New York Art."

Montano shares his capacity for self-discipline and his attraction to ordeals. An ex-nun, her performances have included drumming six hours a day for six days, handcuffing herself to another artist for three days, and living in a sealed room for five days as five different people she found in her personality. Over a fifteen-year career, she has lived in galleries for days at a time, calling it Art. She has lived in the desert for ten days, calling it Art. She has danced blindfolded in a trance, done astral travel events and once, dressed as a nun, "danced, screamed, and heard confessions."

Montano's attraction to Hsieh's work led her to call him, just as he had conceived of the rope piece and was looking for someone to col- laborate with. They had never met before. "We feel strong to do work together," says Hsieh. "When we're feeling good, we're like soul- mates," says Montano.

But they do not touch. As Hsieh says, the piece is "not about cou- ple." Montano says the fact that they're male/female can make them look like a couple, but the fact that they're different races, different ages (he's thirty-three, she's forty-two), and different sizes "throws everything into some strange balance."

Hsieh talks of how they're "married to Art," that they are sacrificing sex, not denying it. They could, in theory, have sex with other people, but, says Hsieh, that would just be a way to try escaping the piece. And, says Montano, it would be kinky, an impossible thing to do to someone else. She says it's a vacation not to have the choice, that not having sex is as interesting as having it, and allows her to see where else she can relate from on the astral or imaginative or visual level.

They ate and dreamt a lot when the piece began, says Montano, because "we were doing something very difficult and repressive. Food was our only pleasure and dreaming was the way the mind processed the new information and brought some ease." Dreaming was the one privacy, Hsieh said, and for him food was important because while living on the street last year, he was never able to eat well.

Montano made a sound, barely audible, when the Walkman ran out of tape, and they both got up to get a new one. She said they were communicating with sounds now—"it's regressed in a beautiful way"—for they had started with talking and yanking the rope, then moved to gestures, now to noises. They were down to about an hour of talking a day.

By the time the piece ends, they will have something like seven hundred of the ninety-minute tapes, each dated on the red and white label that reads: "TALKING." If they have a show of their documentation, the tapes will be displayed along with the photographs they've made, one-a-day, since the performance began. Most show them engaged in some daily activity. For a few days—days when they were fighting or thought of nothing to photograph—there are only gray green blanks. On several days they photographed the word "FIGHT."

"Eighty percent of the year was an incredible struggle," says Montano.

"A lot of ego issues to struggle about," says Hsieh.

They spent most of the winter in the loft, taking away each other's permission. They simply said NO to anything the other one wanted to do outside of the jobs they had to do for money. At one point, the fight went on for three weeks, till they finally just quit, they said, from boredom. In the spring it began to get more physical, pushing and pulling on the rope without touching each other, until Montano insisted they get help from friends. Hsieh still insists this wasn't necessary, because if they fought, it was just part of the piece. They never considered "divorce," since, as Hsieh says, they are not like a marriage, more like a business. Montano says, "It's being done for Art, so the emotions are withstood, no matter what they are."

Eight days before the piece was to end, I met them to go to the park and sensed that they were fighting. They didn't say so, but it was in the air. They were straining at each other, not walking easily—one would start off before the other had noticed, and pull. Weeks earlier, Linda had described how the piece accentuated the negative and "brought it up to the rim of Art . . . the frustration, the claustrophobia, the lack of privacy . . . to surrender to the chosen and to call it Art— I've always had that as an ideal."

Tehching said the cage piece had been easier. He could focus on Art. This was too much Life. Once, in a better mood, he had said there was little difference for him between these pieces: Linda was his cage. Now, as we sat on the grass, he said Linda was his mirror, and he could see his "weakness part." He couldn't hide. It was "much struggle."

After a year of constant exposure to each other, they're obviously tuned in on a nonverbal level. On a day when we were going out for dinner, I'd been sitting with them at the kitchen table when suddenly they were both walking around getting things, putting chairs on the beds to keep the dog off, and I began to figure out that we were leaving now. They hadn't said a word.

This would be my chance to see how people reacted to them on the street. We stood on the sidewalk discussing restaurants. Tehching asked if Chinese food would be okay. Then I realized I'd already forgotten that they were wearing a rope. As we crossed West Broadway, a woman approached and said, "I must ask why I always see you attached." Linda answered, "It's an experiment." That's become their standard response to the question, Linda said, because calling it Art "plays with that definition too much for a lot of people and then they get angry." It may also play with their definition of Life.

I was most surprised by the Oblivious Ones who passed us. And by the Frightened Ones, with the seen-a-ghost look about them. The Perplexed Ones, I expected. In Philadelphia, where they'd gone to teach a performance art class, they found it much more difficult and abrasive to be public. In New York the heightened level of strangeness absorbs some of the attention they don't want. On a recent visit to Area, people stared at them, Linda thought, not because of the rope but because they weren't dressed right.

I asked if we could visit the art world together sometime. No, they mostly avoided those places. Just recently in Soho, they could hear everyone talking about them as they walked down the street, snatches of "tied together for one year" floating by, and it made them feel like they were giving a show. They didn't want to give a show. "Too sensationalize," Hsieh says. They've turned down *That's Incredible, Entertainment Tonight,* and *Ripley's Believe It or Not.*

Dinner and a kung fu movie was more like what they normally did. The ushers at the kung fu theater looked worried when they saw us, while I was forgetting more and more that the rope existed. I made myself look at it and thought, God, they have guts to walk down the street like this. We watched something astonishing whose title Hsieh couldn't translate: a grandmother fighting five villains, men jumping magic distances, girls twirling swords, pairs and groups testing each other to the death. The ritualized fighting looked as powerful, perfect, and hard to choreograph as a wave crashing off a rock. Then we sat through the next movie on the bill, *Boat People,* without subtitles. I never did figure out what was going on, but watching it gave me a chance to contemplate the fact that I had chosen this, and that sitting there was Art.

July 1984

The body mounted a platform. Eighteen fish hooks pierced the back of his naked frame. He positioned himself face down below a pulley with eighteen rings. Calmly he instructed two assistants to connect the hooks and pulley with the cord. Thirty or so spectators around the platform were tiptoe-silent. The body suddenly gasped with pain. "No worse than usual," he winced. "I just keep forgetting how bad it is."

He began instructing his assistants about removing the platform from below so he'd be left hanging by the hooks, his skin stretching and causing him excruciating pain. He was prepared for that. As he'd written about an earlier piece, "Stretched skin is a manifestation of the gravitational pull. . . . It is proof of the body's unnatural position in space." Once the pulley carried him out the window, he would be demonstrating this to everyone out on East 11th Street between Avenues B and C.

He would be amplifying the obsolescence of the body out there, the need for it to "burst from its biological, cultural and planetary containment" in the post-evolutionary age. With more than twenty other "suspension events" behind him, this would be the most public one he'd ever tried. So one more precaution had to be taken: his assistants would lock the building against the possibility of police intervention. We were asked to leave, and I was the first one out. Hadn't wanted a close-up of that horror show of stretched skin—I mean "the gravitational landscape"—anyway.

Stelarc (born Stelios Arcadiou) would not have understood that. The body doesn't respond emotionally to his own self-mutilation. Why should others? He thinks people misunderstand him. They obsess about the hooks. They ask if he's a masochist. They think he has some spiritual goal. They are all wrong. "I am not interested in human states or attitudes or perversions. I am concerned with cosmic, superhuman, extraterrestrial manifestation."

Stelarc lectured on evolution three days before "Street Suspension." He told 40 of us sitting in the sawdust of a raw loft lit with three bare bulbs that we are on the threshold of space. But we're biologically ill-equipped. It's time to consciously design a pan-planetary physiology. Stelarc thinks the artist can become an evolutionary guide. To illustrate this, he demonstrated his "third hand," a prosthetic device on his right arm. He opened and closed its "fist" by contracting his rectus abdominus muscles. Electrodes on his skin connected these muscles to the mechanism. Some day, he added, it would be nice to have them surgically implanted.

He showed slides of other work, fierce projects described quickly and modestly, most of them done in Australia where he grew up or Japan where he now lives. (He is Greek.) The first slide—the inside of his stomach—had been made by swallowing a gastro TV camera, during a "visual/acoustic" probe of his own organs. Other early work: lying on pointed stakes, lying still for ten days while a huge steel plate hovered over him. Many slides of "stretched skin" suspensions: the body suspended horizontally through a six-story elevator shaft by the insertion of eighteen hooks into the skin.

It reassures me to see that "the body," as he calls himself when discussing the work, stands apparently undamaged in front of the room. He describes a piece for body and ten telephone poles, all suspended from a gallery ceiling and then spun over twelve tons of rock on the floor. Just two weeks before this lecture, the body'd been suspended in a condemned building in Los Angeles and swung like a pendulum. A tree suspension near Canberra had attracted 350–400 spectators. Stelarc told us he had asked them to leave after fifteen minutes so he could experience the "symbiotic relationship of the body and the tree" without being distracted. "They drove away in their cars. It must have been beautiful to drive off leaving the body there."

Someone in the audience asked if he was "motivated by pain." Stelarc laughed. He'd read in an essay about his work that all performance art is masochistic but he didn't agree. He said women did not give birth in order to experience pain, and he did not make art in order to experience pain. "Everything beautiful occurs when the body is suspended."

Then Stelarc showed us a videotape of "Trajectory," an event in which the body was connected sideways to a pulley that slid down 120 feet of cable in twelve seconds. Wouldn't movement put more stress on the hooks? I glanced at the monitor where the body had a drawn, pinched look on its face which I associate with pain. Someone asked Stelarc why he'd gone from ropes and harnesses to using hooks. Because of "the physicality," he told her. And it was less "visually cluttered." Meanwhile, the body on the monitor had taken off down the cable and was applauded. Stelarc smiled. "That one felt so good, we did it three times."

Later, he elaborated: "It felt good, yeah. The idea of the body as this projectile propelled by desire to transcend its evolutionary limitations. The idea of the body attaining planetary escape velocity. . . ." He asked somewhat sheepishly if I could mention his book, *Obsolete Body/ Suspensions,* in my article. It wasn't selling well, and he didn't know why. Apparently he hadn't considered that hooks stretching skin out like rubber might not appeal to many people. But perhaps I was just not evolved enough if what I noticed was not the gravitational landscape but the body in distress.

We'd gone to a restaurant near MO David Gallery, which was sponsoring the event. Stelarc was agreeable, polite, sort of a regular guy from Yokohama, married, two kids, teaches art and sociology. Sitting there telling me how he amplifies the sound of his blood flow by constricting an artery, then relaxing and opening the artery and the blood rushes out . . .

I hadn't expected to feel nauseous. There weren't any hooks in him. He was perfectly pleasant. He was telling me about sewing his lips and eyelids shut, then having two hooks inserted in the skin of his back and connected by cable to the wall of a gallery for one week. And we'd only started. I dug my fingernails into the palms of my hands.

During a suspension, he told me, the body was always at the threshold of catastrophe. At times the body had been on the verge of passing out. At times the body had hallucinated. During a seaside suspension, facing sideways over the incoming tide, he'd begun to feel that the surface of the sea was an extension of his skin stretching out to the horizon then back, a membrane that began pulsating and finally bursting in the form of waves.

I asked if he called himself "the body" to dissociate himself from the experience. Was that a help in doing something so stressful? He said no. "If I referred to myself all the time it would personalize the experience too much. It's not important that it's me. It's important that a physical body suspended in space has these experiences."

"Aren't you ever afraid?" I asked. "Well," he said, "in terms of our evolutionary development, reflective thinking is essentially a positive thing. But when thought is always reflective, it leads to inactivity. Sometimes you have to switch your mind off. You set up a situation. Then you do it."

Stelarc told me he did nothing special to prepare himself on the day of an event, just kept busy. When I arrived on the day of "Street Suspension"—Saturday, July 21—he was chatting with friends while someone shaved his back. Puncture wounds from the Los Angeles event were still visible on the front of his body. "Why the shave?" I asked. He said there would be bandages back there later. And if they're pulled up from hair, they hurt.

At the front of the space, the assistants finished mounting the pulley. On a table nearby: a bowl full of sterilized hooks, two bottles of rubbing alcohol, cotton swabs, gauze, somebody's half-drunk beer. "I hope it rains," said Stelarc. He'd never worked in the rain before.

The insertions would take about half an hour. As more people crowded up the stairs, Stelarc showed two men what to do with the hooks. He had made a drawing for them to follow, like an acupuncture diagram with hooks instead of needle points. They would be avoiding any major blood vessels or nerve endings, inserting into skin instead of muscle to minimize bleeding. One would pinch the skin up. The other would insert. He'd had trouble finding assistants, but finally recruited two sympathetic performance artists. "Start with the elbows," he told them. "Go through quickly . . . pinch the skin more tightly . . . faster . . . get it symmetrical . . . grab more flesh. . . ." Across the street I could see a little girl in Mouska-ears sitting on the windowsill with her Dad.

It was 7:08 P.M. when Stelarc emerged from the window of the building. A shout went up from the street, from the art people who were expecting him and the neighborhood people who weren't. "Holy

The "landscape" of stretched skin over East 11th Street. (Photo by Andy Freeberg.)

Shit!" "THAT GUY'S FUCKIN' CRAZY!" A woman covered her eyes. Soon the "landscape" of stretched skin stopped over the middle of East 11th Street. A Hell's Angel stopped his bike and parked. A woman said she didn't know what the world was coming to. Motorists craned through windows. "A man called hawse," yelled one. Probably two hundred people milled below, photographers and children in about equal number. And then, at 7:13 P.M., the police were there too, six of them standing on Avenue B trying to figure out what to do. They would clear the street. "Move back! Move back!" They'd get the traffic (three cars) flowing. Then they'd yell up to the assistants on the fire escape. "Pull him in!"

Stelarc disappeared back through the window at 7:18 P.M. He'd gotten ten minutes out there. He'd hoped for fifteen.

The officer-in-charge tried to enter the building, but found the door locked. A shout came from the crowd: "Officer, this man is a world-famous artist!"

"GIM-me a BREAK!"

A filmmaker pointed his camera at the cop. "You don't want to interfere with someone's freedom of expression?"

"Sure I do!"

The six cops retreated, then regrouped in a more conciliatory mood. "Look, I just want to talk to the guy," the officer-in-charge insisted. "Why couldn't he do this inside? Let's be sensible."

Mike Osterhout, the director of MO David Gallery, appeared. I could hear the top cop saying, "I won't arrest him, I promise. I just hafta give him a summons. That'll satisfy the city."

Finally, two cops were admitted and found Stelarc lying face down on a piece of plywood with white bandages over his wounds. They charged him with disorderly conduct.

"What a circus!" he sighed. "I would've loved to have seen it from the street. Could you see the skin coming up?"

The event had been so different from what he expected. "How?" I asked.

"The expansive feeling of the space. People in their cuboid rooms. The interaction of all the people below, then the police clearing a path so I could see traffic flowing. That was great. And, probably the most beautiful thing, the naive reactions of the people on the street. There's an innocence about it."

A friend asked if he shouldn't be resting. "Theoretically I should be lying down. But I'm hungry. Let's get dinner." By now, 11th Street was empty, except for a woman who must have heard about the event. Was she looking for evolutionary synthesis? Or the potential for planetary escape velocity? Apparently not. She rushed by Stelarc, hardly noticed him, and called out, "Where's that naked man?"

July 1984

The image most emblematic of seventies body art has the rough panicky blur of a news photo. Faces are unrecognizable. So is the rifle. And the artist's description of the action is a simple dispassionate observation: "At 7:45 P.M., I was shot in the left arm by a friend. . . ." Chris Burden took his risks in the manner of a scientist—one who decides that he must test a new serum on himself alone, who later declares that he always knew it would work. When he stopped performing, Burden began to exhibit machines and war toys and installations. The project, however, had remained the same: to demythologize certain choices, to deromanticize certain symbols, to get real.

He says he had himself shot so he'd know what it felt like, though he didn't mean the physical pain so much as "getting ready to stand there." There could be nothing theoretical or metaphoric in knowing that the gun was loaded, that the trigger would be pulled. Burden's performances created a context in which it was possible, though not probable, that he would die. That context itself was the art. In *Prelude to 220, or 110* (1971), for example, he had his wrists, neck, and legs bolted to a concrete gallery floor with copper bands. Nearby sat two buckets of water with live 110-volt lines submerged in them. Had any visitor chosen to spill the water, Burden would have been electrocuted. Typically, he was forcing himself, the audience, and the sponsoring institution to face an elemental and harrowing reality. So too, in the photodocumentation of *Shoot* (1971), we can read the trace of a shudder.

Indeed, the culture seems to have shuddered through some crisis of the body then, beginning in the late sixties. Or was it some crisis in authenticity? Or some trauma surrounding the object's "dematerialization?" Analyzing the emergence and disappearance of body art is beyond the scope of this article. But the fact remains that during the seventies in particular, some artists risked injury and death in a manner unprecedented in the history of art. For example, there was Gina Pane climbing a ladder with cutting edges—barefoot (*Escalade sanglante* [Bloody climb], 1971); Dennis Oppenheim standing in a circle five feet in diameter while someone threw rocks at him from above (*Rocked Circle-Fear*, 1971); Marina Abramovic and Ulay running naked and repeatedly colliding at top speed (1975); Linda Montano inserting acupuncture needles around her eyes (*Mitchell's Death*, 1978). And Burden was no doubt the most notorious of them all, at least in America. His risks were more dramatic than the others, but also more calculated.

Often, his disturbing actions were misread as exercises in masochism or as way stations along some spiritual path. Hadn't he crawled nearly naked through broken glass (*Through the Night Softly*, 1973), pushed two live wires into his chest (*Doorway to Heaven*, 1973), had himself crucified on top of a Volkswagen (*Trans-Fixed*, 1974)? But he denies any interest in either pain or transcendence. As he explained it in 1975, "When I use pain or fear in a work, it seems to energize the situation."[1] That "situation" was the relationship between him and the audience. It was their fear and distress as much as his that "energized the situation." Burden's work examines physical phenomena in their natural context, the land of human error. And *Prelude* wasn't about electricity's potential to kill, but the audience's. It wasn't a symbol, but a real catastrophe waiting to happen. Through his body, Burden (who studied a good deal of physics in college) could investigate an energy that science can't measure.

When he did *White Light/White Heat* (1975), remaining out of sight on a platform at the Ronald Feldman gallery for twenty-two days, his "fantasy" (as he put it) was that the gallery would not reveal his presence, but that people would somehow sense it when they entered the room. *White Light* was Burden's refinement of an earlier experiment in inertia, *Bed Piece* (1972), in which he'd remained in bed in a gallery for twenty-two days, visible to all, but communicating with no one. As he recalled it in 1975: "In *Bed Piece* it was like I was this repulsive magnet. People would come up to about fifteen feet from the bed and you could

1. Quoted in Roger Ebert, "Art of Fear and Pain," *Chicago Sun-Times*, April 8, 1975, p. 31.

really feel it. There was an energy, a real electricity going on."[2] He'd become a generator, and normal human interaction had ceased.

Before he began performing, and while still an M.F.A. student at the University of California, Irvine, Burden made interactive sculpture. Even then, he wanted audiences to *do* something. But it frustrated him when people failed to understand that his objects were not the art; the interaction was. For his M.F.A. thesis in 1971, he decided to circumvent the problem by using a two-by-two-by-three-foot locker already present in the exhibition space—and his own body. For that first performance, *Five Day Locker Piece*, he just expected to curl up and endure for five consecutive days. But to his surprise, people he didn't even know came unbidden to sit in front of the locker, to tell him their problems and the stories of their lives. Was the appeal merely his status as captive audience? Or is it that artists who break taboos and take on such ordeals are perceived as having special powers? Certainly, those who came were projecting something onto him. And Burden's been extremely conscious of audience behavior ever since.

Burden's work exposes real power struggles—with real consequences—between performer and audience, or artist and art world, or citizen and government. Traditionally, an audience wants to sit passively and expects the performer to "take command"; they will attack if the performer doesn't. Burden began to play with this dynamic— traditional theater's unarticulated mise-en-scène. In *Shout Piece* (1971), done soon after *Five Day Locker Piece*, he sat on a brightly lit platform, face painted red, voice amplified, ordering the people who entered the gallery to "get the fuck out"—which most did, immediately. His third performance was *Prelude to 220, or 110*, in which he became the passive one, his life depending quite literally on the behavior of each gallery visitor. While masochism was not the point in Burden's work, there was often a dynamic of dominance and submission. And probably because dominating (as in *Shout Piece*) simply drives an audience away, Burden usually chose to submit, making their decisions much tougher. In *La Chiaraficazione* (1975), he sealed off a small room with particle board at the Alessandra Castelli gallery in Milan and persuaded the 11 people inside to collaborate with him on staying in the room till someone broke the door down from outside. The majority of the audience (about 150 people) remained outside, and no one knew what

2. Quoted in Robert Horvitz, "Chris Burden," *Artforum* XIV No. 9, May 1976, p. 25.

he was doing. They finally broke the door down after an hour and a half.

Burden's actions earned him a sensational media reputation. The *New York Times*, for example, ran an article in 1973 called "He Got Shot for His Art," illustrated with a photo of Burden in a ski mask. The artist had worn this mask for a piece called *You'll Never See My Face in Kansas City* (1971), but in the context of a mainstream newspaper such a photograph suggested that this man was a threat to society, a criminal. Burden went on to work with this public image as with a found object, sometimes undermining it, sometimes exploiting it. (But eventually, it helped convince him to quit performing.) In *Shadow* (1976) for example, he spent a day at Ohio State University trying "to fit people's preconceptions of an avant-garde artist" by remaining aloof and wearing opaque sunglasses, black cap, and a fatigue jacket stuffed with notebooks, film, and a tape recorder. In *The Confession* (1974), on the other hand, he revealed intimate details about his personal life to a specially selected audience of people he'd just met, "imposing on them disturbing knowledge which had to be reconciled with my public image." In *Garcon!* (1976), he served cappuccino and espresso to visitors at a San Francisco gallery and "my attire and demeanor were such that only a handful of people out of the hundreds who attended the show recognized me as Chris Burden." He could create tension just by sitting in a room. In *Jaizu* (1972), Burden sat facing a gallery door, wearing sunglasses painted black on the inside, so he couldn't see. Spectators were unaware of this. They assumed, then, that he was watching, as they entered one at a time and faced him alone. Just inside the door were two cushions and some marijuana cigarettes. As Burden described it, "Many people tried to talk to me, one assaulted me, and one left sobbing hysterically." The artist remained passive, immobile, and speechless—the blank slate to whom each visitor gave an identity: judge? shaman? entertainer?

Burden invited only a small group of friends and other artists to witness actions with the most shock potential, like *Shoot*. But whether performing in public or private, he never made things easy for those who came to watch. These pieces were too real: either too horrifying or too everyday. Spectators at *Shoot* might ask themselves the same question as the spectators at *Working Artist* (1975), a piece in which Burden lived and worked in a gallery for three days—and that is:

"what made me want to watch this?" Audiences found themselves implicated in their voyeurism. "Art doesn't have a purpose," Burden once said. "It's a free spot in society, where you can do anything."[3] Burden established his art as that territory outside the social contract where either the artist or the spectators might do what they would otherwise think inappropriate.

This unpredictability brought a tension bordering on hostility to his pieces addressing the art world. For *Doomed* (1975), at the Museum of Contemporary Art in Chicago, Burden reset a wall clock to twelve and lay down beneath a sheet of glass tipped at a forty-five degree angle, then did nothing. The audience began to throw things at him, but still he did nothing. Eventually they calmed down and some kept vigil with him—for forty-five hours and ten minutes, as it turned out. Like his other performances, *Doomed* was sculptural, in that it was "built" for a particular space and circumstance—in this case, the curator's request that he not do something "short" because the museum expected a large crowd. "I thought—OK, I'll start it, you end it. And that's what the piece was about," Burden said.[4] He decided that when museum officials interfered with the piece in any way, it would end. He never told them this, of course, and never expected them to let it go on for days. When someone finally set a glass of water next to him after forty-five hours, he got up, smashed the clock with a hammer, and walked out. *Doomed* was a classic gesture of passive aggression. By conceding that institutions and business people, not artists, have the power, Burden forced the museum officials to act as the authority figures they really were.

In smoking out who actually has control, Burden has driven some of the art world's most charged taboos out of their hiding places. In the process, he made nerve-wracking demands. For *Tower of Power* (1985), for example, he asked the Wadsworth Atheneum museum to borrow a million dollars worth of gold bricks. From this he built a pyramid for exhibit—to make this fantasy number literal. (It was quite unimposing, as it turned out.) But the museum, of course, had to hire extra security. And *Tower* made its point: if art is about money, why not just show the money? In 1981, with his materials budgets from the

3. Quoted in Donald Carroll, "Chris Burden: Art on the Firing Line," *Coast*, August 1974.
4. In a conversation with the author, April 28, 1989, New York City.

Centre Pompidou and the Ikon Gallery in Birmingham, England, Burden bought a little over an ounce of gold and a small diamond. In Paris, his performance consisted of melting and molding the gold into a small Napoleon figure that could have passed for a cheap souvenir (*Napoleon d'Or*, 1981). In England, while keeping the real diamond in his pocket, Burden suspended a worthless replica, spotlit, in a large light-tight room (*Diamonds Are Forever*, 1981). Viewers, who had to enter one at a time, did not know it was fake. This was an exhibition about exhibitions, in which the "duped" spectators collaborated to ask some blunt questions. Is the artist supposed to play alchemist? Can a fake diamond, by virtue of its presentation, become more valuable than the real jewel hidden away? (And in *Napoleon d'Or*, was the "cheap" figurine, by virtue of the artist's touch, now worth more than its weight in gold?) Does something become valuable if you're told that it's valuable? And is it even more valuable if you're told that it's art? Contributing their own unwitting coda to the diamond project, the angry board of directors at the Ikon Gallery who financed it met to determine whether the artist had defrauded them. According to Howard Singerman's account, "The board it seems, expected Burden to purchase materials that would be worthless until he had transformed them." Burden, for his part, attributed the board's ire to the fact that he didn't display the real diamond. In any case, as Singerman continues, "The curator finally received special permission to issue a check to a local jeweler; no such permission would have been necessary for the local lumberyard."[5] Naturally, Burden kept the real diamond.

As the artist increasingly removed his body and presence from the performance, he continued, at times, to wage psychological warfare with the institutions that sought his work. In 1985, with *Samson*, he created a sculpture with the potential literally to destroy a museum. *Samson* connected a turnstile, through intermediate gears, to two massive timbers pushing against the bearing walls of Seattle's Henry Art Gallery. (Burden had first proposed the piece to the Oakland Museum, which turned it down.) Every visitor had to pass through the turnstile, whose movement increased the pressure on the 100-ton jack between the timbers. If enough visitors passed through, the accumulated pressure would actually bring down the building. Crude and clunky, its

5. Howard Singerman, "Chris Burden's Pragmatism," in *Chris Burden: A Twenty Year Survey*, pp. 24–25.

gears exposed, *Samson* looked less like art than the insidious machinery it really was. Burden had nicknamed it "The Museum Buster." In *Exposing the Foundation of the Museum* (1986), Burden did exactly that—to the architectural foundation at the Temporary Contemporary building of the Museum of Contemporary Art in Los Angeles. He took away a fifty-two-by-sixteen-foot section of the concrete floor and dug down, installing three stairways so visitors could descend to the spot where the concrete footings met earth. A visitor might be reminded that the rest of the floor could go just as easily: dust-to-dust, what-goes-up-comes-down. Or the visitor might find comfort in the evidence of how deep the artist had to dig to find the "raw" elements that supported the institution. In either case, *Exposing the Foundation* disrupted the conventional museum experience, and made the viewer complicit with this project.

That's what Burden did in projects outside the art-world: brought a little jolt to an unsuspecting audience. In *Dos Equis* (1972), he blocked a road in Laguna Beach, California, with two giant Xs he'd made from sixteen-foot timbers soaked in gasoline. He set them on fire and left, creating a powerful image for one driver to encounter. In *Coals to Newcastle* (1978), he flew a model airplane—its cargo tiny marijuana bombs and some messages (e.g., *Fúmenlos Muchachos*, or "smoke it, kids")—over the fence separating the United States from Mexico. And he bought television advertising time to run, over the course of one month, a ten-second clip of *Through the Night Softly* (1973), the performance in which he had crawled through broken glass. In each of these pieces Burden looked for the "logic" ordering the system (highway, border, television), then disrupted it in order to make it visible. With the first two, that was easy. But television can absorb anything it's fed. At the same time, television has codes, even in terms of how scenes are lit. *Through the Night Softly* must have looked like an aberration. A man is injuring himself, but there's no narrative, no editing, no packaging, no moral—and nothing for sale. We, like Burden, can only fantasize about the reactions of the "audience" for such interventions. But if anyone looked up and said, "What was that?" the art succeeded. Burden hoped to crack the veneer of official reality, if only for a single individual in a single moment.

Burden has consistently examined the power of the individual to control his own destiny—or to have any impact at all—in a corporate

high-tech world. At perhaps the height of his performance-art notoriety in the mid seventies, he built himself a working one-person car
(*B-Car*, 1975), and literally reinvented the first crude television (*C.B.T.V.*,
1977). Burden sought to demystify these objects that most people
couldn't make but can't live without. He'd "solved" the car and the
television, one-on-one. But so what? What meaning does individuality
have anymore? A one-man factory has no impact on the corporations
that manufacture cars and televisions. Of the tiny matchstick men surrounding his *Tower of Power*, Burden says they illustrate that "our lives
are transient and consumable in relationship to the ascribed lasting
power of gold." In *747* (1973), he fired several shots with a pistol at a
passing airplane, the Lilliputian gesture of one man against the world.
The shots were more ridiculous than menacing, and this fantasy
skyjacker-without-a-cause didn't even have a demand—his act was
pure frustration.

Since 1981, Burden has been creating his own huge strike force of
model planes, ships, and submarines. In *All the Submarines of the United
States of America* (1987), he's back to concretizing a quantity, this time
the total number of subs ever launched by the government, all 625 of
them. His 625 cardboard miniatures suspended from the ceiling look,
from afar, like a large school of tiny fish. Up close, they resemble a
flotilla of floating toys. Does this make the U.S. submarine fleet more
real to us, or less? Paradoxically, works such as this, including *A Tale
of Two Cities* (1981)—a massive installation of warring city states—cannot create an atmosphere of risk commensurate with the risks they
address. One needs time, for example, to study *A Tale*, a piece so large
in area it can be viewed in detail only through binoculars. Here, Burden has elaborated a whole history of military technology, from prim-
itive canoes to sophisticated robots. But ultimately, this display of the
obsession, organization, money, time, and imagination devoted to war,
since the cave, doesn't arouse fear. The corporate and military powers
still seem faceless and remote, and we encounter them indirectly, not
through the gut. For most Americans, tanks and robots *are* most real
as childhood toys. It's difficult, then, when confronting these pieces,
to overcome the sensation of nostalgic pleasure, and the fascination
that attends looking at almost anything in miniature.

Certain fictions still rule us. When Burden built his installation
called *The Reason for the Neutron Bomb* (1979), he showed us exactly what

the Pentagon's reasons for that weapon looked like. He laid out fifty thousand nickels, each with a matchstick "cannon," each representing a Russian tank. Along with the numbers, he was exposing a whole ideology of power, a belief in deterrence and ultimate weapons. When he had himself crucified across the top of a Volkswagen, he took the West's most hallowed industrial and religious icons and conflated them, producing an image both terrifying and absurd. The artist became one—not with the universe—but with the machinery, which ran its motor at full-throttle *"screaming for me."* It was heresy.

And Burden's work *is* terrorism. One can read the whole resume that way, with its brinksmanship (*Prelude*), top secrets (*The Confession*), surveillance (*Jaizu*), camouflage (*Garcon!*), ambush (*Dos Equis*), hostage-taking (*La Chiaraficazione*), infiltration (the TV ads), raids (*Coals to Newcastle*), and time bombs (*Samson*). But this is terrorism with an R.S.V.P. For as we, his spectators, contemplate the turnstile or the bucket with the live wire, we know our decisions will have real consequences. While Burden's work exposes power without judging it, his project is not amoral—it forces the moralizing onto us. Sooner or later, we will have to decide. And usually sooner.

It's an emergency.

September 1989

■ ■ ■ A Great Wall

The country which is nowhere is the real home.

—Lao-tzu

Last March 30, artists Marina Abramovic and Ulay set out to walk the length of the Great Wall of China.

They began at opposite ends, some 3,700 miles apart. In the east, Marina stepped away from the Yellow Sea and onto the wall at precisely 10:47 A.M., the auspicious moment chosen for her by those Chinese officials who'd come along to bear witness. In the west, Ulay (Uwe Laysiepen) planted a flag honoring Moroccan explorer Ibn Batouta at the canyon where the Great Wall ends; then he turned to follow it east into the Gobi Desert. The artists would simply walk toward each other until they met.

Ulay and Marina's performance work had always forced them into unknown and dangerous territory. And the work had always illustrated and depended on their own relationship, as it supported them through terra incognita. Crossing the Great Wall would take the project to an epic dimension. "The Lovers" they'd called this piece originally, meaning lovers of each other, lovers of the world. But eight years had passed between the dream of walking the wall and the first real step onto its crumbling remains. The epic they'd intended had become impossible. Another would unfold in its place.

From half a world away, Marina and Ulay were metaphors crossing a symbol. The Great Wall is said to be the only human artifact visible from outer space. Chinese mythology describes it as the body of a sleeping dragon. Ulay had stepped off on its tail, and Marina on its head. In pictures, the Great Wall runs snakelike over mossy hills. In pictures, Nixon strolls along it with Mao. But as I prepared to visit the

artists last spring, I couldn't picture what they were going through—
what vistas, what struggles over mountains and deserts, what people
met along the way. Then, in May, I received a "letter" from Ulay—a
page from a daily calendar, actually. On it he had written the words:
"stranger than innocence."

Going off to find the artists on the wall was a trip that I'd saddled with
some do-or-die meaning. I suppose I thought it would change my life.
Certainly the artists expected the walk to change theirs. In art and
myth, that's what happens on the perilous unpredictable voyage: the
sea change. Into something rich and strange. I could be the next pil-
grim in the long brooding line. So, if I went through months of anxiety
over money, if I didn't know how to plan because I didn't know where
they were, if I had to delay leaving a dozen times—what were these
little traumas compared to the artists? It had taken them five years just
to get permission to walk.

I think of Ulay and Marina as exemplars of those who make the inner
journey, who use their art to sculpt the self. Typically, they place themselves in some precarious circumstance, facing not just the unknown,
but the unknowable. At first, the risks they took were always physical.
Their shocking or bizarre actions pushed the artists to their limits,
while making some primal experience real for an audience.

In a piece called *Three* (1978), for example, they crawled over a floor
on their stomachs with a python who hadn't eaten in two weeks, both
of them making sound vibrations to attract it. The snake went straight
to Marina ("like in the Bible") and followed her intently for four hours
as she slowly backed away from it. When it finally broke eye contact
and turned away, the artists declared the piece over.

In the seventies, they created classic Body Art pieces they called
Relation Work: sitting back to back with their hair tied together for seventeen hours; breathing each other's breath until they felt faint; slapping each other till one of them chose to stop; moving mobile columns
by repeatedly hurling their naked bodies at them. They chose difficulty
and risk for their art, uncertainty and insecurity for their lives. For four
years they lived in their car, nomads with uncompromising, self-
imposed rules: permanent movement, transcending limitations, no
fixed living-place, no rehearsal, no predicted end, no repetition. They
have since described this period as one of the happiest of their lives.

By 1980, however, they felt they'd exhausted the possibilities of such work. They turned their attention from the unarticulated voices of the body to those that layer the mind. In the meditative *Nightsea Crossing* series, the artists sat motionless for seven hours at either end of a long table, trying not even to blink. And they did this ninety times in museums all over the world, completing the series in 1986. Both have called *Nightsea Crossing* the most painful and difficult work they ever did. Marina once said that she reached a point, as her muscles cramped in each of the ninety performances, when she felt that she would die. She'd tell herself, "Okay, then. Just die. So what?" Ulay described states of near-catatonia and panic on that edge before the body locks. He said he was "permanent on a brink."

When I watched *Nightsea Crossing* for three days at the New Museum in 1986, I thought of Ulay and Marina as two people balanced on a seesaw over the abyss, as if both would fall if either of them moved. Each knew, however, that the other was unmovable. The piece was trust—and will—made visible. The content was the artists' inner life; the body was mind. "We believe in the art of the twenty-first century," Marina once told me. "No object between the artist and observer. Just direct transmission of the energy. When you develop yourself strongly inside, you can transmit your idea directly."

I could almost see their connection, like some filament between them. Here was a performance in which nothing happened, yet I found it very moving—because of the artists' courage, and the image they created of mutual empowerment. I suppose the relationship-as-tableau represented some ideal of love and work, of trust and acceptance, that I despair of attaining. Like *Relation Work*, *Nightsea Crossing* addressed feelings not easily forced into language—as difficult to describe as emptiness.

Motionlessness, said Ulay, was "the homework." When he spoke of his birth in a bomb shelter in what is now West Germany, of spending the first years of his life among the ruins, or when Marina described her early performances in Yugoslavia, cutting herself in front of an audience for the simple reason that she was afraid to bleed, I would think—they've been preparing to walk the wall all their lives.

I had to prepare, I decided, by entering into the spirit of the work: Take a look if you must, but leap. I converted my life savings into travelers checks, and flew. The artists' heroism, the epic walk, the Great Wall—it was really much larger than life to me. I felt small. When I looked down from the plane and realized that that was China—just an endless undulating brown prairie, really—I began to cry, overwhelmed because I'd come so far, and I don't mean geographically. It was June 1 in the Year of the Dragon. Entering Beijing, I was dazzled by the everyday—the cliché herds of bikes all pedaling in the same heartbeat rhythm, the young guys playing pool on a table in the street, the sign wishing me to become "one of the two hundred lucky fellows," the language that sounded the way it looked, all big blocks. It was a relief to tune into the details and think small and get real.

The young woman who'd met me at the airport announced that in another day I would accompany an official to somewhere in northwest China. To Ulay. In other words, the leap of faith that had brought me there had just been a practice jump. I'd have to do it again every day. I wouldn't know where I was going, what I'd find there, or (usually) who was taking me. And the plans were ever-changing. There was no choice but to flow with it.

The next day, during an unexplained five-hour delay at Beijing airport, I tried to get a grip on my first fit of Western impatience. Or maybe it was pride. I'm not used to feeling so helpless. I speak no Chinese, and my traveling companion, part of the sponsoring Chinese Association for the Advancement of International Friendship (CAAIF), spoke no English. I would point to the line in my Mandarin phrase book: "When does the flight take off?" and Wang Yunfeng, solicitous and paternal, would tell me: "Yinchuan, no." Yinchuan was a destination too far off the tourist track to merit more than a sentence in my guidebook.

Sometime after 7 P.M., we finally taxied off in a plane that vibrated hard and smelled like a hundred years of sweat. There were no safety tips. The stewardess handed out kiwi sodas, then a square gray box of snacks: two dry rolls, two pieces of cake, a chocolate wafer cookie, and peanuts ("the tasty food of tourism," it said on the packet). I had to laugh at myself, at my snack for a sea change. Outside I saw craggy spooky mountains, thin peaks like frozen waves. I hallucinated a dragon in flight from a patch of river golden with sunset. I looked up the word "beautiful" to show Mr. Wang, but it wasn't in my phrase book.

Such a strange and ambitious project as walking the Great Wall wouldn't have been possible in China until recently—until the new policy of *kai fang* (opening to the West), instituted under Deng Xiaoping. The Chinese had been building walls for over two thousand years. Qin Shi Huangdi, called the first Chinese emperor because he unified the warring states, connected existing border walls into a Great Wall between 221 and 210 B.C. Subsequent dynasties built more walls as borders shifted. And the project culminated during the Ming Dynasty (1368–1644), whose emperors connected and added to everything constructed before, giving the Great Wall the course it takes today. Ostensibly built for defense, it never worked in defense. The wall, Ulay would tell me, was "a groove in the Chinese mind." Beyond it, throughout their history, lay foreigners and hell.

Ulay's and Marina's performances, with their elements of ritual and ordeal, have no counterpart in China outside religion or politics. Commitment, struggle, pilgrimage—that was the Long March. Before the artists sent their first formal proposal to Beijing early in 1984, no one in China had ever walked the length of the wall. No one had run it or crossed it on horseback (as Westerners have now done, more or less, in the first few years they've had access to it). No one in China, apparently, felt compelled to do such things. Then in 1984, Liu Yu Tian, former railway worker, suddenly became the first person to go the distance on foot. The artists thought this was no coincidence. Ulay called it "plagiarism." But the artists weren't crossing the wall to enter the *Guinness Book of World Records*. They were surrounding themselves with the unfamiliar in order to find the unimaginable.

That's what they always did. In 1980, for example, they spent six months in the central Australian desert. This experience was the pivot that turned them from aggressive physicality to motionlessness. Forced into stillness by heat that rarely dipped below body temperature, they discovered the "nightsea" of the subconscious mind. And it was in the desert that they decided they would someday walk the Great Wall of China.

They became world travelers, seldom at home, based in Amsterdam but not Dutch citizens. They had no wish to be anyone's citizen. They performed *Nightsea Crossing*, for example, in Brazil, Japan, Finland. In one episode, they sat with an aboriginal medicine man and a Tibetan lama. And they began a series of videotapes, one for each continent, further exploring the spectacle that unfolds in motionlessness. In the three completed tapes—set in Thailand, Sicily, and Boston—local people pose in tableaux that are saturated with things to look at, saturated with the tension of remaining still. Some detail in each, like a gently billowing dress, makes time visible. The artists' self-imposed rule: one take, no second chance. They also began a series of life-size Polaroids, some featuring themselves as archetypal figures or anthropological objects, others capturing their shadows.

At the heart of all the work, still, was their connection and commitment to each other. The artists themselves described their relationship as lovers, brother/sister, husband/wife. And the work was an "energy-dialogue," which created a third entity they labeled "That Self." Three was "their" number. They had it tattooed on the middle fingers of their left hands.

They had met in Amsterdam in 1975 on what happened to be their mutual birthday, November 30 (Ulay was born in Germany in 1943, Marina in Yugoslavia in 1946). They had immediately felt confidence in each other. "Like we knew each other before," Marina once told me. In their work together, with their somewhat similar profiles and sometimes similar haircuts, they became the image, at least, of the ideal couple. Or the symbiotic one. They sometimes designated themselves UMA.

In walking the Great Wall, crossing mountains and deserts to reach each other, they wished to experience at their meeting "the apotheosis of romantic love." They thought they might get married at that meeting, right there on the wall. They planned to camp as they went, exposing themselves to nature as they had in Australia, conditioning themselves to make new work. They shipped a year's supply of freeze-dried tofu and seaweed to China. They bought tents and camping stoves. They would study the wall and make paper rubbings from its stones. They'd be retracing the earth's "geodetic force line," for the wall's coiling path (rarely ever the shortest distance between two points) had been determined by geomancers, ancient diviners of the earth's energy, and they felt that walking this force line might change them. They thought the walk might take a year.

Sometimes I wonder what the Chinese made of that initial proposal. Some ultimate expression of Western individuality and ego? The bureaucracy in Beijing will not even deal with individual artists. In 1983,

Ulay and Marina had to create the Amphis Foundation to represent them. Ironically for two people so interested in Eastern philosophy— who had originally speculated that the piece could become a walking meditation—negotiations turned their way only after they proposed doing a film about the wall for China Central Television. They would be walking its length, then, to *study* it. Finally they were talking the bureaucrats' language. The adventurous CAAIF agreed to sponsor them. The Dutch government then declared the walk a cultural exchange and kicked in some much-needed funding.

But by the time Marina and Ulay began walking last spring, almost everything about the project had changed. Where they once thought they would walk singly, each now had an entourage; the Chinese feared for their safety. The artists had wanted to cover every inch of the wall; but the Chinese restricted them from military areas. (For these detours, among other things, each artist got a jeep and a driver.) Where they once thought they'd camp on the wall, they often ended up in villages, even in hotels, because the Chinese do not camp. The Chinese estimated that the project would take four months and demanded the sum of $130,000—more than $1,000 a day. The artists sold work they hadn't yet made in order to raise the money. Walking the wall had become something they just had to do.

But the most startling change of all was in their relationship. They could no longer call the piece "The Lovers." Less than a year before starting, they separated. Marina told me she wouldn't have expected their relationship—so unique—to end just as badly as any other, but it had. Marina felt that everything had broken between them. Ulay insisted their connection would continue, though it had changed. They would still work together after the walk, he said. They would *not* work together after the walk, she said.

Despite their mutual unhappiness, not walking was something they never considered seriously. They would surrender to the situation. They had always shared this unwavering resolve, the voice that said, "Okay, then. Just die. So what?" That was what had made their work so compelling to me in the first place. Yet their split confused and saddened me. I even wondered if they *should* walk. Was the project still valid? When a mutual friend suggested that the connection between them went deeper than the vicissitudes of romance, though, I agreed.

The artists had traveled along parts of the wall by train and car in

1986—to get some sense of what they'd encounter—and when they told villagers living near it what they were doing, those people had understood it immediately as an epic love story, something right out of mythology. Of course, the project had always been more than that. But it was still, in its way, a love story made real. Ever interested in testing the limits, they would now have to contemplate the limits of love—an emotion more complicated, harrowing, fragile, and imperfect than most epics allow.

The artists considered starting at the middle and walking away from each other, but decided not to. In their very first piece, *Relation in Space* (1976), they had moved toward each other repeatedly for one hour, naked, first touching shoulders as they met, then accelerating the intensity till they were colliding head-on at full speed. Walking the wall would duplicate this action in arduous slow motion and would seem to mark the end of their extraordinary twelve-year collaboration, even as it demonstrated what they'd once called "the impossibility of escaping one another."

I wondered how far we were from Ulay, as Mr. Wang and the Foreign Affairs people and I left Yinchuan by van. The day Ulay had finally begun to walk, he'd sent me a postcard with the message: "I go now." On the back, barely visible, were some faint blue lines. Under a magnifying glass, I recognized the second century Chinese poem called "Confessions of the Great Wall" that he and Marina had found years ago: *The world is small and blue. / I am a little crack in it.*

Now, presumably drawing near, I noticed a billboard on which the winding wall of legend had been painted into the center of a Great Wall Tire. We drove honking and weaving into the bike and donkey traffic, past the rickshaw piled with slaughtered sheep, into the country, past the mud-brick medical office with a gingham curtain for a door. Everything familiar was now strange, and I didn't know where I was. Couldn't tell what direction we were going. And it was raining as we entered the Mao Wu Su desert. Mr. Wang pointed to a jagged reddish rock formation (I thought) on the horizon. "Ulay has been there," he said. *That* was the Great Wall of China.

That little chunk of it must have been thirty feet long. Here in western China, the wall was built from clay. It had eroded, and so had the other ruins we passed. A broken beacon tower. A crumbled compound. Everything deserted but for the odd sheep or shepherd. "How old are these things?" I wondered. The Foreign Affairs people told me, "It is difficult to measure the time."

Finally, after four hours of driving, we entered the village of Yan Chi. Where the Great Wall of China runs through a carpet factory. In a new but already shabby hotel covered with bright yellow tile, we found Ulay.

As he came striding down the hallway, where the dirty strips of red carpet never quite met, Ulay looked happy. As if he were home. In two months he had walked through two provinces, through desert most of the way. He'd seen camels pulling plows. He'd found people living *in* the wall—in caves—in the most clever way. He'd crossed the Yellow River on a sheepskin raft. He was filled with enthusiasms. And with complaints. There'd been so many detours, so many "tough quarrelings" with authorities. They would insist on hotels instead of camping. And when they did let him camp, they would sleep in the van. Often his crew couldn't keep pace with him. And they would tell him that areas were restricted when, really, they were just inconvenient, he thought. It had been impossible to carry out the pure concept, to be one of two tiny humans moving toward each other over this broken but monumental path.

I began to see how the piece was really unfolding, as my first twenty-four hours with Ulay became an ongoing social event. He was not walking merely the Great Wall, but a line threaded through the gears of China's infamous bureaucracy. Crossing a provincial border like this one between Ningxia and Shaanxi was a political event, a time for meetings, banquets, speeches, and a complete change of crew.

"Walking is the easy part," Ulay told me that night, after the first of three banquets we would eat in two days. "All the people involved in the project are bureaucratic, administrative-trained people. There is no great spirit for exploration, for sportive behavior. They like to be nicely dressed. They like to have their dinners on time. They like to sleep." To the bureaucrats, accompanying Ulay was hard work. To Ulay, being accompanied by them was like dragging a heavy tail. They had pulled each other in different directions, and in this tug-of-war the Chinese had taken control of the project.

The only struggle Ulay could hope to win was the ongoing struggle with his temper. Occasionally he'd become so angry that he had "choiced wrong." For certainly he was no tourist wanting China to be a museum—new sights with the comforts of home. Ulay can become absorbed in a culture completely. Rootless and mobile, he is not much attached to his "world of origin." At one of the banquets in Yan Chi, he told the officials and the crew that he had been born in Germany during the war and had lost most of his family then, but here in China he had found a new one.

Yet, two months into the walk, he was still fuming over how "their waterproof security system" had changed the concept. His frustration over this seemed to enter every conversation we had. He'd nearly come to blows, he admitted, one day in Ningxia province when two members of his crew physically restrained him from walking farther into the mountains. They told him he'd come to a restricted area. He didn't believe them. He guessed that they simply didn't want to climb. In his rage, he broke the staff to which he'd tied a knotted white flag—a private signal meaning "remember to surrender." That day, when he'd done neither, had been the worst of his journey.

I recalled his distress when, in 1987, the Chinese had inexplicably postponed the walk (for the first time). He'd described his state of mind then as "so disencouraged, so desperated." At that point, he said, he'd been living on the wall in his thoughts for five years, and "already I have walked it ten times. Already it is worn. It is polished." So when he finally climbed onto it that first day to see the long-anticipated plan "bent into a different direction," he began trying to bend it back.

Not covering every foot of the wall, not camping near it every night—these were the changes that vexed and preoccupied him, the ones he would talk about. The altered relationship with Marina he didn't talk about, and I sensed that I shouldn't press him. He said only that this was the first time he and Marina had worked so separately. They hadn't even communicated. And he didn't know what it meant. He'd decided it was "not important" at the moment. Meanwhile, he continued to speak in the plural: *we feel, our work, important to us. . . .* He asked me if I'd heard anything about how she was doing.

The artists had speculated that they might meet where the Yellow River divides the provinces of Shaanxi and Shanxi, and he wondered aloud one day which of them would make the crossing by boat—but, really, he did not want to think about the ending. When he'd see Marina again. He wanted to have no expectations.

Ulay craved the first light of day, so good for photographs. He always set out between six and seven and walked until noon or one, averaging twenty kilometers. Walking became so mechanical, he said, that the earth moved beneath him like a treadmill. He was measuring the Great Wall with his body.

This was not the picturesque stone wall that beckoned from the travel brochures. *That* wall ran through the eastern mountains, and somewhere Marina was crossing it, headed in our direction. The clay wall Ulay followed through the west had been more vulnerable to both humans and the weather. Obviously it inspired no awe among the people who lived with it. One day it snaked through a village where we discovered homes and stables built in beneath our feet. Hours before in the countryside, we'd found it spread out into two gentle slopes and plowed.

Since the wall had been built from the best available clay, peasants occasionally made off with whole chunks of it. "Mao killed the dragon," as Ulay put it. Mao had encouraged the Chinese to make use of this cultural relic, to take its clay for topsoil or its stones for building. Reeducating millions to leave it alone again was not so easy. At Jaiyuguan where his walk began, Ulay had seen workers restoring the wall for tourists, while eight kilometers farther on, peasants dismantled it.

Even during my first excited walk, I had to remind myself sometimes that I was crossing the Great Wall of China—from afar the stuff of legends, a giant sleeping dragon; up close, a hill to climb. That day, when we picked up the wall at the Ningxia/Shaanxi border, it was scrub-covered at first, an uneven ten to twelve feet tall, but rounded like an earthwork on a battlefield. An hour or two later, we hit desert and began crossing its perfect shapes. Here the wall became a rough clay trail, often too broken to walk on. We were alone in a blue and yellow world where all centuries had been the same, scuttled over by scarab beetles.

As I skirted some large holes in the top of the wall, Ulay, walking below, reported that they opened into one-room caves. Here, the crew told us, soldiers from the Red Army had dug in and lived during the thirties. An hour later, we found a beacon tower converted into a temple, where two old men in gray lived and worshiped a war hero from the time of Three Kingdoms (220 to 265 A.D.). History was just part of the landscape. No drama. No theme park. We were dots moving over the dunes.

Back when the walk was still an idea, Ulay had considered going the distance in silence. He is reserved by nature. He'd always said he was "no talker," leaving the art-world social chores—openings, lectures— to Marina. Now, here he was officiating at banquets, wanting to mix, always the center of some group. If the people he passed wanted to gawk, Ulay was more than willing to be seen. He was their new information. He wanted to connect, even while surmising that "my smile comes from a different muscle than their smile."

He had come to feel that he represented foreignness. He hated the VIP treatment usually accorded everyone who is not Chinese, which so effectively separates them from everything that *is* Chinese. Foreigners travel most often in groups of foreigners, staying in hotels just for foreigners. The Chinese authorities seem to want it that way (and, of course, so do any number of the foreigners). There is, in other words, a great wall.

Ulay said that in all his travels to the remotest parts of India, Australia, and North Africa, he had never experienced such "fear for a person who has two eyes, two ears, and a mouth." Here he had been so many people's first foreigner. Again and again he'd observed in their eyes that "moment of doubt and strangeness." Tall and lanky with a brown mustache and ponytail, carrying a staff, wearing baggy drawstring trousers, big hiking boots, and sometimes a flowing overcoat—Ulay was a sensation.

All of our walks ran through territory closed to foreigners, and for four days, we stayed in the closed village of Dingbian. "A *real* Forbidden City," Ulay called it. Soon after arriving there, we decided to take a stroll and a crowd materialized around us within steps of the hotel. People had stared at me since my first day in China, but in Dingbian they were mesmerized. As though we were movie stars. Or monsters. On their faces I saw joy, fear, hostility, disbelief. We were no longer ourselves, but spectacles of ourselves. I was learning how racism feels, how frightening it is to be Other. Soon we were leading a large blue and green parade through the heart of the village, everyone silent but open-mouthed. When a hundred people followed us back into the hotel and watched as we climbed the stairs, Ulay joked that in all his years as a performance artist, he had never had such a big audience.

"Alien," said Ulay, referring to our Alien Travel Permits. "They use the right word." He did a lot of theorizing about China. He'd come to love it and wanted to understand. "The Chinese have been isolated for such a long time. Deliberately. And if a large group of people isolates themselves from the rest, something strange has to happen. You have a circulation throughout your body. Take a rubber ring and put it around your finger. The circulation becomes disturbed and something starts rotting. And if you take it off, you poison your own system. Maybe that's why they generate one wall after another."

This was what he thought "stranger than innocence." Not that the Chinese were innocent of the world but that for many of them, the rest of the world simply didn't exist. He'd discovered that people who lived along the wall often didn't know it was a wonder of the world, and many had no idea that it crossed most of China. The translator who'd traveled with him and Marina in 1986 said she'd grown up thinking that the moon belonged to her village. "They have a non-ability to look out," Ulay told me. "They are unable to see there is one sun and one moon which is touring." He thought China womblike, thermal. He pointed out that people constantly drank boiling water (of necessity, for there's no potable water anywhere), and that even in June, men wore long underwear. "They live like they're preparing for hibernation."

Often as we walked, Ulay pointed out tools used by the peasants, used for centuries and so ingenious. He would roam from the path of the wall occasionally to explore, wanting to know the history and customs of the area. He'd lit a fire in one of the beacon towers, because signaling in that way had once been their function. And when we found pottery shards along the wall, he could often identify the dynasty from which they came.

For Ulay the walk had become a study of China, and there he had focused his emotional energy—rage for the bureaucrats, love for the yellow earth of the northwest and for the peasants' way of life. So,

Ulay at the end of a day's walk, resting at a xiang in the village of Zhuan Jing, Shaanxi Province. (Photo by C. Carr.)

while his walk was no longer romantic, it had acquired a touch of ro-manti*cism*. It was about another sort of yearning.

In the countryside, he'd observed a bare-bones and, to him, idyllic life. He'd observed that those who lived it had no complaints. "There is contentment, which I find a more reasonable term than happiness." Such a room as one found in a commune—with a brick bed, bowl of water, two chairs, and a table—it was all one needed, really. His first translator had called him a "voluntary socialist."

To the men on his crew, however, this simple life wasn't necessarily ideal. Ulay hadn't understood at first what rigors of exile some of these people had suffered during the Cultural Revolution. Now they'd man-aged a better life for themselves, and the hardship he craved reminded them of old horrors. He told me in Dingbian that he now thought his problems were *his* problems.

He thought maybe the explorer's nature was a sort of greed. Critic Tom McEvilley had visited him in May and observed that he was "greedy for authenticity," and Ulay thought it was so. On our last after-noon together, we discussed what it meant to be blocked so thoroughly from language, trapped without an alphabet. "The search for authenticity is where you are exposed to a different world and have to rely stronger again on intuitive intelligence," said Ulay. "We look to traditional cultures to sound into that intuitive intelligence. Where your sharp senses get a holiday."

Ulay was looking for more by looking for less. Paring things away—technology, comfort, habit, even language. I was reminded of the existential drifters who appear in the work of Ulay's favorite writer, Samuel Beckett. Molloy saying of his journey's aim: ". . . the most you can hope is to be a little less, in the end, the creature you were in the beginning, and the middle."

From June 9 to June 12, from Ulay to Marina, I made a slow, U-shaped arc by jeep, plane, train, and car. I was still an impatient Westerner, ignorant of the difficulties involved in getting tickets or making phone calls, therefore outraged that I had to stop for a full day in the city of Taiyuan. And I still became paranoid over conversations like this one:

"Where's Marina?"

"Maybe she's here."

"Can I see her?"

"Maybe she just left."

"Can you find out?"

Silence.

Though no one in Taiyuan told me so, Marina had come through town the day before, detouring a large military area. By the time I caught up with her at a *xiang* (commune) north of Datong a couple of days later, I felt—as I had with Ulay—that I'd arrived at the end of the earth. I'd also brought with me certain expectations. But no, Marina had had no trouble with bureaucrats. And for her, walking had *not* been the easy part.

The eastern half of the wall, built from stone and famous in pictures, runs across the spine of a mountain range. One small piece of it, fully restored, is open to tourists near Beijing. There they can buy a T-shirt declaring, "I walked the wall." There the wall is most clearly a symbol, like the Eiffel Tower or the Taj Mahal. And there Marina had refused to walk—because it was too short, too fake, and too easy. The rest of the eastern wall is now a trail of loose rock ascending and descending the peaks. Hers was more arduous terrain than his, but in choosing sides, the artists had been concerned only with symbolism. According to Chinese mythology, hers was the male part of the wall and his the female. Their work together had always balanced these polarities.

Each morning Marina had had to climb for two hours just to get to the wall. She would reach it exhausted. Then it would take all day to do twenty kilometers, then another two hours to climb back down. She'd never once camped. She'd descend to find a place in the nearest village or xiang. There she would ask the people to tell her stories about the wall. Not its history, but its legends.

Marina is affable and vivid, the poetry of her rather ungrammatical English only adding to her charm. She was even on a first-name basis with her quiet young interpreter, Han Dahai, and the crew that accompanied her throughout the mountain trek had affectionately dubbed her "Pa Ma Ta Je" (Big Fat Sister Ma) because of her bulky clothing. "I wish new Chinese name," joked Marina, who's fairly slim. Like Ulay, she wore big hiking boots, baggy trousers, a multipocket vest, a flowing overcoat. More importantly, like Ulay, she had an iron will. But they had reacted as opposites to the changes in the walk. Where he had struggled with the authorities and lost, she had yielded and gotten her own way—by incorporating their changes, making them her changes.

But then, Marina didn't really care about the camping. To her the big change was in her relationship with Ulay. She'd even been reluctant to start. "Before was this strong emotional link, so walking towards each other had this impact . . . almost epic story of two lovers getting together after suffering. Then that fact went away. I was confronted with just bare Wall and me. I had to rearrange my motivation. Then I always remember this sentence of John Cage saying, when I throw I Ching, the answers I like the less are the answers I learn the most.

"I'm very glad we didn't cancel the piece because we needed a certain form of ending. Really this huge distance we walk towards each other where actually we do not meet happily, but we will just end—it's very human in a way. It's more dramatic than actually just having this romantic story of lovers. Because in the end you are really alone, whatever you do."

She'd insisted that she had to walk directly *on* the Wall at all times, and the Chinese allowed it. In the mountains, this meant ascending or descending on unsteady piles of rock, climbing to "the border of human possibilities," up peaks where even the local guides would not

Marina Abramovic walking on the Wall north of Datong, Shanxi Province. (Photo by C. Carr.)

go. To avoid a fall, or an avalanche, she'd had to concentrate so hard on every step that she could think of nothing else. She couldn't think about Ulay.

Before we left the xiang, she described the drama of her fourth day, when she and Dahai had nearly fallen to their deaths. They'd been descending the mountain at the end of the day, when it suddenly dropped off at a ninety-degree angle, the rocks "polished like ice," below them an abyss. "We were hanging there on the tips of our fingers." They had, of course, no climbing equipment. It had taken two perilous hours to inch back up.

Where I met her, the Great Wall had been built from clay. She complained that walking was so easy here her mind could wander. She'd come to love the stone wall, its dangers, its "continuous falls and ups like real life." While never foolhardy, Marina appreciated danger. "Is danger what wake you up, and that's what I like so much." With months of this behind her, she had the survivor's conviction that she could face anything.

Marina had permission to cross just one of four counties in the province of Shanxi (not to be confused with neighboring Shaanxi, where Ulay was). As we started down the wall behind the xiang, I pointed out that we were going east—the wrong way. Marina was taken aback, then shrugged her shoulders. The new crew had driven her to the starting point the day before, and she'd started—that's all. I couldn't help but think of Ulay—his precision in estimating where he'd stop for the day, calibrating the mileage, his U.S. Air Force map, the most detailed he could find, always tucked in a vest pocket. Marina rarely consulted maps, wouldn't think of carrying one, and didn't plan her days. It was one of their differences: "his practicality, my chaos."

We set off down the border of Inner Mongolia, for this was one of the rare places were the wall still served that function. And at the end of the day, we came upon a network of ruins. I was sure it had been a massive fort. In the field south of the wall, where peasants were weeding on hands and knees, sat two ancient greenish stone lions, and beyond them a walled city. I figured this had been the passage to Mongolia, heavily armed back when the wall was supposedly stopping the hordes. Marina wanted to spend the night in that ancient city, where I could learn the history and she could get a legend. We bounced through the same gate that once saw chariots—I was sure of it. I was overwhelmed by it. The buildings were yellow mud; their windows were oiled paper. Our jeep was the only vehicle there. Dingbian, in comparison, had been the picture of urbanity.

The jeep dropped us at a shabby old house festooned with pink paper—the village radio station, half its area filled by a brick bed wide enough for six people. "The sheets," Marina laughed, pointing to the dirty corrugated cardboard on the bed. She was excited, for what she liked most was staying with peasant families in villages like this one. She disliked the xiangs. (They now function more like county seats than communes, but there's no exact equivalent in English.) Laid out like cheap motels, in straight brick rows one story tall, they embodied order. They were always the same. They were too much like Yugoslavia. "These straight lines. This socialist aesthetic," she would sigh. "Bad light and hospital green. Why they choose this form of expression?"

I, however, felt a sort of vertigo in the village, an irrational panic I couldn't explain to her. Perhaps I was simply more alien(ated) than I had ever been before. Perhaps when nothing fits a single groove in your memory, you're like a newborn. I would remember this later as a most valued moment.

But at the time, I took notes as if a list could help unravel *my* "doubt and strangeness": a couple of sheepskins, the door of a jeep, a telephone so old it might have rung during the Long March. Women and children began to sit down in silence across the dusty yellow yard from us, to stare, while an old man came in and, without acknowledging our presence, began broadcasting into a mike with a red cloth tied over it. He was calling the head of the village, said Dahai. Or trying to. None of the ancient equipment seemed to work.

Yet the head of the village arrived soon after. A middle-aged man with Beatle bangs and a Mao jacket, he told us several times that "conditions" here were not so good. Marina assured him several times that "conditions" did not matter. But no foreigner had ever stayed in this village before, and he clearly didn't want us to be the first. We left for a xiang.

There we were able to discover that the village, over 2,100 years old, had been there before the wall was there. But no one knew anything about the ruins. No one knew any legends.

We set out the next morning around nine or nine-thirty. Marina never began earlier. She followed the habit acquired in the eastern mountains of walking all day, with a break at lunchtime.

"Here is like Ulay wall," she complained. She didn't like it—this ragged line of baked clay surrounded by plowed fields. "This like the endless tail. Like the burial ground of the dragon." It was a day of blazing heat. At noon, Marina asked about the jeep—since of course she had made no plan—and the security man with the walkie-talkie said, "Six kilometers." Insects and heat shimmered off layers of brick scraggly with grass—the Great Wall. Apart from this enigmatic line built by unknown hands so long ago, the landscape could have been Iowa.

Two hours later, we still hadn't found the jeep or even a road. Now the security man was telling us, "Just over the hill." But it wasn't there either, and we'd run out of water. "Kafka is good literature here," said

Marina, who now felt sick with headache. She, Dahai, and I sat down across the river from a factory belching chemical fumes, while the crew went on ahead. Around three, Dahai pointed to a stick figure atop a distant beacon tower. They were telling us the jeep couldn't come.

We spent the night at a nearby graphite factory, where all the offices had brick beds. When a blackout hit around 10 P.M., someone appeared with candles almost instantly, suggesting that this might be routine. In the hallway, a tallow burned on the handlebars of the bike parked just below the portraits of Marx, Lenin, Stalin, and Mao. We joined the workers who'd drifted into the yard with their thermoses and teacups. A voluble middle-aged man in a white T-shirt made some little speeches (through Dahai) about how welcome we were.

People always talked to her this way, Marina said. It was so hard to get past the platitudes. The workers went on to say that "conditions" weren't so good, then he asked us to please sing. Marina had soon persuaded *him* to sing instead, and in a beautiful tenor he sang bits of local folk songs. I went in for a jacket and returned to find that Marina had assured the group *I* would now sing. A dozen workers watched me expectantly, as Marina suggested I do "Strangers in the Night." Mortified, I gave them my best Sinatra. They only looked baffled and stunned.

In every village she'd come to after descending from the wall, Marina had asked to meet the oldest resident. She would photograph that person and ask for a legend about the wall. The oldest person was always a man. She had never been able to get a woman to tell her a legend. She hadn't been able to get a woman for her crew, either, though she'd requested one. Holding up half the sky they may have been, but the women I'd seen (in rural areas especially) stayed shyly in the background and were rarely included in the official dinners or meetings. Marina must have seemed doubly strange—not just a foreigner, but a female on an incomprehensible mission. In one mountain village, people had gathered to watch her fall asleep. A different group was sitting around the bed when she woke up.

Judging from the legends she'd heard, Marina believed the wall's origins were connected more to mythology than to defense. The legends spoke of marvelous fierce dragons. White, yellow, and black. Mountain dragons. Sea dragons. They fought. They caused earthquakes and tidal waves. Where she'd started, at the Yellow Sea, the builders of the wall had sunk ships—representing, in some legends, the sea dragon; in others, the head of one giant dragon slain by the emperor of the air. To control the creature's energy, peasants had designated "energy spots" along the Great Wall, like acupuncture points along the dragon's spine. There they placed copper pots, then covered them with heaps of stone. When Marina found these places along the wall, she stopped and spent time. To absorb the energy.

She was convinced that the geodetic energy line was alive in the mountains (while the clay wall, much of it older, felt dead to her). That was why she'd insisted that she couldn't leave the line of the wall. She'd come up with a phrase that described her process: "boat emptying, stream entering." She would empty her mind as a meditator does—the danger she faced forcing her to stay in the moment, to stop thinking of past or future. The stream was the energy of the wall, the force line, nature.

Marina had made the walk an inward journey, a way to strengthen herself for the new life ahead when she would work, she said, without Ulay. She called it "a broom for my soul." Art should be done, she believed, from that extraordinary state of mind one could only get to physically, through exhaustion or pain or repetition. This was what attracted her to hardship and risk. "I put myself in a circumstance where all my defense is broken and all my habits don't exist." Every day of the walk in the mountains had exhausted her and caused her pain. She'd had two months of that. She thought it essential to push herself for a long time. Then—"is like gate to me, when the body give up."

The morning that we left the graphite factory, we soon came upon steep velvety hills. The wall ran up the sharpest incline, at the angle a ladder takes against the side of a house. It was no mountain, but it looked impossible. Marina scrambled straight up, exhilarated. Winded after toiling to the top of the first stretch, I could see that this was nothing to Marina and Dahai. The wall here was stone, unsteady beneath my feet, and dropped off sharply on the left. Wind snapped my hat off, began strangling me with its cord.

Finally the wall leveled off on a barren plateau that stretched toward what looked like forever. It was so empty. Not even a tree. Just to the north was a breathtaking vista of treeless, silver green hills: Inner Mongolia. I began to imagine that we were the first humans who'd been here in centuries.

One of the crew sprinted over the grass behind a rabbit. "He thinks is dinner," said Marina. We'd brought a lunch today, again uncertain where we would eventually find the jeep. Again, the sun was scorching. We had to settle for a foot-wide patch of shade in a little gully. In our lunch bags, packed by the crew, we each found six hard-boiled eggs, some cucumbers, and one tomato. We ate it all. Marina thought that, given the heat, we should rest until three, and we moved on to find better shade. There was one thin tree. There was one tiny cave. In a beacon tower north of the grass-covered wall, I eased into a cranny big enough for one human and watched the ants.

When we began walking again, Marina said that I must tell her exactly how I felt. I knew that I had two feelings. Everywhere we looked was the beauty that language can't describe, the primordial landscape, naked gullies forking into soft hills. This grass was the only jade I'd seen. And here were these amazing ruins. Not just the Great Wall of China, but walls that were once houses or stables, built long before the country I came from was a country, and over there some obelisk, all so mysterious. So I told her that I felt exhilaration. I would leave China having seen the massive Buddhas back in Datong, having seen the terra cotta warriors near Xi'an. But nothing would compare to this walk on the wall, because there I saw the things I didn't know I would see.

But my second feeling was a great anxiety. I told her that we didn't know where we were or where we were going or how big this plateau was or if we'd leave it by nightfall or where the jeep would find us again. I'd noticed that the security man couldn't get through on his walkie-talkie. I supposed we were up too high. And look what had happened yesterday. Marina smiled at this, my fear, as she put it, "that jeep is somewhere and we are nowhere." She told me that this, actually, was the ideal journey. When nothing is fixed. She got happiness from this openness, from not knowing. This was why she wanted no plan. This was where she found the "edge that make you wake."

"In this way," she said, "I find my destiny."

On June 27, having each walked well over a thousand miles, the artists arrived at Shenmu in Shaanxi province. Ulay had just endured the most physically difficult part of his journey, crossing the Mao Wu Su Desert with its nearly three-hundred-foot sand dunes and canyonlike east–west cracks. It had been two steps forward and one back the whole way. Marina had had to make another giant detour around a military area, resuming her walk at the Yellow River, at the place where they'd thought the piece might end. The day before meeting with Ulay, she'd passed through a kilometer of human bones.

Chance set their meeting at the site of two hundred small Taoist, Buddhist, and Confucian temples built into the hills early in the Ming Dynasty, dedicated to the warrior hero, Er Lang. The crew had found musicians to play traditional instruments. They'd hung banners to fly in the breeze and exploded fireworks. By chance, the artists were both just rounding the corner of a temple when they saw each other. By chance they had traveled for exactly ninety days, the same amount of time they'd spent doing *Nightsea Crossing*. And by chance, they finally came face to face at the center of a stone bridge. "Over the abyss," as Marina put it. They embraced. She experienced a flashback of their twelve years together. He whispered something about how much they'd accomplished.

I had left China before the meeting, unable to extend my visa. But the meaning of the walk was no longer hinged there. Over the telephone, each complained a bit about the other's first reaction. Marina had started to cry, which Ulay thought inappropriate. Ulay's first words were something about her shoes, which Marina thought inappropriate. Marina couldn't wait to leave China. Ulay said he could have walked on forever.

They discovered that they had both written the same little poem along the way: "Cloud in the sky / dust in the eye." But in no other way had their journeys been the same. "For the first time in twelve years, we had separate experiences," reported Ulay. "There will be no way to fuse it."

From Shenmu the artists went right to Beijing to hold a press conference. The Chinese media has never published anything at all, however, on the journeys made by Ulay and Marina across the wall. The artists returned, separately, to Amsterdam.

Their walk had been much like the Great Wall itself, which never accomplished what it was built to accomplish, yet it became a wonder of the world. It was both an absurd and a glorious project, a bit of a failure yet an overwhelming success. Like the aspiration to love, to transcend, to risk everything, it was too too human.

February 1989

■ ■ ■ Underground

■ ■ ■ The Hot Bottom

Art and Artifice in the East Village

The first time I saw Pat Hearn Gallery I was walking home down Avenue B around midnight. Perhaps that was what made the gleaming, astonishing, almost absurdly out-of-place Light Thing on the corner of 6th Street and Avenue B seem so like an apparition. Like "I have seen the future of Avenue B and it looks like a maximum-security shopping mall."

The art world baby boom in this nabe continues to be the story of the season. Twenty-six galleries have opened in the last year bringing the total on my list to thirty-two—although Nine has now closed, I never found the Runners Club, and I stopped adding new names a month ago.

Suddenly, it looks like everybody wants a piece of the neighborhood. Amsterdam had a "Best of the East Village" show last fall. Some of the "hot" artists are popping up in Barcelona, Tokyo, Queens. . . . "In Berlin," Deborah Sharpe of Sharpe Gallery tells me, "they all wanted to know about the East Village." Back home, Gracie Mansion has doubled in size and Civilian Warfare's looking for a building to occupy. The buyers are here—European collectors who use the Whitney Biennial as a shopping list, and upwardly mobiles who are part of an expanding market for art. The highly publicized "energy" of the scene feels something like gold rush fever.

"The hot bottom to the art market" is how Jay Gorney characterizes the East Village—a place where collectors come to "drop their change." Gorney, who will curate the "Evolution" show at East 7th Street Gallery in April, was associate director of Hamilton Gallery on 57th Street for seven years. He points out that the top of the market is very active as well, with collectors just itching to plunk down tens of thousands for something like a Salle or a Baselitz, while the middle of the market is "closing down." Uptown, "you can get a print by trendy artists like Elizabeth Murray or Jennifer Bartlett for $500–$4,000. In the East Village, you can get an *original painting* for $600–$800, and most galleries have work in the $150–$200 range." Local artists who now have a rep—Futura 2000 and David Wojnarowicz, for example—can sell for $6,000 to $8,000 tops but, as the legend goes, you'd pay more for it uptown. The highest figure I'd heard in the neighborhood was $10,000 for a Richard Hambleton, but just the other day I heard $20,000 for a Kenny Scharf.

Money and status are the elephants wandering through the art world we're all supposed to pretend we don't see. An unspoken etiquette attends to the clumsy things. One day, I witnessed a beastly blunder at the old Mary Boone gallery, when a rather plain, unfashionably dressed woman approached Boone and bellowed, "How much is that painting?" Boone handled it well, murmuring something like "it's sold." She sells selectively, of course, to the Right People.

I can't imagine this scene taking place at an East Village gallery. As Deborah Sharpe put it, "Our spaces are not intimidating." And prices are usually posted on a typewritten sheet at the desk. C.A.S.H. Gallery addressed the issue head-on with a show called "25 cents to $25,000." At Sensory Evolution, dealer Steven Style asks artists to give him work he can sell for $50 or under, $250 or under, and $500 or under. Many of the dealers say they like having cheaper work so artists or young collectors can buy. The sold-out Rodney Alan Greenblat show at Gracie Mansion, favorably reviewed in *Art in America,* had work starting at $5 (ranging up to $3,500). The Sue Coe show at P.P.O.W., favorably reviewed in *ARTFORUM,* included prints for sale at $20.

I could even afford that, and I began to think how wonderful it was that these were MY galleries in MY neighborhood serving MY needs. Then, later, on a Saturday night, I squeezed into an opening at some ex-bodega where typically half the crowd had to stand out on the sidewalk and a "waiter" in tails twirled by with drinks on a tray, and I saw the same people in tall hair and lizardskin pants who'd been at an opening in Soho just hours ago, everyone dripping attitude and on the make. Maybe the hideous pictures on the wall had put me in a cynical mood, but I couldn't help thinking that the problem in coming full circle from a gallery where they won't tell you prices is that sometimes they offer you nothing *but* prices.

In Soho or uptown, an artist who thought of paintings as pure product certainly wouldn't brag about it. But in the East Village we have Mark Kostabi—who says his middle name is "et" (as in "Mark-et")—telling the *East Village Eye*, "Paintings are doorways into collectors' homes." In Soho or uptown, artists labor toward that one show a year, bring in the work, and there's a hushed moment. In the East Village, certain painters, like Kostabi, are getting massive exposure, appearing in dozens of shows simultaneously, working with three or four dealers, and showing at the art bars—Kamikaze, No Se No, The Cat Club, Beulah Land. . . .

When I talked to Jay Gorney about the market, he said he thought a lot of the work shown in the East Village was "mannered." One artist I talked to used the same word but took it further and pointed out that you usually see mannered work after something good has come along and everyone's trying to copy it. "In the East Village, it's happening backwards. It's starting at the decline stage—derivative, commercially oriented, and decorative. Everyone's waiting for it to get good."

"It's depressing to see what people are making," says Peter Nagy of Nature Morte, "but neo-expressionist figuration is good for the market." Nagy shows conceptual work at his gallery; he expressed distaste for the East Village "look." What people seem to mean by that is cartoony figuration, painted quickly, probably meant to register quickly, often helped to that end by simple shocking imagery. Often the paintings are small in size. I might use words like "crude" or "garish" to describe them. Work like this is shown at just a few of the thirty-odd galleries but it's what people associate with the neighborhood.

Last year I would have said East Village art was street art taken indoors, like the best "East Village show" I ever saw: the abandoned Pier off Canal Street where David Wojnarowicz, Mike Bidlo, and others painted images on the damp crumbly walls and worthless fixtures. I also appreciated the Pier as a lesson in how trendiness can ruin an artist's intention. When I visited last fall, a fashion photographer was using the space for background, much of the art had been stolen or destroyed, and the artists had long since stopped working there.

Rene Ricard's article on Fun Gallery in the November 1982 *ARTFORUM*, the first insightful writing about the East Village scene, was really an article about "making it"—about stardom, illusion, the future (the bomb), and the art world socializing one is usually too discreet to talk about. But a young artist hustling slides around to galleries is going to talk about it. "Slides are not cool—you should go to parties and try to be friends with the right people," one dealer told an artist who told me. As Rene puts it, ". . . one's behavior, one's merest gesture, too much muscle, the wrong shade of lipstick, a casual word influences and can ruin the campaign of a lifetime."

I ran into Rene at an opening for Lee Quinones and Kathleen Thomas at Barbara Gladstone and asked if I could interview him about the new East Village gallery scene. "Never! I won't talk about it. I don't believe in the East Village! Wait, I'll write it down." He took me into the gallery office and began to write on a card: "I don't believe in the East Village. The idea is vulgar and corrupt, a journalist convenience term that has nothing to do with art. Great art surfaces and to relegate it to neighborhoods is the nadir of vanity." He told me to say that he had refused to make a statement. I had the card in my hand and told him I thought this *was* a statement. He took the card back and wrote, "Rene Ricard refused to make a statement because" and said to put that at the beginning of his quotation. He said he wouldn't even go to the new galleries, except that he had that very afternoon because a millionaire came down and took him around in his limo. He told me that JULIAN had bought a painting at an East Village gallery but when he hung it over his Twombly, the Twombly *blew it out of the room* so JULIAN took it back. He said it was inside stuff and I could quote him.

The events Rene reported on just a couple years ago are now legends—how it all began in Fun (gallery), with artist Kenny Scharf naming the place and dealer Patti Astor thinking maybe they'd rename it every month. The first galleries were like the plot of a Judy Garland/Mickey Rooney musical. "Hey, let's start a gallery. . . ." As Gracie Mansion relates it, "I was created by the media." When she started showing work in the bathroom of her apartment, she wasn't committed to dealing art; but a reporter from the *Voice* showed up and asked, "What's your second show?" Civilian Warfare was Dean Savard's studio, open only at nights and on weekends because he and his partner Alan Barrows had to work regular jobs; the gallery didn't sell even a poster for fourteen months. These three galleries are now acknowledged by many as the most successful in the neighborhood, though oddly, they each appeal to very different kinds of collectors. Civilian sells mostly to Europeans, Gracie sells to "the same people who buy from Mary Boone and Charlie Cowles," and Patti Astor told me a month ago after the Fab Five Freddy show that she had sold work of his to Francesco Clemente and two banks.

New ideas of what a collector, a dealer, an artist, a gallery can be—they're all being tried out here. Take the simple matter of presentation. When I went to Sensory Evolution, I walked through a vestibule that had been draped in black plastic; a strobe light blinked at my feet. I struggled to find a way into the gallery through the plastic and eventually asked what was going on with the door. Steven Style informed me that I had just passed through a "sensation chamber" because this was, after all, a show called "1984." A month earlier, I'd been to Gracie Mansion. She and her partner Sur Rodney Sur had just opened their "Salon," a group show. They had moved in some chairs, redone the floors, painted the walls hospital green, moved in a rug and a refrigerator. She said they liked to change the feel of the place for each new show, right down to the color of the walls.

Maybe only a dealer who'd started out as an artist—as these two did—would go to the trouble. All the first galleries here were opened by artists showing their friends or other unknowns whose work they admired. But nearly all the new galleries are run by people who've always wanted to be dealers. They're in the East Village because it's the only neighborhood in town where they could be part of a gallery scene and still afford the rent. The landlords are happy to have them, in some cases providing a new dealer with one of those hard-to-find East Village apartments. Steven Style mentioned that his landlord was going to let him paint a neighborhood gallery guide on a wall near Avenue A.

"We're raising the property values," said Nina Siegenfeld of New Math, taking me up to the apartment she and Mario Fernandez share a door or so down from their gallery, because "people always want to see how we live here on the Lower East Side." She'd taken some people from an Indianapolis museum up there just the other day and they'd found it so interesting. She and Mario had a lot of work up on the walls, a mattress on the floor, a broken-down couch in the living room. The place was filthy. "Instead of living better, we're using our money to buy ads."

Turns out Nina moved here months ago from the Upper East Side. Poverty, apparently, was just a cool new lifestyle. While Mario had moved from a "really bad neighborhood" at 4th Street and Avenue D (my old block!). Their gallery had been a Puerto Rican social club closed by the cops after a shootout. The landlord was very fair and had even taken a painting instead of rent for the first two months. Nina feels "a responsibility to the neighborhood" and has organized a show at the candy store on the corner; all the people in the building will do art on matchbooks and the winner will get ten dollars. I have an impulse to think they can't know any better—they're too young. A year ago, Nina was an sva student; now she teaches there, a course on how to present work to galleries.

Lately I've seen flyers up all over the neighborhood soliciting work for some antigentrification, antigallery show apparently sponsored by p.a.d.d. (Political Art Documentation and Distribution). But I haven't been able to determine the where, when, and how since someone's deliberately torn this info from every one of the flyers. I think this means something, dear p.a.d.d. members. I think it means you're too late.

April 1984

■ ■ ■ Country Clubbing

The pig had been cooking on a bed frame since midnight, its 250 sauce-red pounds suspended over a pit. Biggest porker 8BC had had in three years of Pig Phests. During last night's *Tarzan* performance, actors had carried the pig out of the club, trailed by the entire audience. Trussed in Reynolds Wrap, it began cooking in the fire-lit vacant lot as part of "Tarzan's" plot. Seems the pig had been gentrified. The club was the jungle, decorated in garbage bag vines. And the neighborhood was Africa. As the villain put it to another victim of the real estate boom, Tarzan's mother: "We're evicting you! Africa's getting nice!"

Now the pig still needed a few hours of fire time in the gunpowdery air of a July 4 afternoon. But the miniature golf could begin. Back in the tough flora and cracked fauna behind the club, facing 9th Street, a demented vision of suburban leisure had materialized in ten holes of art golf.

So the ironies could begin too. Pig Phests and theoretical golf greens can make a neighborhood in ruins so charming, so newly valuable, so far from what the artists wanted it to become. 8BC had just made *Vogue* along with the rest of the East Village "scene." But what they intended was to celebrate a disappearing Loisaida with their third annual pig-roast, inviting both the clubgoers and the folks from the block to bring a covered dish.

8BC's Cornelius Conboy, Phest organizer, walked through the "green" with me, marveling that almost every club, gallery, or artist who'd promised to build a hole had really come through, for no reward except a good time. Sure, he said, there was rivalry among the clubs. But they were also a community. He hoped he didn't sound like the Kiwanis. That transvestite-from-outer-space mannequin was the Pyramid Club. That loop-the-loop tire and carpet construction was the Life Cafe. And the sonic golf hole—where a ball went up a ramp, into a wok, through a vacuum cleaner hose and pipe, over a xylophone, into a kiddie pool full of silver bowls—*that* came from P.S. 122. Player after player tried it, lofting balls everywhere but up the ramp, while Cornelius began drawing up a scorecard, a list of par whatevers. Soon he tossed it away—what with the distractions and the realization that a lot of these holes were at par 1,000: unplayable.

Carmelita Tropicana, the performer who reigns as "Miss Loisaida," pointed out, for example, that the wow Cafe's little roller coaster of pink and green tubing and orange stairways had a wiffle ball stuck to the cup, making all putts impossible. She proclaimed it a rhetorical hole. Holly Hughes, its architect, said she realized it was all pretty tasteful for her, but she'd decided there was already "enough doll mutilation." A reference, I guess, to the adjacent Club Chandalier fairway, where a baby doll sat in a little blue swimming pool, red liquid pumping out of a hole in her head. "Look! Blood!" squealed a couple of neighborhood kids who ran over to scoop some into their hands. With a satisfied look at someone using a putter made from a fly-fishing rod and a piece of spray-painted cardboard, Hughes continued, "It's the Lower East Side's first country club."

Cornelius hadn't provided any golf clubs. Because what if someone wanted to use a basketball instead of a golf ball? There were no rules here! (Spirit of the East Village and all that.) Back at the hole constructed by Carol Black and Julie Hair of the band Bite Like a Kitty, a neighborhood artist tried pushing the ball over a blue bone and into a tiny coffin, using the club they'd provided—a cardboard skull stuck to a stick. "Too much like croquet," he muttered.

Everyone had come to play. Or to get what they could get. A panhandler on a crutch waved a fur hat full of small change at Cornelius, who told him, "Come back in an hour. You'll get a free dinner." The guy wearing a huge Hershey Kiss over his baseball hat said he was looking to get noticed and had brought his fur-covered BMW Isetta to the "car art" show over on the 8th Street side of the sizzling pig. Sure, this was his everyday car. Used to be purple till he'd repainted the fur in fluorescents a couple weeks ago. He'd sleep there, right in the zebra-skin interior. And people's heads would turn.

Hundreds were milling over the green now in church-social grins, mellowed out like the tree branches that waved through windows of an abandoned building across the street. Five children had solved the sonic golf problem by making it basketball, leaping to toss balls right into the wok. Nearly pig time now, volunteers began tossing chicken pieces onto the grill around the fat red carcass. I walked to where a crowd had gathered on a bluff of fractured dirt. Here Howard Taikeff, assisted by Timothy Greathouse, had spent three days inventing a multitiered Rube Goldberg contraption, half-billiards, half-golf, complete with plaster of Paris masks and flags, sand traps, and elaborate twisting causeways, painted in Pollock drips. "It's a tribute to the New York School," Greathouse announced. Looking over his shoulder, I saw the neighborhood lined up for pigmeat.

Last night's Tarzan with Pig performance had delighted the club-goers with its surprise ending in this very lot. Poor old Cheetah'd been gentrified when a car stopped abruptly out on 8th Street, and the villain, screaming, "We're going to drown you in the East River!" had pushed the monkey into the hatchback and it squealed off. Two neighborhood women, ripe for gentrification themselves, happened to be passing by and stopped in astonishment. They didn't know what to make of this death threat and this guy in gorilla fur and a nightgown. But then the play wasn't addressed to them. *Tarzan* is the African show about white people.

July 1985

■ ■ ■ To Thine Own Self Be True

Ethyl Eichelberger thinks that at this point in his life he should play both women and men. So when he hit forty two weeks ago, he did his own variation on *King Lear* at 8BC. *Leer* he called it. With a cast of one. That way he got to do Cordelia too, which "made playing a man easier." He knows some women find drag offensive, but he doesn't know why. This bothers him, as though he'd been accused like Shakespeare's Lear of having "ever but slenderly known himself." He believes he sees the world through women's eyes.

I'd never seen Ethyl out of a dress before. But when the curtain rose on *Leer* last Saturday, he stood there looking like Mark Twain—the white hair and mustache, the white suit, the bitter funnybone. Pinned to his jacket was a jeweled red and gold fly as big as a piepan. The set indicated that a nineteenth-century road company had wound its way into the club, what with the painted trail and mountain backdrop and strong footlights enclosing a small portion of the stage. Ethyl was even starting on time (a circumstance so unusual in East Village clubs I'd missed the entire birthday show the week before), and the pit of 8BC kept filling with standees as the plot lurched tragically on.

This was Shakespeare boiled down to a nubbin of Leer, Cordelia, and Fool—all thrashing it out over what you owe to someone you love. Ethyl fleshed it back out with Southern Gothic ambience, bits from *Hamlet* to *Streetcar* to kids' games, and sentimental songs sung to accordion or piano. "Getting up there in years, fighting back all my tears . . ." Leer's losing his grip, and wants to divvy up his kingdom: an Ozark mountaintop.

After planning on a cast of three, Ethyl took on all the roles when one performer had to drop out. Enter Cordelia, the good daughter, played by a dress—a long black filmy thing with a red tutu. It's hanging

Ethyl Eichelberger as Leer (and Cordelia and Fool). (© Dona Ann McAdams.)

from a wire and Ethyl runs behind it to speak her lines. "Daddy, you're as dotty as a Bloolip." She'll love him but won't give him presents, while the other two daughters are "too busy" to appear in this production. (Thank god. It's already a frenzy up there.) But they've sent their pathetic chocolate-bar gifts to stage right, and these turn Leer's head. Like Lear before him, he's hard to warm up to, a dimwit about human relationships. Enter the Fool on another wire, a Raggedy Andy doll wearing yard-long children's jeans.

After Leer died of his broken heart, I talked to Ethyl in the corner of the stage that serves as a dressing room. He showed me that his Mark Twainish suit had a skirt to it as well "so it wouldn't be so jarring." I asked about the song they'd been playing over the PA as the curtain fell. A rare 78 by Bert Williams, the black blackface performer, Ethyl told me. He sees himself as part of a whole long vaudevillish and disreputable tradition.

A couple of nights earlier I'd stopped in at the Pyramid Club to see a drag version of *A Midsummer Night's Dream*, written in Cliff Note chunks by someone named Joey. I stayed only for the thirteen-minute first act, in which Ethyl played Queen Hippolyta, and I couldn't always catch what was on the somewhat muddy prerecorded tape. ("That's to prevent improvising. We have to keep it short," the doorman told me later.) But the style was pure pose, a distanced mocking comment on all the characters. That manages to ridicule the women just for being women.

Ethyl's "Minnie the Maid" performance at 8BC the weekend before, on the other hand, was a completely different sort of theater. That both were "drag" describes nothing. Minnie had finally appeared to a thinned-out crowd at three in the morning, wearing a short black dress, fishnet stockings, and huge silver wig entwined with black feathers. Accompanying herself on accordion, she sang about love, about how she's "never said no" but never found the right man either. Would she never find the One?

Suddenly Ethyl himself came into focus. Said probably we thought we were gonna see some *classy* drag act. And he reeled off a line each from Bette Davis, Diana Ross, Mae West, et al. But no. Ethyl's never been a female impersonator, just an actor who wants to play great women. And men.

He shifted back into Minnie, who did another verse on love lost. She told of finding happiness at hairdressing school, because the teacher was a queen "nellier than me. Who said, 'The hair has no brain,' and I thought, 'I'm home.'" Actually that was Ethyl, licensed hairdresser, talking. (He did the hair for *Cloud Nine* and *Einstein on the Beach* and does Charles Ludlam's wigs.) Minnie/Ethyl sat down at the old upright piano next to do a song on what her/his mother had told her/him about love—that friends were the most important thing—and then s/he pointed out the people in the audience who were friends, saying *why* they were friends. Ethyl said later, "Minnie is me." The style may be retro but she's authentic and tough and not available for ridicule.

The first time I saw Ethyl—a few years back at a benefit for P.S. 122— he came striding out before his act because the sound technicians were having trouble with his equipment. This was a startling figure: tall guy with tall hair in a long dress and giant angel tattoo across his back carrying a big red accordion. He fixed the mikes, and then bolted off-stage, only to poke his head back out at us: "Pretend you didn't see me."

Ethyl has a genius for transforming the awkward moment into art. He loves the artifice of theater, loves gleefully reinventing the classics in the Ridiculous tradition of tawdry preposterousness. He proves that transcendent drag is really art about art.

August 1985

■ ■ ■ Sex Gods, Ekstatic Women

The pompadour deserves a place in the history of great ideas. No one realized this till John Sex sharpened his hair, exaggerating the outlandish essence of the sex god. It crests a foot above his forehead like a wave about to crash. Last week at the Pyramid Club, in this hair plumage like a courting bird's, in a broad-shouldered tuxedo jacket encrusted with little lights, John Sex hit the stage singing no one does the shing-a-ling like he does. Small leap of faith to ask in the face of so extravagant an image, even if the music was—well, less than memorable.

This was Las Vegas from another planet, Sex working through eight songs of either awesome schmaltz or vulgarity—from the *Mary Tyler Moore Show* theme to the X-rated "Hustle with the Muscle." He dropped the electric Liberace coat, asked us to applaud it, continued in a sparkly red suit that looked wet under the lights, and danced loose as a go-go boy in front of his three-woman back-up group, The Bodacious Ta-Tas.

"I *want* what I've got!" he sang. That's the secret of his sex appeal. He called it the story of his life. His act celebrates a pansexuality even though a few songs reaffirm everything Frankie Avalon ever believed. This teen dream is a freak, delighting in his sexiness and everyone else's: "I've got it and it's allright. She's got it and it's allright. Sex appeal."

Days earlier I'd seen John Sex descending from the heavens into the frenzied hi-tech baroque at the Palladium, as the finale to a depraved Hollywood Bible pageant called *Pagan Place*. In big white wings and feathery leggings, he crooned a teen angel sort of song. But nothing much works for the over-stimulated audience at the Palladium after

Sharp hair and hustle: John Sex
in performance. (© Catherine
McGann.)

the first moment of impact. As a one-man spectacle John Sex was rather
wasted here, as were the other singers, Ann Magnuson and Joey Arias.
The crowd shrieked louder at the parade of outrageous costumes, like
the "bull" wearing nothing but suspenders and spotted leggings that
ended at the top of his thighs.

I'd seen the same phenom a week earlier when Nina Hagen appeared during Ekstasy Night in what was once the Palladium's loge,
surrounded by white balloons, saying something fishy about religion,
singing four bars of "Don't Think Twice, It's All Right." Then good-
bye. We didn't think twice. 'Twas all right. We'd lost our attention
spans. We'd experienced mash media in the palace of excess. The walls
were changing color with every beat. Clusters of lights plunged and
gyrated over the dance floor. A mini-14th Street descended for ten minutes, then two banks of twenty-five video monitors, swooping and
blinking out a series of feverish non sequiturs: baby hippos and news

headlines and computer-generated cubes. Performances here have to be honed to sharp edges. Either that or bounce right off the glassy-eyed.

Hours after Hagen's five minutes, the two women who call themselves Dancenoise (Anne Iobst, Lucy Sexton) ascended over the dance floor on pulleys, flinging glitter at the crowd, wearing black tights and bras and haphazard red war paint with styrofoam mannequin heads on top of their own heads. Always abrasive, tearing baby dolls limb from limb or dousing themselves with "blood," their emotional intensity feels right in a raw-looking space like 8BC's. They embody and parody female rage, an illustration for *Of Woman Born* one minute, for a cavegirl flick the next. At the Palladium their crudeness was a knife in the high-tech gloss. They dropped rough paper banners (like "Baby! Go! Baby!"). They made a mess up on the catwalks around the central stairway, swigging "blood" from old coffee cans, tearing up dolls, breaking open big bags of shredded paper. A surly crowd returned the hostility with yells and whistles.

A friend said she supposed this was all intended as a sample of the East Village for those afraid of the real thing. Certainly the Palladium has the ambience of an Upper East Side come late to punk, alienated in its cocktails and business drag, crying an unconscious anthem of "Gimme. Gimme. Shock treatment."

August 1985

■ ■ ■ The Revolution That Won't Be Televised

Mike is mega-mellow. You listen to the Muzak he talks. You look at the freeze-dried color of his clothing. You think here beats the white-shoed heart of the supper-club host. Then with the comalike calm of Mister Rogers introducing a vocabulary word, he trots out one peculiar downright un-American entertainment after another. You have to say, "Jeez."

Last month Mike brought *Mike's Talent Show* to Danceteria so Manhattan Cable could tape it. Bits of it could have been quirky Ed Sullivan: a magic act with attitude (Robinson's Mysteries), a surly standup wit (Margaret Smith), a tap dancer who told us when to applaud her during the hard part (Jane Goldberg). But as usual, Mike had the drag queens, the bad-mouths, and other talents you really have to turn off a television to find.

Mike's band, the Feetwarmers, would grease the transitions with talk show oom-pah-pah and fragments of ancient pop. He'd stand stage right—near the cheap hunk of wood paneling meant to represent, I guess, a manly den. And there he might do the water-drinking trick he once did as a Cub Scout. Or sing a bland little ditty ("public transportation, what a situation"). He was the great tranquilizer so necessary around acts of outrage.

He'd really have to make like the valley of the Valium that night. Because the paradox in Mike bringing his guerrilla gueststars to a television taping is that many of them play off TV in their club performances. And work at restoring everything television took out.

Harry Kipper (Brian Routh) emerged with three dolls stuck into his undershorts and rang a schoolbell, oven mitts on both hands. Once he'd thrown the black cloth off his upper body, you could see the centurion hat, and the string forcing his nose back into a pig nose, and the big silver bowl taped to his torso. First doll: "Like her Dad. A true Nazi." And the others: "When they get together—and you leave any milk out, any blood out—it's gone the next morning." Pulling a statue of Jesus from his crotch, he said he liked pretending it was his penis. He squirted milky liquid from its head, and then, as though worried someone might still be unmoved, pulled a turd from the back of his shorts.

So they were gonna take this transcendental grossness to the tube. As Mike would say, slowly, "It's amazing."

He introduced Karen Finley as "a very sensitive person from the Windy City" who always brought him a present. She walked out in leopard-skin top, heels, and running shorts, and threw a pair of underpants to the floor. Mike's present, she announced as he retreated. She'd forgotten to bring him one this time so she'd just taken these off. Mike stopped in his tracks looking sheepish. "Pick 'em up, small boy," she commanded.

Then she shifted decibels and launched into a wail of male lust— ". . . I'm an ASS MAN! . . ."—so intensely obscene it gave people the fidgets and the ever-present din of talk and beer bottles turned into a pin's drop. She was men lusting for women, men lusting for children— ". . . ooh I just wanna TOUCH that young chicken meat. . . ."—like it was a cry of glory from the pulpit of manhood.

Pat Oleszko came on right after and turned parts of her body into bad Europop singers. With a little TV she framed, for example, Ivan— eyes painted on her stomach, his beard her pubic hair. She turned around to frame Galena, painted on her ass. Grinding all the while to make their mouths move.

Mike, played by Michael Smith, had mentioned an air date during the taping and implied that this was going to be a series. But for several days after, he and Manhattan Cable both pleaded confusion and refused comment on whether the show would run or on anything that had happened. The show's obscenity might be a problem, but it was just "one factor—the easiest one to deal with," according to Smith, who reached an agreement with Cable last Friday. "Mike's Talent Show" will air at some point in the fall as a one-hour special.

Smith said Cable had been confused over what they were going to get. "They were looking for MOR."

I suppose Ethyl Eichelberger will qualify even though drag queens aren't in the middle of anyone's road. Ethyl's was a tragic love story, and television's full of them. Eric Bogosian's character study in self-delusion should be familiar as well. I mean, the guy's life was perfect.

But in general, club performers can't be MOR and expect to hold a stage. Paul McMahon had crooned in a lonesome cowboy voice, "I'll never understand these forces that command my emotions." So thoughtful and poetic hardly anyone listened. Beyond the front rows, the audience was a horror show.

Fran Liebowitz had figured out the necessary approach by the time she took the stage. Said she realized she wasn't a real performer because she didn't have dolls taped to her stomach. She read from one of her books about "People," a group that, in her opinion, had attracted an undue amount of attention.

They kept right on attracting it too, jabbering and hooting away like a party of animals in the back of the op and paisley-painted room. "What happens if you *lose* this Talent Show?" she snarled. "Where do you have to work *then*?"

September 1985

■ ■ ■ R.I.P. 8BC

or one last night we engaged in "unlicensed activities." Like watching Ethyl Eichelberger. He strapped the accordion on around 4 A.M. and announced from 8BC's stage, "This is a song about loss." An unscheduled gig for Ethyl, who'd hurried over in full mascara from the Pyramid Club where he has a job dancing on the bar. But shutting down hadn't been scheduled either. The city had fingered 8BC as an "unlicensed cabaret." And owner Cornelius Conboy wanted Ethyl to do the swan song. It was magic. The song over, the much-publicized East Village club scene had shrunk before our eyes.

Just last spring, *The Drama Review* published an issue on "East Village performance," but among the venues it describes, only P.S. 122 and Club Chandalier carry on as they did a year ago. The wow Cafe and Limbo Lounge have changed from clubs into theaters. The Pyramid Club seems to be booking a less experimental range of performance styles—and more music. Darinka never reopened after it was fined for operating without a liquor license last summer. And 8BC, arguably the neighborhood's hottest club, is now gone. Did high visibility in the likes of *New York* and *Vogue* get them the wrong kind of attention?

Nothing is certain except that a whole new audience has developed, some of it with less interest in the work than in Making the Scene. Trying to appeal to this new audience could easily change the art. Blunt it or slick it up. "Everything's more formal now," one performer commented. "People realize they can get famous. Remember how playful it used to be?" I can't imagine Karen Finley, Brian Routh, Tom Murrin, and other 8BC regulars compromising themselves to make it with the *Vogue*ites, but now they may have a problem finding a place to work. In the sixties, LaMama's Ellen Stewart was closed by the city countless times, and just kept moving. But in today's real estate crunch, no one has that kind of mobility.

In the new era of what's hot/what's not, things get very serious very fast. It's easy to forget how naively, how precariously, the clubs began, run for artists by artists with little business sense among them. Who bothered with legalities? Who could afford them? Dennis Gattra, Conboy's partner, said they'd "juggled one step ahead of a bust" right from the start. In the olden days of a mere two years ago, 8BC had a log cabin ambiance—dirt floor, no heat—and didn't meet a single licensing requirement. The plan was to get legal gradually.

Twice last summer I arrived to find the fire trucks there, waiting till the place cleared of all but seventy-five people (a third or fourth of the normal crowd). *No sprinkler system. Inadequate exits.* It was all true. Conboy and Gattra hadn't taken the fifteen-hour "food handling" course required of those who keep lemons and limes at the bar, either. But they *had* won a Bessie Award "for their late hours and enlightened leadership in the DMZ of the never-ending talent show."

This would not impress inspectors from the Department of Consumer Affairs, who showed up on September 20 and filed an oddly sinister report about "a raised stage with a curtain and a disc jockey and persons dancing to recorded music." The partners were cited for unlicensed activity and fined $300. They chose to shut down. Consumer Affairs could have closed them if they'd chosen otherwise.

By their last day in business, October 12, Conboy and Gattra were apparently one piece of paper away from meeting their requirements. But that one was a biggy—a certificate of occupancy, which would have required a zoning variance. In a four-page statement he issued a couple days later, Conboy declared that they could have never become legal without changing 8BC—raising prices, perhaps removing the bar or cutting back on the number of shows. "I think it's best to close while we're at our peak." In its two years, the club had staged 1,500 performances.

Conboy said it took closing the place to make him realize it was too small anyway. He and Gattra will eventually reopen somewhere else—with backers.* Probably more at a loss are the performers who no

---

*In 1986, Conboy and Gattra became the creative directors at 4D, a short-lived uptown club.

longer have access to the neighborhood's biggest proscenium stage. Canceled most notably this month: Kestutis Nakas's spectacle, "The Amazing Spear of Destiny," designed specifically for 8BC. It would have opened there last week. Even "too small," the club had luxurious space compared to the rest of the neighborhood's cramped corners. Japanese performer Poppo Shiraishi was perhaps the most exciting of those who moved their pieces through the space and into the adjoining vacant lot on this mostly abandoned block.

Closing night, in fact, began outside with Ellen Fisher's rendition of *1001 Nights*. With Scheherazade preparing to tell her first tale, the club emptied into the amphitheater in the back yard—the way through the rubble lit by torchbearers—to where some people from the neighborhood were already sitting in anticipation, watching the exotic dancers and the ornery fake camel running around on four human legs. While the piece seemed to go on forever, I watched a few more spectators climb out onto their fire escapes. Perhaps something like this would have died in the real estate boom anyway.

Later that night, near 3 A.M. and waiting for Ethyl, I left the claustrophobic nightmare at 8BC and walked to King Tut's Wah-Wah Hut. They were turning everyone away at the door. Too crowded? Who *are* all these people? Of course, long lines outside the Pyramid have been a weekend fact-of-life for years. When Ann Magnuson or John Sex performs there now, they don't even advertise. A full house gathers on word of mouth. Kestutis Nakas, who did all his early stuff there, now regards it as a "tourist trap." He wants to see the "Spear of Destiny" open in a theater space. Denise Lanctot at Limbo Lounge told me she thinks the clubs are dying out. Or course, constant change is the only constant in the club world.

Holly Hughes, whose hilarious lesbian soap-opera, "The Well of Horniness," had one-night stands at five different East Village venues, said she hates theater in pristine white places. Though she also appreciates not having to deal with an audience of drunks. In a club, performers have to *encounter* audiences who may be talking back or otherwise crossing the genteel borderline people observe in theaters. For example—admittedly an extreme one—Hughes mud-wrestled at 8BC the night it opened and eventually jumped, naked and dirty, on top of a heckler. "There's something about my aesthetic that clashes with blonde wood. That sort of burnt-out rec room feeling the clubs have is just more appropriate. 8BC was funky and not precious, the kind of space I don't think we'll see again."

October 1985

t's as if the city had just discovered its fringe art, hanging there like a ghastly little thread from the real estate brocade. Wherever I turned, bureaucrats were enforcing bizarre building codes and applying red tape in the wings. The week's theme became Illegal Performance.

Signs of life. I'd gone to the Downtown Film Festival at the now-defunct 8BC—liquorless and leased out for the occasion—and found the place packed to the bricks. It would be days yet before *The New York Times*'s Michael Gross discovered "club fatigue" and "Palladium fallout," informing us that "there is a waning interest on the part of upwardly mobile urban dwellers in these smoky late-night dance halls and demimonde cabarets. . . ." Took me ten minutes to squeeze within view of the stage.

Jo Andres appeared midway through the evening's dozen films and slide shows for an "expanded cinema" performance. This is dance for people who hate dance. Her work's impact comes from its startling visual elements. Last summer I saw a piece at 8BC in which Andres and a partner danced with their hands coated in blue paint, slapping each other with color. Then suddenly their hands were coated green. Then brown. The source of this color remained a mystery. Back pockets, I guessed. At the Film Fest, she worked with slide projections on four layers of tulle-like fabric, fat human outlines in red yellow green blue, stretching and playing with the figures, lifting the veils to show that only one color was visible on each layer of "alternative screen." Later I asked her how she'd done that. "I don't want to tell you," she replied. The piece ended with Andres, Steve Buscemi, and Cynthia Meyers squiggling over their black clothes with phosphorescent liquid as they danced, splattering phosphorescence over the stage and out into the audience, covering the first crowded rows in glowing spots.

And death. If that's your thing. The next night, that first row was in danger of more indelible spots, when a naked and shrieking Brian Moran poured a bucket of blood over his head. It was Cinema of Transgression night, a real droolfest of current underground gore, plus two performances. Filmmaker Nick Zedd, wearing a black dress, Cleopatra wig, and the gaze of a dying starlet, drifted across the stage, accompanied by a schmaltzy soundtrack that might ordinarily signal the entrance of a mutant B-movie crab. Richard Hell narrated. ". . . *She* savors even the tiniest joys allotted her too seldom and always in the dark where the dirt does not show . . . Maneater, homewrecker. . . ."

The next week, Zedd had moved this female victim/victimizer nonsense down to the Collective for Living Cinema, appearing once more as "Nichole." This play ended in a bloodbath, Zedd shooting a couple of "plants" in the audience who collapsed at their seats, bursting little blood bags. Smoke from the cap pistol hung in the air throughout the screening of Zedd's *Geek Maggot Bingo.*

It was probably fortunate that no inspectors happened by in the midst of this juvenile spectacle. The Collective, which screens all sorts of independent experimental film, has had its own problems with the city lately, and the program might have been tough to explain. When the Department of Consumer Affairs suddenly stumbled upon them last April—during a film called *Love Stinks*—the inspector thought they were showing pornography. That was straightened out, of course, but then Consumer Affairs came back and padlocked the place for operating without a motion picture theater license. In August, the city dropped charges but restricted audience size to fifty spectators. The Collective will now have to move after operating at its current location—unnoticed by the bureaucracy—for ten years.*

Un-altared. On the day before my Geek Maggot evening, I had planned to visit another universe entirely—in which Donna Henes would collect personal talismans and food for the hungry on her "Autumn Altar." But the project wasn't happening. Henes told me on the phone that the city (this time, the Parks Department) had said no at the last

*The Collective did move, but folded for good in 1991.

minute to lending her the parade-route bleachers she needed for the altar. Two years ago they had said yes, and she had collected an entire truckload of food, living outside with the altar for three days at the Municipal Building. "This is a personal tragedy for me," said Henes, who describes herself as an "urban shaman and ritual artist." Earlier in the week, she'd spent a whole day chanting for peace. It's an art form that gets more support in California, she admitted, but that's why she feels her work is needed here. "In New York, no one even knows if it's the longest day of the year or a comet's going over." She hopes to reschedule this event, but by then the autumn equinox will have passed.

Ex-heeled. On Friday, October 25th, police entered the Greene Street Café in Soho, brandishing the establishment's *Voice* ad with its little photos of scheduled entertainers. They pointed out that there were three people in the picture of the High-Heeled Women. If those three women took the stage together that night, the police were going to padlock the place.

Greene Street does not have a cabaret license. Therefore, by law, only one performer at a time is allowed onstage. The next night, the police came back to make sure this law was being obeyed. The High-Heeled Women had been playing the Green Street Café for two and a half years.

Revealed. So Vito Bruno has a timely idea. Just incorporate the police into your work.

On Halloween, the former owner of Pizza-a-Go-Go threw his sixth Outlaw Party. Bruno's parties happen in illegal spaces—a Hudson River pier, for example, or a deserted stretch of Westside Highway. The invite is strictly word-of-mouth. And the arrival of the police is the much-anticipated highlight.

That night the site was an abandoned amphitheater in East River Park across from the projects. Hundreds entered through the broken wall at the back of the stage. Bruno had moved a whole sound system in, along with candles and a set of klieg lights. Someone dressed as a monk swayed in front of the turntables on the balcony, while others in more exotic costume danced through the rubble on the dirt floor. But once I'd taken in the concept and medieval ambience, I was ready for it to end. There's never a cop around when you need one. When I left at midnight, someone was announcing that this would be the longest Outlaw Party ever given. I suppose the police are busier than usual on Halloween, what with all the revelers. And crowded cinemas and folks standing two to a stage.

November 1985

■ ■ ■ Loisaida Talking Pictures

There's a scene in *Bubble People* where the spectral Jack Smith, looking like a drag queen biker, has a little encounter with the filmmaker Ela Troyano. "I am the Bubble Goddess," he intones, then pauses. "Tell me the truth. Has the camera started?" Close-up on his beads and beard and orange wraparound shades. "We can get better results if we're honest with each other, and you tell me when the camera has started. Depicting what a great actor I must be."

Just the sort of odd moment Troyano wants—where the movie artifice shows, the performer is not pretending, and she as the filmmaker is clearly just an equal participant. Someone tells Jack the take *has* started, and he begins to read a script—"skid-proof mayonnaise helps you enlarge the size of your breasts"—as Muzak plays, a man's head in grass-skirt headdress bobs into the frame a couple of times, and a soft off-camera voice repeats, "the angle of the bra." Jack claims his breasts are growing already. This scene has a weirdness and sparkle to it that can't be rehearsed, that remind me of performances I've seen in East Village clubs, particularly wow Cafe. It can only be improvised. It's very playful. Rapport and then some sort of energy build up between audience and performer—who may be sliding in and out of character. And suddenly you're watching something so inspired and ephemeral no one ever could have planned it.

Troyano's first two films—*Bubble People* (or *UUlua*) and *Totem of the Depraved*—are the closest things I've ever seen to film as performance, where someone is trying to do this from behind a camera. Which isn't to say that it always works. *Bubble People* is a Happening, excessive on every level: two unedited reels side by side, two projectors, two soundtracks. Performers carry scripts or improvise around exotic plastic sets, and they're all playing Marilyn Monroe, and they're mostly men. Jack

Smith and Phoebe Legere share the role of the Bubble Goddess. The film begins out of focus in big blurry splotches of color. Someone is reading to us about the war between men and women, how the women traveled together through the cracks in the wall. "Linked to each other, they traveled through time until She appeared." (That's Marilyn.) "And multiplied."

It's a wild vaudeville hippie mess. By choice. The aesthetic is to "transgress" formal filmmaking codes, and *Bubble People*—done in three days during 1982—is part of the current underground "cinema of transgression." Troyano placed her camera in the middle of a loft where there were four sets—a volcano, a classroom, a beach party, and a stage draped in lamé. She wanted the actors to choose their own sets and props, and the camera would pan. She wanted someone from the crew to enter the frame occasionally, holding two extended sticks, and the camera would zoom in to this new frame. She wasn't interested in doing a film where the director made all the choices.

Troyano has no prints of *Bubble People*, but it's not exactly in demand. I watched original footage projected over white drapes on a wall at Club Chandalier. There just aren't too many venues around for "transgressing" films—apart from the clubs. Last month at 8BC, I saw most of the three-night Downtown Film Festival, organized by Troyano and filmmaker Tessa Hughes-Freeland. This was not a Transgression Fest, but a place to see all kinds of movies that had fallen through the cracks. From this crowded cave, a place as far out of the mainstream as Millennium really looks like the establishment.

Troyano describes Millennium, a showcase for experimental film, as having "seventies minimalist structuralist concerns." (As far as I know, only films by the team of Bradley Eros and Aline Mare have "crossed over" from the Downtown Festival to Millennium.) Less kind is filmmaker Nick Zedd in *The Underground Film Bulletin*, a xeroxed 'zine he edits under one of his many pseudonyms. Here he promotes the Cinema of Transgression and rails against "pompous compounds of cinematic exclusivity" (i.e., the Collective for Living Cinema, Film Forum, and Bleecker Street Cinema), the likes of "Squat Theater, Films Charas, the Kitchen—totally mired in the past," and the "critical-myopia" of the press.

The goal of the all-but-invisible Transgressors is to shock, and the best-known perpetrators—Zedd and Richard Kern—rely on gore and gross-out. They've made what look to me like B movies, which don't exactly break new ground except that they're grislier and dumber than anything Scott B or Beth B ever did. And who says gore is shocking? Or the degradation of women? Isn't *that* the mainstream? Troyano, though, is fiercely supportive of these filmmakers and says this new underground has no one who can speak for it with understanding and sympathy, the way the sixties underground had Jonas Mekas. The shock in her own work is in her anti-illusionism, her impulse to blur gender distinctions, her choice of performers ("people like Phoebe Legere shock people and they don't even mean to"), and her willingness to relinquish some directorial control to them. It's an approach different enough to have sparked a struggle one night at Danceteria when Nick Zedd tried to pull *Bubble People* off the projector—scratching the Jack Smith section—because he thought it was "too arty."

On the last night of the Downtown Film Festival, Uzi Parnes suddenly went berserk in dress, wig, and buzzsaw, attacking the smallest of three screens onstage (a sheet suspended from the ceiling) and reducing it to a ribbon. The slide show in progress was his and Troyano's— images of Loisaida, Rome, and club performers like Poppo and Ethyl Eichelberger flashing on each screen, including the one that was now a rag. Then Uzi lunged at the big screen with his saw. "I won't perform unless I can transgress," he said later. "One of the most delightful moments I've ever had was when people came up to me at the film festival—even Ela—and told me they thought I was really going to chop up the big screen. I was ecstatic." (Troyano, who'd rented the screen, hadn't been.)

Parnes, who was *Bubble People*'s main Marilyn, has collaborated with Troyano on her third film, *Loisaida Lusts,* on numerous slide shows, and on running Club Chandalier in the East Village. Transgression in a film, he said, meant "transgressing the reality of the script by making references to everyday life." He thinks this is characteristic of both club films and performances on the downtown circuit—what's left of it. "Ethyl Eichelberger, for example," he said. "One of his most interesting moments is when he's transgressing from his character to his person." Another style common to the scene is putting some real figure in a hypothetical context.

This is what Troyano does in *Totem of the Depraved.* She wanted to work the way Warhol did in his films with Edie Sedgwick, and the plan was to pair Nick Zedd with three different partners and get them to do something in bed. The first was Gia Gamba, a young woman Zedd and Troyano had just met in a pizza parlor. "I wanted to mix the film with real life," Troyano explained, "so when somebody approached us and said, 'Hi, I know you,' I said, 'Great. Let's take her. That's an actress.' I think she was coming on to Nick. But the idea was to use whatever was happening."

Totem opens with Zedd talking to Troyano, who is behind the camera. "Where's Ela? Someone told me something about a film. I'm supposed to be playing a stud." Troyano said that she felt her choices in the film were to turn the camera on or turn it off. Her plan was to shoot one roll of each encounter, but Zedd sabotaged that immediately by leaving with Gamba before the first take was finished. He'd intimidated Gamba, and his Mr. Attitude persona never cracked. In the next encounter, however, we get the "real moments" Troyano was looking for, when Zedd encounters the musician Phoebe Legere and begins in his I'm-so-bored monotone, "You remind me of someone. A passive local singer." She laughs at him. "You smell revolting." She opens his shirt. "Show your pimples to the camera. What kind of sex do you like?" He looks dazed and mutters, "I have no preferences."

Zedd hated working without a script and insisted that Troyano film him and Phoebe reading a five-minute dialogue he'd written. It has all the emotional charge of two nonactors rehearsing a TV sitcom, while the improvised piece is funny and tense and shocking. In the last— and actually depraved—section of the film, he tells the blue-and-crimson-haired James Richardson that he'd like to be gay because women never make enough money to support him very well. But he's completely ill at ease with the patient Richardson and finally grabs a dog visiting the set and pretends to fuck it. The last thing we hear is the disgusted filmmaker telling him from behind the camera, "Kiss the dog. If you're going to insist on doing a bestiality scene."

Since Totem, Zedd has referred to Ela as "the late Troyano" in his Bulletin because she won't give him a copy of the film. He wanted to use it to apply for a grant, because it was "artier" than his own work. In fact, he always lists himself as its co-director. "He believes essentially in stealing. Being bad is part of his aesthetic," she explained, adding that she still backs him as a filmmaker.

Loisaida Lusts premiered unedited at the Downtown Film Festival. In this collaboration, Troyano and Parnes are trying to adjust their styles to each other. They have a script. Parnes even rehearses people.

It was a shock to walk in after the previous night's bloodbath and misogyny (Kern and company) to the sight of three old women fondling some young love-slave or art object or whatever he's supposed to be. (*Lusts'* plot is a bit opaque.) These are the Weird sisters, who have lived through the ages and are now on the Lower East Side making "kings" in the art world. "They're vampiristic in terms of constantly needing new art," Parnes explained. Later we see them dancing around some crunched-up garbage can in a rubble-strewn lot doing the *Macbeth* witch incantations.

While it's the most conventional of her films in its format, *Lusts* has a lush bordello texture and is populated with the usual unusuals. Principally Carmelita Tropicana, the alter ego of Alina Troyano, Ela's sister. Carmelita is one of the club scene's most thoroughly-realized personas, sort of a low-rent Carmen Miranda (no fruit), adept at improvising within her character. (Alina also plays Fernando, a butler who worships Carmelita and wishes to serve her.) Perhaps Troyano's films are so performer-oriented because she's been a performer herself—with Richard Foreman (*Rhoda in Potatoland*), in Michael Kirby's Structuralist Workshop, and most recently in wow's *Saint Joan of Avenue C.* And if Jack Smith has been her biggest influence as a filmmaker—along with Jacques Rivette and Russ Meyer—she's been informed just as much by Smith's performance work.

Some films happen without ever making it onto celluloid. I hesitate to call them "slide shows." Jack Smith was doing them in the seventies for an audience of practically nobody. Maybe folks thought it was "visual aids." Whatever you want to call these unrepeatable movies made on the spot, Troyano used to do them regularly at the Pyramid Club and in performance with musician John Zorn, usually showing three-dimensional objects, color transparencies, and homemade slides through several projectors at once and manipulating the images by hand.

At Chandalier one night (she and Uzi live over the club), Ela showed me a box of her materials: colored gels, little rubbery critters, a chain-mesh cigarette case, crystals, etc. A black cubism-descending-a-staircase image on the wall turned out to be a hunk of tape on a glass slide that she'd been manipulating in the projector: "You're just making a movie out of very simple materials." Troyano learned photography in the first place because of Jack Smith; she wanted to work with him and he needed someone to take the photographs for his slide shows.

She also appeared in a few of his slow-moving performance epics with titles like *Impacted Croissants of Outer Space*. Smith extracted a rich exoticism from the banal. His version of Ibsen's *Ghosts*—retitled *The Secret of Rented Island*—featured a cast of stuffed animals and one NYU professor seated in a shopping cart, with Smith doing all the voices. I saw him perform on a Christmas night around 1980 and remember most his mood—the irritation in which he arrived (an hour late), donned his trademark sheikgear, and began the hesitant rearrangement of props and exotic draperies. He played schmaltzy records. Limbo. Mambo. He threw talcum powder in the air—"dust of the desert"—then stared with displeasure at the spot it made on the floor. After more than an hour of this, he began to read some lines, but kept stopping to further rearrange. "Lines" weren't the point.

Troyano describes these performances as "visual art—not theater." She finds them beautiful and subtle. They have that go-with-the-bizarre-flow quality common to all her influences—Zorn's willingness to let his musicians change the direction of his piece (within his structure), Warhol's willingness to let a character like Edie Sedgwick get in front of the camera and be. Even the carnivals she remembers from her childhood in pre-revolutionary Cuba. There's a faith that something interesting is going to happen—you just don't know what it is yet.

Troyano described a performance she did at the Pyramid in 1983 that sounded much like her film work: James Richardson making a set. Ela and Uzi doing projections. Carmelita Tropicana and Holly Hughes cavorting in the background in pig masks. Nick Zedd reading from his journals, "something radical and disgusting" (as Parnes put it) about his breakup with Donna Death. And Jack Smith, wearing a lampshade, emerging to destroy the set, wrapping himself in it. Troyano remembered with admiration that he had destroyed it quite beautifully.

December 1985

■ ■ ■ The Queer Frontier

About a year ago, I watched Holly Hughes and another woman rolling around on the bar at Club Chandalier tearing most of each other's clothes off during the "Russ Meyer Tribute Night" Holly had organized. The all-woman crowd had just watched *Faster, Pussycat! Kill! Kill!*, and we'd been promised "killer go-go girls." The friend I was with said, as we were leaving, "Remember ten years ago when we were making those posters that said 'Women Are Not Chicks'? Now we just went to something that proved women *are* chicks."

It gets confusing in that uncharted land where lesbians are trying to create something out of the nothing that is their birthright. And do it with verve instead of the sappiness that runs rampant in Womyn's Culture. There is, for example, simply no precedent for much of the work I've seen at WOW Cafe over the years—and not just because it often deals openly with queerness, female branch. What's fresh is the often playful improvisatory style. (I speculate that it's the old lesbian "community" ideal made usable as a basis for ensemble work.) Anything that injects new dimensions in queerness into the culture is vanguard labor, even when it remains invisible to the mainstream.

A couple of weeks ago, coincidence brought three different dyke-u-dramas to stages in the East Village within days of each other—work by Hughes, Carmelita Tropicana, and the team of Robin Epstein/Sarah Schulman. I've been acquainted with both Holly and Carmelita for a couple of years, so I'm a partisan observer of this scene on several counts. But what keeps me coming back is the energy of people who are publicly redefining the thing that labels them. "Not shrinking back from the word 'queer,'" as Hughes puts it.

Denizens of the "dumpster for love's leftovers" in Holly Hughes's *The Lady Dick* at WOW. Hughes is second from right. (© Dona Ann McAdams.)

"It's time for perverts to take a good hard look at themselves." That's Hughes. She thinks some of them are trying to get normal in the Age of Reagan. So the characters in her new play, *The Lady Dick* (currently at WOW Cafe), are brazen queers and hard-boiled ones at that. They hang out in a lesbian bar called the Pit that looks like the interior of a fish tank. ". . . a dumpster for love's leftovers. You bet it's crowded," growls Garnet McClit (Sharon Jane Smith), the "dick" of the title.

"I don't think the lesbian world is a beautiful place," says Hughes. *The Dick* creates a lowlife pulp fiction ambience with its Billie Holiday songs, butch/femme style, detective patter, and rapid-fire double-entendres. But there's no plot. And no crimes in this bar except the patrons' unnaturalness. These aren't the dykes who make it to the *Donahue* show. They wear society's contempt like a badge of honor, but it costs them. Cynics, backbiters, and braggarts—the assembled tough cookies argue and tell stories, insult and proposition each other. Sis-

Carmelita Tropicana prepares her classic chicken sushi during a "Cheet Chat Seis" at Club Chandalier. (Photo by Uzi Parnes.)

terhood is surly. Danger and claustrophobia radiate into the audience, trapped for the duration (like the characters) by the fact that the theater's door is onstage. *The Dick* ultimately felt too grim to me. But Hughes's writing is quite funny, which pulls it back from the precipice. This is the first attempt I've seen at a dyke theater of queerness, a play in the wicked and ridiculous spirit of Charles Ludlam, the Hot Peaches or Jack Smith.

"I don't know how to stand the fascination." That's Carmelita Tropicana assuming a lesbian world in the "Cheet Chat Seis" shows she hosts irregularly at Club Chandalier. Dancing in her flowered sarong, singing an off-key "You Light Up My Life" (her signature song), preparing her infamous chicken sushi, or interviewing "famous" guests, Carmelita is a Latin bombshell of great self-possession.

Her most recent show, spontaneous and improvised as usual, featured "people who sing, people who are in the rodeo, people who have long hair"—in other words, the "Great Women in Herstory." Carmelita had announced that it was "time for the womens to take over," and the audience was to choose a leader from among Annie Oakley, Nancy Sinatra, and other Greats (nearly all played by wow regulars). If it had actually come to a vote, I might have cast mine for Margaret Mead (Lisa Kron), who kept photographing the audience with an Instamatic ("Just act natural!") and asked someone if she usually *sat* in chairs ("I don't take anything for granted. It muddles the results").

This was a more informal "Cheet Chat" than usual, even eliminating the "controversial section" Carmelita likes to include, in which guests discuss current hot issues—like wife-swapping in the lesbian community or special friendships between nuns. Taboo presented as routine Merv Griffin fare.

"Go ahead. Adore me." Epstein on the Beach was the latest in the Adventures of Robin Epstein, who perhaps only *seemed* to play the same character this time as last (in *Whining and Dining*) because of the nonacting acting style this company favors. Parts of the show were quite funny—especially a parody of *Quarry* which managed to recreate and mock many of the visual high points of Meredith Monk's classic within a few minutes. But the gist of its story—that "hypocrisy is the spice of life" and lesbians will sell out as fast as the next person—made it the most cynical of these three pieces. (It was also the most conventionally made.) "No one is immune from what's happening now politically. The gay community is depoliticized, and there's a push to assimilate," explained Sarah Schulman, who co-wrote the play. She describes the work she's done with Epstein as "community theater." In the two productions I've seen, it's also a theater in which everyone outside is the enemy.

A risky "Dyke Theater" which transcends this defensive position is more to my taste. The territory Hughes and Tropicana have started to carve out—rude, wacky, politically incorrect, sleazy, and overtly sexual—is a place where lesbians, suddenly confident in their inappropriateness, are allowing themselves to roam for the first time.

December 1985

■ ■ ■ Disenchanted Evening

Often these goddess events happen at some ungodly hour like five in the morning, as determined by the relationship between earth and sun and the Farmer's Almanac. But this year winter solstice fell at a sane moment, 5:08 P.M. Donna Henes, urban shaman and ritual artist, mused later that perhaps that's why everything went wrong.

Henes assured me that every solstice event was a test. She said that hours before the police arrived. Back when we were still on a yellow school bus, decorating ourselves with tinsel, glitter nail polish, and white lipstick. We were an hour behind schedule at that point. The "tranceportation" had been stuck in Brooklyn, unstartable in the bitter cold, and some would-be celebrants had already bundled off to warmer pastures. In defiance of rational thought, I huddled in the Bowling Green subway station with the other die-hards, not knowing what to expect, and wondering how much of a fool I was for joining this beach excursion on one of the coldest days of the year.

Suddenly the school bus rattled up and Henes stepped out in white-face, white jumpsuit, white wool hat with white bangles, white boots, orange and gold accessories, with four small woven bags around her neck. "We had to jump-start it," she announced. No signs of winter suffering here, and she didn't even have a coat on. The two friends I'd brought along agreed with me later that at this moment we knew it was going to be good. We didn't know how we knew that. We climbed on board and began to pin sleighbells to our coats.

Henes was philosophical about the fact that we'd probably still be en route when the Solstice Moment arrived. She'd just been reading Buckminster Fuller—the part where he points out that species grow extinct because of overspecialization, while survivors adapt to their

circumstances. As *we* would. When the bus rolled into the Staten Island Ferry, its innards like a big orange car wash, we were 13 women
glittered up and ready to go.

From a stack on the front seat, we each grabbed a long cardboard
tube daubed in fluorescent color and walked to the tongue of the boat.
Gliding hard through a fierce bitter wind, everyone raised her tube.
"WHAT ARE WE CHANTING?" I yelled to a friend. "YOU MAKE IT UP!" she
yelled back. I tooted some noises into the gale. A few drivers who'd
come up to the front for the ride quickly retreated. Sunset in Antarctica.
With 13 tinseled women chanting over it.

As we bounced off the ferry, someone proclaimed it "4:56 Staten
Island time." All my glitter had blown away. A bag of noisemakers
circulated through the dark bus, and one woman set up a snare drum
that filled a whole seat so we'd be ready for the Solstice Moment. Then
suddenly we had arrived. At Fort Wadsworth, U.S. Army. We were
lost, and the Moment was upon us. The bus shook with our noises as
we began to circle the blocks. Circling was appropriate to the solstice,
one celebrant pointed out.

So we stopped at a pizzeria for directions, then a liquor store, and
noisily advanced. South Beach turned out to be one of those urban
deserts festooned with signs like "Water Polluted" and "No Picnick-
ing," with a great view of Brooklyn. We all carried the wine and
noisemakers and rotting, nail-infested boards from the school bus and
found other women and men waiting for us on the beach. They'd
passed the time by constructing an altar of found objects—kewpie dolls
and driftwood.

We built the bonfire near the altar, and Henes lit ten flares along the
edge of the water, one for each year of her solstice celebrations. Soon
a healthy blaze burned into the cold, and she began chanting to the
beat of the snare drum: "Rev-er-ence, rev-er-ence, rev-er-ence to Her,"
invoking "the female forces in the universe present in all people."
Some chanted and some danced and some clapped their noisemakers.
This was supposed to go on for a while, till all the wood, then all the
fire had died. While it still roared, we were given little packets that
would color the flames. Henes tossed the first one, saying, "To that
power which exists in all beings: survival. Reverence to Her."

Moments later we heard a noise behind us—two dirt bikers, one flat
on the sand next to his capsized bike. Henes and several others ran

over to ask if he was all right, and this seemed to propel him to his feet. He looked through us as though we were ghosts and rode off with his pal. We wondered later if perhaps they had called the police.

Because there was just enough time for someone back at the fire to figure out how to pull the pot of mulled wine from the heat with a long stick, for Henes to begin ladling it, when the New York City Park Rangers popped up behind the crowd. "Who's responsible for this fire?" one of the Smoky Bears demanded. Henes came forward. "I need to see your ID," he said. She had only what she'd brought in the little bags around her neck—"her entire identity," as she told me later. But pictures of her family, personal artifacts, and amulets of past solstice events would not satisfy the Ranger's thirst for ID, so she told him she had none. Someone showed him a flyer for the event and explained that winter had arrived at 5:08 P.M. "You need an open flame permit," he replied. "Someone has to get a summons." He asked the people documenting the event to turn their spotlights on his ticket-writing book.

Back in 1975, nine cars of law enforcement officers—federal, state, and city—had descended on the first of these celebrations and forbidden Henes to light the fire. So in '76 she got a permit. She said the head of the Cultural Affairs Commission told her that two hundred years ago she would have been burned at the stake. Then in 1981 she was arrested in Los Angeles on the autumn equinox for "defacing public property." Specifically, for hanging orange streamers with the word "peace" in all the UNESCO languages from light poles in Pershing Square.

Two more Rangers had arrived from the opposite direction. To surround us, I realized. Then a celebrant tossed more wood on the fire, and this sent the guy writing the ticket into an authoritarian tizzy. "Put it out!" he bellowed. A woman explained that if the fire burned into ashes, it would blow away, biodegradable, and wouldn't leave any garbage. "NO!" he shouted, and grabbed the shovel Henes had brought to cover the embers. A woman in the crowd called for everyone to grab a handful of sand and throw it on the fire, so putting it out could become part of the ritual. The Ranger began stomping and kicking at the boards, showering sparks all around us, while Henes and others chanted "Peace on earth! Peace on earth!" When he finished, he told her she could just mail in the $125 fine. "But I'm not guilty," Henes said. She told him she had a permit at home. "Merry Christmas!" the Ranger replied and walked off with his little squad.

With the fire gone, it was unbearably cold. I couldn't feel my feet anymore. As we headed for the school bus, one of my friends observed that the world wasn't really designed these days for "sacred events." Especially if they were just appreciations of the calendar and the natural world and the facts of life. "Yeah," someone remarked. "Winter is here."

January 1986

▪ ▪ ▪ Big Bang Theory

Universe Viewed as Sea of Bubbles
—*New York Times* headline January, 1986

T he little pink pig steps daintily off the stage to sniff, first my foot, then the other feet cramped into lotus positions. Piglet tugs at its white leash and harness. I barely note the white-clad performer who's just crossed the stage on his back, holding that leash, because a woman in black swimsuit to his right is "bouncing" eggs. Hard. The front row dodges the splatter that continues when— all her eggs broken—the woman dives into the gook and slides. At the back, a naked woman rises from a silver tub. Here in the center piece of *A New Model of the Universe*, the blueprint for the future is not clear. But the contradictions are.

Poppo works with contradiction at every level of performance. That's why he'll stage cosmic spectacles in rubble-strewn lots or ramshackle spaces on the Lower East Side. That's apparently why he calls his mostly female troupe "GoGo Boys." That's why he sends a clean pig onstage to be the crowd pleaser while a nuisance performer scrambles eggs out into the audience. This is more than a theater of images. Poppo's work suggests alchemy, the process of purifying, perhaps transcending contradiction.

Poppo Shiraishi was trained as a Butoh dancer, though he adds on his press release that he's "shamanized people with his mysterious power." His performances at the now defunct 8BC were like neighborhood religious rites, the last of them, *Eternal Performance*, drawing some 1,500 people (police estimate) on its final night.

Model of the Universe, staged at the CUANDO Community Center off the Bowery, started out looking almost normal, like some post-

Transcending contradiction: Poppo (right) in *A New Model of the Universe*—with "go-go boys." (© 1986 Massimo Agus.)

Cunningham movement piece (however heavily influenced by tai chi and yoga), but looking whited-out nonetheless. The powdered bodies. The BVDS for costumes. The snowy drop cloth over the stage. This (feminine principle, lunar) in contrast to the near-naked performers painted metallic gold at the end (masculine principle, solar).

In the alchemical universe, the integrated personality is androgynous or hermaphroditic. Poppo danced his first solo in a stiff ruffled skirt, and danced it like it was his last. Holding tension in the bow of his body, then hurling himself at the stage. Leaving a streak of white makeup from his head at my feet. Balancing off his classicism with risk. At the end of the performance—with metallic dancers carrying wooden beams for the night's final polarity—Poppo seems to have painted even his eyeballs with gold, a riveting, revolting image.

John Gernand, stage manager/production consultant for last weekend's spectacle, explained that the performance was supposed to build to a *shotai* state. This Butoh term means the performer's superficial qualities are stripped away. "You see the core of his being," as Gernand put it. Just so in alchemy, which was never really about turning rocks into nuggets but about spiritual transformation, revealing or releasing the gold "immanent in all things" (per mythologist Joseph Campbell).

Poppo apparently doesn't want to discuss what's revealed. And true to form, current and ex-associates contradict each other in explaining his silence. Poppo is either: (a) not verbal; (b) unable to speak English; or (c) unwilling to explain himself. Clues in the program notes hardly make these rituals less cryptic. Last weekend's performance was "a ceremony of prayer for the internal and external in the human being, and at the same time, for the perpetual innocent play of infants." (Hymns courtesy of Damage, hardcore band "of instinctive vibration.")

Goals this grandiose recall Jan Fabre, whose theater of perpetual menace, *The Power of Theatrical Madness*, swelled through on a sea of world tour hype just weeks ago. *Power* was a pretentious criticism of pretension, too formalist, too nihilistic, too militaristic, to compare to Poppo, who has simply decided to change the entire universe without forgetting to amaze us.

March 1986

■ ■ ■ Bad Company at the Love Club

A friend assures me that if I visit EPCOT Center in Florida, I can tour a science exhibit while being tortured by giant Mickey Mouses. This she calls "the second-best kitsch thing to do in America." And it sounds like a multimedia experience, too. But if I never get there, at least I have the *Bad Music Videos* option, now that the program has become a regular feature at the clubs and on cable TV. I mean it's an option if I want a taste of the weirdness out there that's passing for normal.

Last Wednesday, Industrial Strength Productions came to The Love Club to tape the show's second episode. I arrived just in time for the Karen Carpenter tribute—a video "done to her after [pause] she croaked," Karen Finley explained. Carpenter died of anorexia, and Finley urged us to "look at her thin face." The camera crew panned from Finley and co-host Carlo McCormick to the large screen. Here the puppetlike Carpenter sang a medley of her hit, "Close to You," in a set built from all the colors of Jell-O.

We in the studio audience hooted with pleasure. It was transcendently bad, spliced full of pix from the family album (Carpenter meets Miss Piggy, etc.). Cut back to the Jell-O where men in Beatle bangs and white suits—the "band," I guess—swayed among the giant letters "Y," "O," "U." Carpenter herself sat in the crook of the "U," as though trapped already in the cutest circle of hell.

Bad music video is a natural in the clubs, where so many performances have worked the post-television vein, mining the "ironic richness of banality." In contrast to the electronic product (which at least aspires to slickness) and the careful on-air packaging that usually surrounds it, veejays Finley and McCormick are appropriately crude and unrehearsed.

In her own shocking performances, Finley charges through the gross forbidden subtext of everyday life, spewing obscene detail about child molestation, turds, venereal warts, the rapist's desire. It's breathtaking, the way a kick to the gut is. Naturally Finley applies to bad video some of this penchant for telling the awfullest truth.

For example, we watched Philip Michael Thomas journey through the Land of Cheap Special Effects, carried by women in bikinis. He wiggled his torso, lines radiating nimbuslike from his head. "Ooh, he's God!" yelled Finley. When it was over, she concluded, "I think what he's talking about really is that he wants his nipples touched." Moving right along, we saw this stoo-pid Mink DeVille number, weighted with punky clichés. Willie DeVille, strangely unconvincing as a street tough, was kept from his girl by her brother. Finley suggested that they could have improved that tape by adding an incest scene. Comments like this are a public service, really—making visible what's there, like the graffitists who outline penises subliminally suggested on subway ads.

John Cale had canceled out as the evening's Special Guest Star, and just as well. In "tribute," they were playing his bad video, a work so inept it looked like a parody. "There gonna be some changes made," growled the ex-Velvet-gone-Velveeta. He paced awkwardly among crudely choreographed dancers. Animated money fell down behind an animated car. A man's family disappeared from around him while they watched TV. Then three boys had a pillow fight. There's nothing worse than an impoverished surrealism.

Substituting for Cale was performance artist John Kelly, "doing a bad music opera just for us," as Finley put it. Kelly sang an aria from *La Gioconda* in Italian gibberish and his startling soprano. In his own work, Kelly wrings subtlety from these overwrought opera moments, but in the evening's "bad" context the piece was rarified schmaltz.

Seldom is the Bad taken seriously enough, given how much of it there is. A bit of good Bad, for example, rises above bad Bad with its sincerity, inappropriate emotion, and awkward execution. In their first program, Finley and McCormick presented a classic example of the form—David Bowie and Cher longing for each other through clouds of colored smoke. "Take it and ride," they sing. It's the midseventies. Bowie's familiar smugness and Cher's unfamiliar pageboy stroll through an atmosphere of pathos rendered even more absurd by the passage of time. No doubt the Pia Zadora/Jermaine Jackson tape that followed will someday surpass even this effort and become pure camp. Pia, super-cool in glasses that resembled a damaged hunk of plastic, provoked shrieks of appreciative laughter. Things can only get worse. And do. "Pia is a bad name," Finley mused. "It makes me think of pee. I'm crossing my legs now because I have to pee."

The night after *Bad Music Videos*, I caught the infamous purveyor of Bad Taste, Divine, playing the Ritz. What a disappointment. Divine tooled that rotund body around the stage in the usual tortured wig and glitter face, palpitating with self-hatred and hostility toward the audience. But perhaps he just hates the hack work that drag has become for him. "You wanna fuck me, don't you? How big's your dick? . . . I'm so fuckin' beautiful, I can't stand it." He tossed sweaty napkins into the crowd, whose hands reached up to him as if he were B-R-U-C-E. Proof that an orgy of self-loathing can be as compelling as one of self-love. Most scary was seeing someone this weird be mediocre, without the sincerity to be Bad in a *good* way.

April 1986

■ ■ ■ Help Thou Mine Unbelief

Dollars smell funny when they burn—all too suitably like burning sweat. But the "Reverend" Mike Osterhout thought they smelled wonderful. Gussied up in a black suit and dozen or so gold necklaces, he stood inside the door of Darinka greeting his parishioners. "Burn that little green man," he directed. I stuck a dollar bill into the flame and watched it curl into ashes in the offering box, an anti-gift, the price of admission at The Church of the Little Green Man.

The Church lasted for three inglorious weeks during The Holidays, three Advent services without manger or magi, and most of all, without beliefs. At the last of them, four shopping days before the birth of Our Lord, the Rev and the other performers were dishing up theologies both anti- and quasi-. Lo, those who spend their holidays in the Slough of Despond are tempted to sup at the Trough of Cynicism.

When the Reverend took the stage with his church band, the Workdogs, he said he'd heard rumors—"that we are a mean church, mean to our congregation, mean to the performers. . . ." Cries of "NO! NO!" rose from the parish. "And the only way we can react to this is by arming ourselves," he drawled in a Southern accent, no doubt a quasi one. He pulled a twenty-gauge shotgun from its case, as pious organ chords punctuated the moment. The gun was of surprisingly little help in getting the worshippers on their feet for the first hymn, but when half of us stood up it was good enough for the Rev. The three Workdogs swung into "Amazing Grace," and we sang along to the words in our church bulletin: "Amazing Bag, how sweet the stuff/that saved a wretch like me/I once was found but now am lost/could see but now can't see. . . ."

Already a miracle had been declared, as a bottle of champagne sitting among the Workdogs had apparently uncorked itself. To that a few folks muttered matter-of-factly, "Miracle, miracle." Several performers seated in the audience would be coming forward to do "ceremonies." The first of these, Brother Bob Berens, read a quasi-poem (quasi-beatnik) about a previous service and displayed a little green monster or perhaps frog he said had appeared to him while writing it. Even this cheap and useless miracle got a few "hallelujahs" from the crowd. Surely, it's a struggle to make unbelief mean something.

The Reverend showed us the Hand of God he had at the lectern, a big plastic fist on a spring. Gonna be a long sermon tonight, he warned. We booed. Osterhout once studied for a year at a seminary—as an art project, he said. He slipped into the preacher's cadence that sharpens, then softens as it carries a congregation between heaven and hell. This sermon, though, carried us from insult to insult on a wave of poetic nonsense: ". . . you are the squirrelies, the mistakes, the congregation of despair, the helpless pee-splashers who stare at nothing at the Palladium in the delirium. . . ." A collective yelp of approval rose heavenward when it ended. We were by this time at least fifty strong—that's sro at Darinka—and the Rev, warming to his venom, turned to the Workdogs. "Should we humiliate someone now?"

There would be time for that later. First we had some testimony from Brother Gary Ray, who told us he'd been disturbed. He didn't feel right. He'd seen our disbelief. He tried to get someone to come up and get saved. No one budged. He even offered a "special Savior gift." No one stirred. He implored us. Just one of us! Finally someone in the crowd called out, "What's the gift?" The Brother admitted that it was a mimeographed sheet about gum disease. "Doesn't anyone have gum problems out there tonight?" That did the trick. A sinner came forward.

"It's a miracle," intoned the Reverend, who then plucked from our midst both a Saint and a Scapegoat, equally coveted titles in this crowd. To the Saint went a gingham surplice, or perhaps, more accurately, an apron. To the Scapegoat went one of the Reverend's necklaces, and to us a reminder: "Make fun of her tonight; don't let her down."

Certainly, no two unbeliefs were alike. Karen Finley did a ritual with a McDonald's box she'd brought back from Brussels. She'd seen a few "miracles" over there, and tried to set the McRelic ablaze to illustrate that "God is everywhere." It wouldn't burn.

As Osterhout announced the finale, an exorcism by Tommy Turner, a nervous nerdy guy began approaching the stage. The Rev told him he had the wrong church, that the Presbyterians were right down the street. Then Osterhout began singing about the Lord in his Oldsmobile and Mary peddlin' her ass, and again the nerd approached the stage, saying he wanted to "help." "Where's the security tonight, boys?" asked the Rev. "Insurrection vibes here." The guy was acting real twitchy and then began chanting "nam myoho renge kyo" over and over, standing in front of the stage. "Tommy!" called the Rev. "We need an exorcist up here tonight."

Was this a setup? Suddenly Turner was there in his black robe and death mask doing dueling chants with the guy, saying *he'd* win because he was in league with the devil. Turner's chant went: "Mighty phallus, lowly twat, infestation of bodily rot. . . ." One could hope that the two chants would cancel each other out in their mutual inanity. After a few moments of this drama in front of the stage, a big smoke bomb went off, filling the little club with a bilious gray, while Turner and some compatriots near him leaped in the air, shrieking at the nerd, who began to back out with his arms over his face, as if posing as the Unbeliever in a Sunday School bulletin. It was a setup, all right.

"Such a beautiful note to leave the church on tonight," the Reverend declared. "Reminds you of when you were a kid, doesn't it? Christmas was like this at my house."

January 1987

■ ■ ■ Nightclubbing

I
t started before midnight with a ragged little rally directed at the park faithful—the unlucky, the unruly, your tired, your poor. Near the entrance at 8th Street and Avenue A, a plump balding man in tie-dye exhorted about a hundred punks, politicos, and curious neighbors through a tinny speaker system: "Yuppies and real estate magnates have declared war on the people of Tompkins Square Park!" Fliers from the Emergency Coalition Against Martial Law covered a card table nearby, and a young man in black clothing and beret waved a black flag stapled to a cardboard tube. The cops were going to shut the park down as they had every night that week. I overheard some talk in the crowd from neighbors who thought it *should* be shut. *The crime here . . . the noise,* some guy explained to a companion. The grim cops at the gate, the chants of "Die Yuppie scum!," the M8os exploding deeper in the park—all added to the aura of latent violence. Even so, who could have predicted the police riot to come within the hour—complete with cavalry charges down East Village streets, a chopper circling overhead, people out for a Sunday paper running in terror down First Avenue. Running from the cops, who clearly regarded any civilian as a target.

At midnight in Tompkins Square, the motley demonstrators had begun trooping defiantly around the paths with their "class war" banners, returning on each swing past the officers lined up along the bandshell. Most nights, the bandshell is filled with homeless, but they'd been hoovered out to god-knows-where that morning. Now it was police headquarters—focal point for twelve vehicles including vans, eleven horses, and the long blue line. One officer shone his flashlight into the lens of every photographer who tried to get a picture—foreshadowing the more aggressive camera-shyness to come.

Protesters marched by, chanting that hell no, they wouldn't go. But they did go, of course. As soon as the mounted cops pranced out to Avenue A.

It was 12:30 Saturday night, a peak traffic hour on the avenue between Alcatraz, the Wah-Wah Hut, 7A, and the Pyramid—when, as a rule, the skinheads and spiky heads hang out at curbside, neighbors go to-and-froing, and the peddlers set their tattered goods out along the park. But on this night, people were lining the park between 7th and 8th as if waiting for a parade. I could see some protesters pushing on a squad car, jerking it a couple yards closer to 7th. I could see the mounted cops in a line near 7th and the rally "leaders" in the middle of the street at 8th, black flag and card table stuffed in a grocery cart. Fists in the air, they yelled, "It's our fuckin' park!" as another M80 exploded at someone's feet along the sidewalk.

Suddenly the cops had their riot helmets on and clubs out. Someone in front of a bar threw a bottle toward the mounted police massed at 7th Street, and the cops backed up. Protesters and onlookers milled around the avenue, while a long line of honking cars tried to make the turn off 8th. Protesters yelled "yuppie scum" at bewildered drivers. Three Hell's Angels drew cheers. Another bottle smashed on the pavement. And another. The mounted police backed up again. The foot patrolmen stood shoulder-to-shoulder at the park entrance. It was 12:50. Metal gates began to slam closed over the storefronts. Punks were jumping the fence, urging the crowd to follow. But apart from them, it was no longer clear who was protesting and who'd inadvertently walked into this mess or come outside to see what the hell was going on. By now the crowd numbered in the hundreds.

About 12:55, I heard an explosion and the mounted police suddenly charged up Avenue A, scattering the knot of demonstrators still in the street. I ducked behind a car. The policemen were radiating hysteria. One galloped up to a taxi stopped at a traffic light and screamed, "Get the fuck out of here, fuckface!" I walked toward 9th Street, unsure where to go. "Calm your men!" yelled a pedestrian to an officer.

At 9th Street, foot patrolmen in riot gear formed a line along the drive into the park. Across the avenue, some young men stood on the south corner screaming drunken taunts: "Faggot! Pussy! Koch's dogs!" I was on the north corner at a phone booth. I recognized two of the patrolmen, despite their helmets, as the two I'd spoken to just forty-five minutes earlier. Then, they'd told me courteously that they couldn't say why the park was being closed. Now, they were charging me with their clubs raised.

They couldn't be charging *me*.

I just stood there because I was the press and I was wearing my credentials and I hadn't done anything and this was my neighborhood and this was the phone I use to call my friend over there who doesn't have a buzzer and . . . "Run! Run!" screamed a tall young black man, taking me by the arm. "We gotta get outta here!" And I felt a billy club across my shoulder blades, the cop pushing me. Cop pumping adrenaline. Cop yelling, "Move! Move! Move!"

They were sweeping 9th Street and it didn't matter if you were press or walking home from the movies or sitting on your stoop to catch a breeze. You were gonna move. At First Avenue, I watched two cops on horseback gallop up on the sidewalk and grab a guy by his long hair, pulling him across the street between them. Minutes later, the same guy was down on the sidewalk in front of Stromboli's, bleeding.

The cops seemed bizarrely out of control, levitating with some hatred I didn't understand. They'd taken a relatively small protest and fanned it out over the neighborhood, inflaming hundreds of people who'd never gone near the park to begin with. They'd called in a chopper. And they would eventually call 450 officers.

By 1:30, I'd taken all the notes I wanted to take. I wanted to go home, so I walked back to Avenue A, where I was soon trapped, as were many others. "Can I cross the street?" I asked a policeman at the corner of 7th, showing him my orange press card.

"If you do, you're going to get roughed up!" he declared.

"If you do that, you're going to get some publicity you aren't going to like," I spouted back.

"Hey," he said, "you're trying to stereotype me!"

It had been a big night for absurdities.

Getting back to First Avenue took another half hour. And there, dancing around their grocery cart in the middle of traffic, were the so-called "leaders," bandanas pulled up over their noses so the police couldn't identify them. God. This was gonna take all night. I walked south. Then I heard screams. Cop attack.

Panic-stricken pedestrians ran down the sidewalks, as the cops galloped, clubs at the ready. I tried to duck into a restaurant. "No!" shrieked someone at the door, slamming it in my face.

I kept running.

The next day I walked up to Tompkins Square. It's a foul little park and a symbolic one. I've lived near it for 11 and a half years and have yet to experience a moment of tranquillity in its crummy confines. But I can tell you that the people who go there are, for the most part, the people who've always gone there. The old Ukrainian guys who play chess and the old ladies who go to sit down and the squatter kids, drag queens, Rastas, and junkies. As the neighborhood slowly, inexorably gentrifies, the park is a holdout, the place for one last metaphorical stand.

At the empty bandshell on Sunday, I noticed some posters pasted up by the political comic book *World War 3* and the Rainbow Soup Kitchen weeks before this curfew dispute began. The posters feature a quote from a former resident of the neighborhood: *The uneasy spring of 1988. Under the pretext of drug control, suppressive police states have been set up throughout the Western world.*—William S. Burroughs, *The Wild Boys*, 1969.

August 1988

■ ■ ■ The Triumph of Neoism

There at Chameleon Bar with the other beer drinkers, the neoists had assembled from across the universe—Baltimore, Berlin, Rivington Street. Maybe they numbered only fifteen or twenty. But they were hard core—those who wanted to destroy the existing order, those willing to announce "give me freedom or kill me," those who might wear flaming bread loaves on their heads.

It was the first day of their Millionth Apartment Festival, otherwise known as the APT Festival, otherwise known as the Anathema Party Takeover. Onstage, two artists had amplified a baby with a little mike. Baby cries sounded over the bar din: neoist music. Waiting to address the narrow barroom was Monty Cantsin (real name: Istvan Kantor), founder of neoism, member of the Rivington School, and "self-appointed leader of the people of the Lower East Side."

Any definition of neoism simultaneously reveals and conceals, because that is the goal—to get where "all mechanisms of logic are broken, control is impossible, the great confusion rules." Neoism dates from the late seventies—an ism that swallowed every modernist ism, then puked out the pieces. Jarry's pataphysics, Marinetti's manifestoes, Duchamp's readymades, Klein's leap, Warhol's fifteen minutes, Beuys's alchemy, Maciunas's games—they're all floating in the neo soup now. Neoism is the last little gurgle of what we once called avant-garde. Or maybe it's nothing.

I asked Monty/Istvan about his court appearance the week before. Last August he splashed six vials of his own blood across a wall at the Museum of Modern Art. In court, he said, they'd only given him a new date to appear. He'd intended the blood painting as a gift to the museum. He'd read a manifesto in front of it, protesting gentrification on the Lower East Side. He figured the citadel of modernism would understand such a gesture. "I thought they would leave the blood on the wall. But I was too idealistic." He'd spent two days in jail, one of them his birthday. A good birthday, he said. A good separation from the world.

Monty wore his characteristic uniform: breeches, skinny tie, leather jacket, red soldier's hat, badge with two-headed arrow (symbolizing the neoist slogan, "It's always six o'clock"). With this military look, he told me, he was able to irritate bohemian artists. Onstage, brandishing a flaming steam iron, accompanied on kohl drum by Gordon W. Zealot who had donned the ritual flaming bread loaf, Monty declaimed, "Art is nothing, art is dead, art is living, art is bread!" He cried out his warning that the authorities would soon eliminate urban society, a hiding place for terrorists, perverts, and drugs. No one seemed stirred.

"Monty Cantsin"—an "open pop star"—was a name, an identity, an idea invented in the late seventies by David Zack, a mail artist. Anyone could be Monty Cantsin. The name would then become famous, to the benefit of *every* Monty Cantsin. But the person most identified with the name is Istvan Kantor—construction worker, nurse, Canadian citizen, and native of Budapest. For this, Kantor/Cantsin has taken some neoflack in the neozine *Smile* ("Free to Shoplifters"). In a philosophy where nothing matters, it's funny what does matter.

He turned the stage over to tentatively a. convenience (Michael Tolson), who would introduce the videos. tentatively wore a suit made from dozens of zippers. A tattoo of a brain covered most of his shaved skull. He'd amplified the baby to get people's attention.

I felt a great nostalgia as the tapes began. In my fantasy of the avant-garde I never knew, people all over downtown Manhattan watched things like *Philosopher's Union Member* (by Emma Elizabeth Downing) in their unfinished lofts. I rather liked this footage of a woman's mouth painted in black and white zebra stripes, the mouth ranting about the blood of the lamb, the search for meaning through vulnerability, and other philosophical hoohah.

Most of the tapes were tentatively's. For example, some quasiporn he'd run at a peep show two weeks before anyone noticed. (Vegetables having sex and goofy people in monster masks, spliced with real blow jobs.) Then, a video of him boarding a London bus on all fours, wearing a dog mask, trying to ride free as a seeing eye dog. Most of the rest was tediously self-indulgent. During tentatively's taped document of every book and record he's ever owned, several drunken members of the Rivington School took the mike and began to chant the usual: "Fuck you! Die yuppies!" I went home.

So ended Flaming Wednesday. Next was Painful Thursday— Thanksgiving.

Up at the Stockwell Gallery on East 13th Street, twelve hours had been set aside for wasting time and for the writing of a collective book. I found Monty Cantsin writing alone on a giant newsprint pad on the floor. He'd hung finished pages haphazardly over the walls with red tape. On one of them, Monty had declared his intention to keep writing "even if nobody else comes." Here was true dedication to a philosophy of the false.

On Friday of the Millionth Apartment Festival, the neoists planned to make a monumental blood painting at Stockwell Gallery.

By the time I got there, though, mere anarchy had been loosed. And I had missed the police intervention.

It was about 10:30 at night, and Pamela Stockwell was dragging from her gallery the last of several big hunks of scrap metal, the purported instruments for that evening's concert of "booed music." She was quite agitated, the blue and green strands of her hair sticking out from the red. She said it had been too noisy, and she was glad that I'd missed the fight. The neighbors had freaked.

No, the noise was no problem, Monty told me. Some of the guys had been drinking beer on the street. That's all.

Everyone would tell me a different story. First disappointed that I'd missed the action, I soon realized that missing it was appropriate to the spirit of neoism. Now I would never know "the truth."

Stockwell complained that the Rivington School had wrecked the evening. (They'd been the scrap metal players, while the neoists had planned the blood painting.) I wondered if there was some split between the groups, but I'd noticed that Monty's attitude had always been that whatever happened happened. He belonged to both camps, and both shared the slogan, "Art is shit."

Inside the gallery, people stood talking, but a hostile wiggy energy bounced off the walls, where most of Monty's "collective book" pages had been covered with Rivington School graffiti. *Suckbutt. Die yuppies.* The usual.

"Smells like they're boiling a rat in here," said a friend who'd come with me, only half-joking. Someone was cooking on a hot plate, and I peered into the kettle. Eggplant.

Monty had had five doctors coming to draw blood for the collective painting, but they'd arrived when the police had, and they'd fled. There'd be no painting.

Whatever had happened at the gallery spilled into the next day, End of the World Saturday. Down at the Rivington School Sculpture Garden, about a dozen people gathered around a bonfire. Monty explained that what the Rivington School did with their sculpture, he did conceptually. I looked around at the tire treads, graffitied bathtub, rusted car parts, unidentifiable wreckage lifted right from the dumpster—all welded into something new and, on the whole, quite ugly. What is the Rivington School? According to festival propaganda: "a bunch of idiots . . . dirty and broke . . . terrorists, revolutionaries, alcoholics, stupid assholes, painters, construction workers, neoists."

Rivington School was the name of an atmosphere, according to its self-proclaimed "dean," Ray Kelly. Kelly dresses like a cowhand. He said, "We started the fight at the gallery as a performance. 'Make shit happen.' That's our motto." In the Rivist headquarters/welding shop next to the garden, graffiti covers the walls, the fridge, the tools, the canoe. The scrawls, like the space, are half frat house ("Beaver Club"), half holdout against suburban blandness ("I'm Too Intense to Die").

Back in the garden, Pamela Stockwell complained that the Rivington School had written all over her windows and personal possessions. That they were disrespectful. Disruption was their lifestyle. She'd been trying to support these outsiders and felt betrayed. Yet, when I left for Mars Bar with Monty Cantsin, she stayed behind while Ray Kelly threw some steaks on a grill over the bonfire. Later she would tell me that she *did* love them. Stockwell Gallery is a holdout too. She'd featured a group show of "attack art" after the riot, for example.

"You don't seem to agree with her that the evening was ruined," I suggested to Monty.

True. He didn't agree. "The people had been very excited to play their scrap metal music because this is music no one wants to hear." Besides, he said, the apartment festivals (which *were* held in apartments years ago) should be chaotic.

Neoists brandish flaming steam irons in Tompkins Square Park to end the Millionth Apartment Festival. (© C. M. Hardt.)

Back at Monty's apartment, neoist headquarters, Gordon W. Zealot was having dinner with Jack Smith, the forefather of Queer Theater, the auteur of *Flaming Creatures*. Smith turned his bony Sam Beckett head to us with a baffled scowl, but said nothing. He was wearing Gordon W.'s pearl necklace. Gordon W., I learned later, had been a Krishna monk in India for two years and currently lives in Toronto, where he works as a caterer. Other neoists drifted in, including tEN-TATIVELY a. cONVENIENCE, Stiletto, an avowed antineoist, and festival co-organizer Matty Jankowsky. In his studio lined with blood paintings, "Stop Misery!" posters, and other neo junk, Monty threw every steam iron he could find into a dairy case, preparing for the day's big event—the Flaming Steam Iron March into Tompkins Square.

I noticed that tENTATIVELY's brain tattoo was, in fact, meant to be 3-D, red lines right next to green lines. "You should be able to see it vibrate right in the middle," he directed as I looked through some 3-D glasses. And his zipper suit had been made by "midget undersea hermaphrodites," he said—giving me, the media, a colorful quote.

Furthermore, he hated *The Village Voice* and hoped I'd write something bad about him.

We all walked to Tompkins Square with the ten irons Monty had found. He'd forgotten the rest at the Rivington School, but, as it turned out, ten were enough, because after waiting half an hour for more participants to arrive, no one did. Monty started the backing tape on his beatbox and began to sing: "Every six minutes, we need new sensations. Every six minutes we need rock 'n roll." The other neoists stood chatting to one side, and a passerby asked me what was happening. "They're neoists," I said.

The man looked frightened. "Nihilists?"

Monty began to rant: "I believe in the power of the imagination to change the world, to release all the prisoners and abolish all oppressing systems for whom the most frightening idea is freedom!" And so on. But this seems to me to be the central message of neoism.

Monty distributed the steam irons, handing one to a dazed-looking park transient since there weren't quite enough neoists. He poured rubber cement over the bottom of each and ignited them. "Just walk peacefully," he said. They did, with Gordon W. on drum and Jack Smith on finger cymbals—sort of. The flames never lasted more than a minute. The motley parade kept stopping to relight, while a mutter ran through the passers-by: "Nihilists. They're nihilists."

A squad car was driving down the park sidewalk. A cop stuck his head out the window and asked me if I was leading this group. "No," I said. "It's just an art event."

"Is it gonna get violent?" asked the cop.

"They didn't plan for it to be violent."

"Okay. Okay. Just asking. Just asking."

Monty stopped at the Faith/Hope/Charity cupola and did some more songs. "Nothing stays forever/the skyscrapers will fall into ruins . . . the day will come/walls will tumble, blood/will overflow the streets." The squad car had turned, pointing its headlights at us. And the Rivington School had arrived. "What is the aim of art?" sang Monty. "Where are we going?" They did one last ritual steam iron flame.

"Fuck you!" Ray Kelly shouted, to end the festivities.

In confusion, they drifted apart, unable to reach a consensus on where to party. "These freewheeling people. You can't make plans with 'em," sighed Pamela Stockwell.

There with the dozen faithful, the curious, the hecklers, all lit by a squad car, I felt I had seen the triumph of neoism. For in a culture where it's increasingly difficult to find the margin, they had found it.

December 1988

■ ■ ■ Don't Make Me Over

laves of New York is the first eighties revival.

Out of sheer attitude, hairspray, and design, the movie recreates that electric moment before downtown "died." That moment in the mideighties when a thousand flashes in the pan flared up at once to illuminate the Global East Village.

Okay, I'm being simpleminded, but that's what nostalgia is all about. Like *Slaves*, I too can overlook the serious artists and dealers who emerged (most of them are now in Soho) and remember the teeny storefronts crammed with neobadness. The East Village was a toy version of the grown-up art world, where those who played were less *enfants terribles* than kids who wanted a slice of mom and dad's pie. And *Slaves* is less about artists than about a group of oddly dressed young entrepreneurs who use bohemianism to sell themselves. As J. Hoberman put it in his *Voice* review, *Slaves* itself is "less a movie than a marketing strategy." Perhaps that's only fitting in an age when consumer culture has replaced the avant-garde.

More product went on display last week at The Gallery on Bond Street: the real paintings by real artists featured in *Slaves*, yours for up to $20,000. Most of them had that funky East Village look, though only a few were by East Village names (Rhonda Zwillinger, Stephen Lack, et al.). Appearing in a film had given the pictures a sort of glamor makeover. Still bad (for the most part), they now looked perfect for a time capsule, some Museum of Downtown. They were the "real" bad thing. I got there early and listened to collectors call them beautiful, watched art lovers/scene lovers shoehorn into the space, big as five storefronts, claustrophobic as just one. Few people wore costumes bizarre enough to suit a bit player in *Slaves*, and I wondered if even those few hadn't been inspired by the film. The scene that once parodied the art world had now become a parody of itself.

Later that night I went down the Lower Worst Side to the place where "East Village art" began. ABC No Rio hasn't changed much over the past decade, though there's no longer a gaping hole in one wall labeled "rat poison." I arrived to find that no one had keys to the front door, so we all tottered into the basement, turned left at the black coffin (a prop? free of its vampire?), and climbed up into No Rio. There, a man apologetically collected two dollars, "if you have it." Eventually twenty-five or thirty people filled the scarred benches for *Guns and Guinness*, a reading—rather, a ranting—by Erl Kimmich and Darius James. Just before they began, the radiator suddenly spewed a stream of boiling water onto a straggler climbing up from the basement, and I couldn't help but think of *Slaves*, with its collapsing chairs and exploding pipes that constantly signified Starving Artist.

Guns and Guinness turned into one of those rough-hewn evenings that you lose all sight of in the Big Time. The poets read as they paced, drank, raved, lay on the floor, twisted themselves over the podium, and drank again. Erl Kimmich is white and lives in the South Bronx. Darius James is black and lives in Jersey. Already juiced up on Colt 45, Kimmich recited his rhymes about the greedy, the media, the usual. They were simple words on hard subjects, addressed with passion, and I was in the mood to see some art, which by my definition is connected with struggle.

Back and forth, pacing like a hothead, Kimmich chanted, "who will feed us?/we will, we will/who will teach us?/we will, we will/who will love us/we will, we will/who will house us?/we will, we will." Hours later, after the reading had degenerated into a half-drunk conversation with the few remaining spectators, Kimmich told me that that section was "the empowering message."

Darius James talked about his writing as a "magical practice." His best work addresses racism, with hair-raising effect, and he's been working for years on a project called *Negrophobia*. This is a text as ugly and gross as racism itself. He said he'd gone to New Orleans to read from it, but the audience there hadn't wanted to listen, wouldn't shut up. So he'd left the stage, then returned to try again with a bottle of brandy. He told me reading from it had never made him cry until that night in the South.

At No Rio, he chose to read instead some of the pornography he writes for a living, including *Penthouse*'s occult sex column, "Ask Dr. Snakeskin." He also delivered a work-in-progress about the trip to New Orleans, his first to the Deep South. He said the racism he'd encountered there was a different strain from the one he'd grown accustomed to. "You ain't on the Lower East Side where we keep our white folks in line and they know they place," he screeched. "With the former Klan Wizard running for State Rep and me going into my arrogant New York Nigger bag, I'm bar-b-que, dig, with tequila sauce flambay. 'Feets,' I say, 'don't fail me now.'"

I got home just in time to catch Tama Janowitz on the Letterman show. Dave was asking Tama if she'll get "a piece of the action" from Bloomingdale's *Slaves of New York* boutique. She avoided answering, but she indicated that she wasn't really rich. Then she mentioned in passing that the clothes in the movie had been based on thrift-store items. The originals, in other words, had been secondhand.

It reminded me of something critic Edit DeAk had written when artists first opened such "anti-spaces" as ABC No Rio. The artists were idealistic, political, and young, and they'd acquired ABC No Rio, for example, by breaking into an abandoned city-owned storefront and installing what they called "The Real Estate Show," aimed at "celebrating insurrectionary urban development." They didn't know it, but they'd tapped into a capitalist mainline they wouldn't be able to control as it led the neighborhood toward gentrification and spilled into Bloomie's. Now DeAk's words come back to haunt: "We are prospectors of slum vintage. We have taken your garbage all our lives and are selling it back to you at an inconceivable markup."

March 1989

■ ■ ■ Just Revolting

Nowadays the East Village seems peopled by ghosts. And it's small comfort to imagine the spirit of beatnik, digger, and yippie flickering through the polished new condos.

In April, the city swept two more squatters' buildings from a fast-disappearing Loisaida. In May, Allen Ginsberg and William Kunstler showed up at a squatters' benefit. Ginsberg triggered a spontaneous sing-along clap-along, creating instant community. We were a tribal gathering of antigentrification holdouts. But it's a short road from utopia to dystopia. Days later, the rock band Missing Foundation roused a crowd to burn garbage and throw bottles in Tompkins Square—bringing "Steal This Park," an all-day Abbie Hoffman memorial, to a sad conclusion.

Missing Foundation comes right out of the old street-brawling tradition, touched with a bit of Dada, as in "Life must hurt—there aren't enough cruelties" (Richard Huelsenbeck, 1918). Anti-art always had this dark sardonic edge, but there's no mockery at all in what MF does.

The day of the "Steal This Park" memorial, organizers temporarily displaced the homeless who camp in the Tompkins Park bandshell—so folks could get up onstage and talk about housing. Such are the ironies in the neighborhood today. The show began with Baron Von Blumenzack's political skit about a squatter hero who battles cartwheeling cops to the tune of "Kung Fu Fighting." Four real-life foot patrolmen watched from the periphery. Out on Avenue A, the homeless formed a long line at a truck handing out lunch—rolls, sandwiches, potato salad.

I never quite figured out the point of this event, which became a parade of neighborhood bands. Between sets, we were urged to think politically, to perhaps form a Green Party. We were the real motley crue—ripped leather, bandanas on the dogs, and nothing vaguely like a Banana Republican. Most of the bands had a studied cool. I felt like I'd seen it all before, like I was watching the young do their oldies acts. Or was it just my 'magination? Every tic and grimace in rock seems learned to me now. Life is so cycle-delic.

Missing Foundation was scheduled to close the show. They were both the newest and the oldest of acts: New as going one up on the Sex Pistols' "NO FUTURE" pronouncement. Old as the cavemen slugging it out around a fire. During a year-long hiatus from performing, the band had grown more and more infamous. Real media monsters. Channel 2 ran an idiotic "special report" last winter blaming them for the Tompkins Square riot. And some people standing behind me at the bandshell relished the rumor that MF had been accused of blowing up a fire extinguisher at the Christodora Building.

So the MC didn't introduce them by name. Just told us to "act natural" for the "mystery band." But I think most of us knew who we were expecting when, just before 10 P.M., a black banner unfurled across the back of the bandshell: "Liberty Under Siege" it read, with MF's upside-down cocktail glass logo ("the party's over") painted on. For the first time that day, a coterie of demonstrators appeared at the back of the crowd, holding another banner: "End Police Brutality and Racism." By this time, maybe three hundred people had gathered, all electric with anticipation.

Peter Missing tossed cans of spray paint from the stage, along with copies of the MF poster/declaration: "We will not act civilized in this fucking city." Then he shouted into a bullhorn, "Welcome to the United States of America! Love every fucking minute of it!" He wore a red T-shirt and dog tags and a backwards baseball cap. He banged on some scrap metal while three band members pounded drums, one crunched in on guitar, and another slammed a lead pipe against a steel plate. Fireworks exploded here and there in the crowd, which began moving convulsively. I could see someone circling through with a rope, pushing and corraling people at the center. Garbage can lids sailed at us from the stage, then more explosives.

I saw a trash can emptied at the center of the crowd. Peter Missing shouted through his bullhorn, but I couldn't hear the words. Somebody lit the trash. Perhaps twenty people were now holding the rope, whipping through the center of the esplanade in front of the bandshell.

From behind them, a man hurtled an empty liquor bottle at the stage. It came hurtling right back. More trash cans were dumped and heaved through the air, to the accompaniment of breaking glass. It felt dangerous, riotous, ludicrous. Again, somebody lit the garbage.

The crowd dwindled quickly to its hard core. The band played for just fifteen minutes—then the sound man decided to unplug the system and haul his board off to safety. Though the band had stopped, it didn't matter. The audience had taken control of the show. Up in front of the stage, a dozen people jumped in unison on the big steel plate. Ten or twelve others stood around the burning debris, hitting the overturned trash cans with anything they could find. (A chain. A stick. A garbage can lid.) Someone ran up into the bandshell and spray-painted "Mug a Yuppie" across the back. Some sprayed doodles across each other's shirts.

The banging went on for half an hour. No police in sight. No band members in sight. Here was a performance that attacked human failings with more failings, that showed us how bad things were by making them worse. Who were they punishing? The three music fans I found later in front of Leshko's holding towels to their bleeding heads? Nothing like bringing more carnage into a war zone.

And then it all ended as if by some mysterious signal. Peter Missing walked into the dying fire, kicked at some burning crud, and suddenly all those who'd been pounding and flailing drifted off quietly into the night. The trash cans lay smoking. Garbage was everywhere. A squad car that had crept up the path near the bandshell moved away.

Stretched out on a park bench was an old, homeless black woman who'd been displaced from her spot in the bandshell for this. She'd slept through all the cacophony, not fifty feet from the stage. I realized that she'd been there all day, waiting for the show to end. And I thought of William Kunstler reading one of Ginsberg's poems at the squatters' benefit: "Hearts full of hatred will outlast my old age."

June 1989

■ ■ ■ **Regenerate Art**

■ ■ ■ Unspeakable Practices, Unnatural Acts

The Taboo Art of Karen Finley

A raw quaking id takes the stage, but at first you don't notice since she's wearing an over-the-hill Sunday school dress or a Sandra Dee cocktail party outfit and she's stepping shyly to the mike looking nervous. But then her pupils contract as if she's disappeared inside herself. She's slipped into that personalized primeval ooze now and the floodgates fly open in a loud declamation: "*No, Herr Schmidt, I will not shit in your mouth, even if I do get to know you. . . .*" Or, "*I go down on that ass with my mouth, my penis still kinda high and hard and I suck suck suck my own cum outta your butt juice with a little bit of yum yum yum yum yum baby liquid shit mixed up with that cum, baby. You can jerk off on my pancakes anytime.*" She might be stealing the male voice like that. Might be spitting on the stage. Tearing at her taffetas. Smearing food on herself. She might say or do anything up there. Onstage, Karen Finley represents a frightening and rare presence—an unsocialized woman.

Finley performs on the club circuit, wafting on to the stage in her polyester good-girl getup at one or two in the morning to wail like some degenerate apparition about incest, priests' assholes, the cum on the bedpost, bulimics up-chucking in their stilettos. The fuck-and-shit vocabulary draws shrieks, back-talk, occasional hysteria from the rowdy drunk crowds. But Finley says, "I'm really never interested in the sexual point in my work. I'm really interested in the pathos." In fact, her monologues are obscenity in its purest form—never just a litany of four-letter expletives but an attempt to express emotions for which there are perhaps no words. An attempt to approach the unspeakable.

Finley began performing in 1979 after her father's suicide. She'd been exclusively a visual artist before that, but "I had difficulty being alone and doing static work when I was feeling such active emotion."

Karen Finley in "Don't Hang
the Angel" at Poetry Project,
1985. (© Dona Ann McAdams.)

She's still working out of the emotional range she discovered in her
rage, the skinless panorama of taboo. She says the charge she gets from
performing balances the pain she feels about his death.

Deathcakes and Autism was an early performance piece based on the
events of her father's funeral, where everyone became preoccupied
with the food brought to the bereaved. "People were actually having
arguments over which ham to eat. Or saying, 'Was it much of a mess?
Did you clean it up?' while they were bringing in two dozen Tollhouse
cookies." In that disconnection between custom and emotion, Finley
felt she'd become autistic. When she returned to college, the San Francisco Art Institute, she felt an "incredible yearning" to spill it, to get
up and tell the awfullest truth in front of people.

The result is both fascinating and horrifying to behold, because audiences can't help but recognize their own most mortifying obsessions

in the fast-flowing bile. Finley rivets, but she doesn't entertain. There's no nonsense here about taking an audience out of itself and into the performer's world. Even an artist like Spalding Gray—whose work tells the ongoing story of his own life—uses an I'm-not-acting persona, removed at some level from a "real" self. Finley doesn't offer such wholeness; she presents a persona that has shattered, a self unable to put a face on things.

Finley told me once that she thought some women performance artists were getting more hard-edged, less subtle, while men were learning to be quiet, more contained and passive. Certainly women have no tradition of foul-mouthed visionaries, as men do—Céline, Genet, Lenny Bruce, et al. But at least women now have a sort of rude girl network that provides a context for outrageous work. Think of Lydia Lunch and that baby-faced dominatrix image so startling in the late seventies, or the obscene and sexually demanding narrator in any Kathy Acker story, or the oddball menace of Dancenoise (Lucy Sexton, Anne Iobst) onstage at 8BC swigging "blood" from coffee cans, tearing dolls limb from limb, shouting, "Give me liberty or give me head!"

Finley, thirty, grew up in the Chicago suburb of Evanston, the oldest of six children in a somewhat bohemian family dominated by strong and troubled personalities. Her father was a jazz drummer who would quit music periodically to sell vacuum cleaners. Her mother ran a sewing business out of their house and would involve the whole family in her obsession of the moment, which might be Wagner or Jungian psychology or health food. There was never much income.

There *were* lots of people passing through—musicians, customers, and people with problems whom her mother would "adopt." For a number of years, a deranged aunt would call them "sixty times a day. . . . So whatever was going on, the phone would be ringing, and she would come over to the house with bird crosses and she once tried to kill me with chairs. . . . We would have the police over at our house all the time." One of Finley's grandmothers believed Martians were sending radiation beams to the house, and when the family visited her, she sometimes had them wear little rubber hats for protection.

Finley began to "perform" as a teenager. Her favorite routine was to stage an epileptic seizure in front of a restaurant—or pretend to vomit—to see whether or not people would keep eating. Mostly, they would. Then, because she and her high school friends had read about Happenings, they created some of their own—again, hardly more than pranks, but like the traditional avant-garde, aimed at interrupting the decorum of everyday life. For example, they covered hallway entrances at school with aluminum foil and waited for people to burst through them. This was the early seventies, "the time of do-your-own-thing," as Finley put it, "so I just pushed it as far as possible."

No one ever discouraged these playful shock tactics. Today her mother is one of Finley's biggest fans. "She gives me pointers. If I'm in Chicago, she always helps me with my stage work. Actually she usually tells me she thinks I should go farther." In one of Finley's more shocking routines she pulls her pants down and smears canned yams on her ass and talks—in male persona—about sticking yams *"up my granny's butt but I never touch her twat, baby."* Even Finley's grandmother has seen this. "I'm really open. I tell people what I do." She showed me a "review" her grandmother had then written on some flowered stationery. "She thinks I'm talented but a toiletmouth."

One night last April at Danceteria, Finley suddenly appeared onstage around 1 A.M. in a tatty satin prom gown. For hours the stoned punky crowd had been juicing up on liquor, hard rock, and the tape loop of slash-and-gore film highlights playing on all the monitors. In her usual confrontational stance, Finley shouted, "You leather kind of folk with your spiked hair, I love to think about you masturbating!"

She told them how she was gonna put some peaches up her cunt, then get one of "you mo'fo's" under her party dress and tell him *"Baby, eat those peaches and cream,"* and then how she'd make a visit to the nuns' house because *"I can't go to sleep unless I hear the sound of pussy,"* which she followed with a fierce declamation on the mung juice torture—pregnant Eskimo women with corks in their vaginas and men beating on their bellies—and then the liquid shit number (*"What I do is, I suck, baby."*) She punctuated the moment by spilling a can of Hershey's syrup down her dress front.

A powerful charge of hysteria ran through the crowd. Two young guys next to me were twitching and squealing and bent double. Finley then hiked up her gown and turned her naked butt to the audience. "This is 'Yams Up My Granny's Ass,'" she announced. "OH GOD!" one of the men next to me screamed. He and his buddy began throwing lit cigarettes at her. They were out of control. Finley cut the performance off abruptly a few minutes later and had the guys bounced.

But the incident depressed her. It wasn't a first. Last New Year's Eve at Danceteria, men in the audience began yelling "Whore!" (She told them, "Go back to New Jersey and stop coming to our nightclubs to get laid.") And one night at 8BC three men dropped their pants to their ankles during her monologue. (They pulled them back up when she declared their dicks too small to interest her.)

Obviously a man doing the same routine wouldn't be confronted like this—nor would the act have the same meaning. A filthy woman (in any sense of the word) has stepped further outside social mores than a man can possibly get. Hard-working men get dirty. They're a common sight in soap commercials, taking their showers. But that kind of dirt on a woman signifies "crazy" or "victim." No positive meaning is possible. Just as obscenity coming from a man asserts a tough manliness, in a woman's mouth it signals a threatening femininity, a banshee.

It's hardly surprising, though, that Finley felt an affinity for the work of two men who had made of themselves monstrous Others— the Kipper Kids. The Kippers became infamous in the seventies for performances that deconstructed every learned nicety into the raw human behavior observable in infants. Dressed in jockstraps and swimming caps, pouring food over each other, the Kippers burped, snarled, and grunted their way toward a state of transcendent gross-out. *LAICA Journal* described a rather typical piece in 1975 as "a Freudian nightmare-comedy of oral and anal obsession."

One of the Harry Kippers, Brian Routh, was Finley's graduate adviser at the San Francisco Art Institute. They developed a personal and artistic relationship and eventually married. "We have a real similar philosophy and both push our work to the limit, so we were very good for each other," says Finley. (They've now separated but remain friends.)

The Kipper Kids were scheduled to tour Europe in 1981, when Martin von Haselberg (the other Harry Kipper) couldn't go. Finley replaced him. She and Routh then touched off a near-riot in Cologne at the Theater for the World Festival, when they appeared as Eva Braun and Adolf Hitler.

According to an account in *Unsound* magazine, corroborated by Finley, she and Kipper/Routh had installed several rotting carcasses of beef in the space, where it was SRO—over eight hundred people—on each of their four nights. Kipper goose-stepped and saluted, naked from the waist down. Finley wore a corset and garter belt, and because she had diarrhea, periodically took a dump on one side of the stage. On one of the nights, Kipper sang a Johnny Mathis hit, then went to the bowl where Finley had been relieving herself and lapped up the shit. (Like Hitler used to do, myth has it.)

The audience became increasingly agitated. Finley stuffed toy sharks with hot dogs and sauerkraut and hung them from her body for Kipper to eat. They began reporting anti-Semitic incidents they had witnessed in Cologne, then began to rub chocolate pudding on each other's asses. Spectators started arguing among themselves. "Get off!" "No, she's right. . . ." "We don't need to hear this about Hitler," and so on. Kipper and Finley crawled around drinking beer out of bowls. One faction in the audience protested that this gesture said Germans were dogs. Finally a Spanish woman, a Nazi sympathizer, ran to the stage and attacked Finley with a mop. Kipper threw her off, but then a couple hundred others got up and rushed the stage. The performers made their exit.

One group in the audience had found it all wildly funny—among them the filmmaker Rainer Werner Fassbinder. Fascinated by the crowd's hysteria, he came back the next night to film the show. Fassbinder died soon afterwards, however, and the film has never been shown.

Earlier this year, Finley got a letter from *Playboy*, asking to film one of her sexy performances for their video magazine. They hadn't as yet seen one. A couple months later, she got a second letter announcing that they'd changed their minds: this was not mainstream sexuality.

Finley offered to read me the letter, but couldn't find it. Perhaps she'd thrown it away. She doesn't like to "harbor badness." As she remembered it, "*Playboy* thought I wouldn't be appreciated by mass culture, which to me says I'm not like a blond sex kitten who deals with passivity and the typical heterosexual way. . . . My work is basically exposing that we as a people really don't deal with that [*Playboy*] type of sexuality."

Then last month Finley was interviewed by someone from *Chic*, a porn magazine. "He asked me these questions like 'Does your lover ever feel you're talking about him?' I mean—really—sometimes I would have to set him straight. I don't feel that my work is pornography at all." As Finley sees it, she's just telling it like it is.

But you can still get censored for that. Police stopped a couple of her performances in San Francisco. Her reputation began to precede her so that when a Los Angeles club booked her, they told her "no four-letter words and don't show your body." She canceled. Then last summer, this performer who once told *Soho Arts Weekly* that "if I wasn't avant-garde maybe I'd have my own TV show or be on *Cagney and Lacey*," was part of the *Mike's Talent Show* that Michael Smith had pulled together for a cable TV taping. But then she wouldn't tone it down for the tube. "I'm an Ass Man" hit the cutting room floor.

Finley plays the club circuit—Palladium, Limelight, The Cat Club—and she's been booked next year for a run at The Kitchen. But right now her only regular venue is the monthly No Entiendes cabaret at Danceteria, hosted by Haoui Montaug and Anita Sarko. No Entiendes revels in the bad. All kinds of bad. In fact, the acts in this mutant Gong Show are *so* bad that Finley thinks its devoted followers must be "a cult of sadists and masochists." She's been a regular there since last August and also works at Danceteria as a bartender.

Given what Finley puts out in performance, you might expect her to be a tough cookie offstage. But that's hardly the case. She has a sensitive, if blunt, manner, and a definite sense of propriety. When she got some clippings together for me about her work, she mentioned that the review that obviously had a piece missing had praised her but had been uncomplimentary to another, better-known performer. She'd cut off that bit, she said, because giving it out to people would be rude.

When Finley watches videotapes of herself, she says, "I have to close my eyes. I don't know who that person is." She performs in a trance and has never rehearsed a piece. She doesn't even like going to sound checks, because it interferes with spontaneity. "I want the audience to see what I'm going through. I want to demystify this process you go through when you're trying to expose yourself. Also, these issues can't be packaged and polished. It's not like a talk about having a nice day. So it's important to have that rawness to it." Not that she's improvising, either. But if you've seen her do "I'm an Ass Man" eight times, you've seen it eight different ways.

She writes material out of what's floating in the cultural ether, stimulated by books and TV. One day at her apartment—neat, "airy," decorated with her paintings of people throwing up and shitting—Finley pulled some books from her shelf to show me how she might work. Take, say, *Psychoanalysis and Women* and *The Function of the Orgasm* and cross it in your mind with *Citizen Hughes* or *My Life with Jacqueline Kennedy*. She read from a random page in the *Psychoanalysis* book: "'Under optimal arousal conditions, women's orgasmic potential may be similar to that of the primates described.' Now *that* sentence I can do a lot with." She also uses autobiographical material, like the bit on that nice, nice man who was *so* nice that before he put the gun to his brain he laid down some carboard to soak up the blood.

She also studies TV for women's fashions and roles. "The way they like to team the chicks up" on *Kate and Ally, Cagney and Lacey*. The women with power who won't really use it—"and they're good women *because* they don't use it"—on *I Dream of Jeannie* and *Bewitched*. Television is the world of kitsch emotion. *The Dating Game, The Partridge Family, Dynasty*—to Finley these are deeply embarrassing shows, but all the more fascinating for that. "I feel personal humiliation for those people. Whenever I see Linda Evans walk in a room, I cannot watch the screen. Or Tony Danza. They're trying to humiliate themselves even more to get at something that deals with emotion."

Finley prefers to dive into the horror, of course. Years ago she even tried out for a *Dating Game* spot, but was rejected. As if to finally exorcise the obsession, she staged her own version of the show at 8BC. Now she hosts *Bad Music Videos* for cable TV, along with art critic Carlo McCormick. "When I see The Captain and Tenille, I get really upset. Some people are like that when they see Ronald Reagan's face. They break out in a cold sweat. Some people are like that with their own parents. It's like an allergic reaction."

One night *Bad Music Videos* taped a religious show at The Limelight—Elvis Presley and others turning spirituality into a Lawrence Welk moment. Finley encouraged us to remember Presley's mother fixation, and to "think about what drugs he might be on." Just as she does in performance, she goes straight to the real dirt beneath the banal.

Finley told me she hoped she could do a cable TV special in the fall featuring women performers. She wouldn't label it a "women's" thing. She'd just exclude those others. "You know, the way men do it," she said.

Finley considers herself a feminist, but is obviously working that red light area where feminists are known to disagree with each other. It isn't every feminist who idolizes Carol Doda, a burlesque dancer and one of the first women to get silicone implants. Finley loves burlesque—"the greatest theater in the world" and, to her, a female art form. "If I had a lot of money, I would open up a burlesque house—a really good one. It would be great, with the piano and women walking around in negligees."

Finley put herself through school working at strip joints in both Chicago and San Francisco. She was a hustler, getting the men to buy drinks at "two bucks a guy." Her career as a stripper had been brief, because she made the customers laugh. She considers herself lucky. Never had one bad experience. Says the men she serves now as a bartender at Danceteria are often harder to deal with.

She did not have the conventional feminist reaction to Judy Chicago's *Dinner Party* project, either. She thought it disgusting—memorializing women's achievements by sculpting their vaginas on plates. "Men would never have a show with, like, Abraham Lincoln's dick on a plate." She organized a party outside the Modern (with Bruce Pollack), to which people were asked to bring plates painted "with their favorite man's prick."

A few months back at a conference held by the Women's Caucus for the Arts, Finley's scheduled appearance on the "Hot and Nasty Humor Works" panel created political controversy when she told organizers she'd be doing "I Like the Dwarf on the Table When I Give Him Head." She considers this a prowoman piece—a woman taking sexual control right there in the title. Caucus organizers asked her to change the title. Get rid of the word "dwarf." Call it "I Like the Person of Shorter Stature on the Table when I Give Him Head." It seems a feminist of shorter stature had complained about "dwarf," deeply offended. Finley said she thought "dwarf" a beautiful word and wouldn't change it. The panel's moderator, Jerri Allyn, refused to drop Finley but agreed to let the feminist of shorter stature present her case—which Finley never heard because she got sick that day. A painful experience all round.

But feminists fight like this over language because they know it controls the world.

Whatever might spew from the wound in the psyche Finley describes in the language of pornography. But she renders the pornography impotent. In this id-speak, shitting and vomiting and fucking are all equal. Desire attaches to disgust. Finley's work moves beyond rage to the trigger for that rage. To damage and longing, the desperate want for something, the hole in all of us that nothing ever fills. The unfulfillable yearning produces an orgy of rage: *"You take your salami and put it up the wrong alley boy, make it all brown and gooey like I wanna take a big brown hot smelly shit. . . ."*

Finley's characters have no boundaries. They flow into each other over the course of a monologue as it moves from one emotional peak to the next, the dislocated genders and narratives held together by a feverish dreamlike logic. The very boundaries of the body collapse. What's inside and what's out when the food is smeared on, not ingested?

It's a big bulimic landscape of consumption and expulsion out there. The constant fetishization of food makes Finley that monster of orality, the devouring woman. *"You aren't throwing up on my tuna casserole, honey; you throwin' up on your own tuna"* becomes the lyrical prelude to sex: *"I mean whenever my child says 'fuck you' I fuck him in the ass. I turn him over and fuck him in the ass. I mean like when I make my husband ooh when I make him his steak sandwich the way he likes it, he turns me over in the kitchen and lets me have it in the ass. He says that's the way you deserve it, baby."* This is penetration as both the desire to connect and the desire to punish. Here sex and rage are virtually the same impulse. And the gender difference based on possession or lack of a dick has disappeared.

Finley often appropriates the male point of view and male desire in her language. Or some woman character starts fucking whoever up the ass, magically acquiring the power of men. Her work returns again and again to oral or anal sex, usually associating them with power, as in the appalling, hilarious passage above (a pecking order of assfuckers). Or the story of Mr. Horse confronting his young daughter's friend in the bathroom one night (*"I need your strong mouth to suck the piss out of my dick or I'm gonna die"*).

Only this girl's gonna tell. She's gonna knock the self-censor down and tell on Mr. Horse, her father, the culture. The tired old vocabulary of abuse has never sounded so sad. It's as if we've never quite heard it before, because we've heard it mostly from men. When it *is* abuse. Finley played me a still untitled song she's recorded with Mark Kamins (who produced Madonna's first album). Here were the usual unholy urges chanted over a downbeat disco track: *"You are fuckin' your granny/ you're fuckin' your sister too . . . suck the dick, bastard bitch . . . I want your wiener in my mouth . . . get me off!"* The music gave it a yearning quality as it blurted out the true language of love.

One night at the Cat Club, Finley followed Lydia Lunch on the bill. Lunch works the sex/anger territory herself. Stalking around the stage in her tight leather dress, she railed at the men in the crowd: "Stick your dick back in your fuckin' pants, you jellybelly looselip absolute fuckin'. . . . Look I know what you want. You are united in your search for that perfect piece of meat, the one that cooks, cleans, fucks, and sucks. . . ." The drunks around me responded with both adoration and abuse. Lunch even singled some out for special put-downs, but her anger was abstract, an idea of rage.

Finley appeared after her in a yellow fifties party dress, carrying a can of sauerkraut ("foetus juice," she said), and launched into a bizarre impassioned fantasy of fucking paralyzed boys. *"And after I had that boy he starts crying cuz it's the first time he ever felt anything . . . ooh baby he says to me all I want is to suck some tit with sauerkraut. . . ."* And here she ripped open her dress, dumped the sauerkraut on her breasts in her push-up bra, raised her arms joyously before the screaming crowd, levitating on the energy of some taboo destroyed.

June 1986

■ ■ ■ The Lady Is a Dick

The Dyke Noir Theater of Holly Hughes

Wherever she goes, it's the wrong side of town, because of what polite folks call her "lifestyle." Though she'd just call it "queer." She'll embrace a stigma faster than you can slap it on her. She's hell on heels, a twisted sister—a character from the timeless, tasteless world of dyke noir as imagined by Holly Hughes.

In her plays—*The Lady Dick*, *The Well of Horniness*, and now *Dress Suits to Hire*—Hughes has gleefully invented herself a genre with little precedent. From the hard-boiled fiction she loves, she's appropriated the toughguy talk, the lowlife mood, the shady shifty operators. What she forgets about is the crime. The *characters* are the crime—women who drive each other to emotional extremes, who put their sexuality upfront where everyone has to acknowledge it. They don't even need a plot, preoccupied as they are with "the killer inside"—rage, lust, love, and pain.

"The meanness was bred into her," one of the characters in *Dress Suits* says of the other. "We just called her a tiger 'cause there weren't words for what she was. Something more than a tiger—half woman, half something weird. French maybe. All cat." The two women in *Dress Suits*, Michigan and Deeluxe, live together in a tiny storefront and complete each other's worlds. They might be sisters. They might be lovers. Deeluxe might even be dead. Maybe the play is Michigan's dream, or memories she can't squeeze out of her mind. Michigan says she always knew what "a hundred and fifty pounds of killer pussy" could do to a man. "What I didn't know is what it could do to a woman."

Hughes isn't sure what draws her to these characters, but knows she isn't interested in "showing straight people how nice we are." The women in *Dress Suits* and *Lady Dick* don't explain lesbianism or apologize for it, or seek society's approval. Their sexuality is a given the way heterosexuality is a given in, say, *Our Town*. However, Hughes's theater toys with three conventions in lesbian lit and culture. First is the traditional tale of anguished abnormality, *The Well of Loneliness* for example ("Like Cain I am marked and blemished," it's heroine declares). Then there's the pulp written for a straight audience, kitsch of the *Hungry Virgins* school in which the women soon meet Messrs. Right and "straighten out." And finally there's "womyn's culture" born out of the gay-is-good seventies with rigid politics and a saccharine worldview—and "just sickening" in Hughes's opinion. Her own introduction to gay life came in 1978 when her car broke down in Wichita, and she wandered into a bar where women were fighting each other with beer bottles.

Hughes grew up in Saginaw, Michigan, the daughter of a GM executive, bent on "rebelling against that Republican stuff, like being forced to work for Nixon at age twelve." She became an anorexic, a Jesus freak, and "town bowling alley slut," admittedly not all at once. "I got saved a lot of times and then I'd sort of revert." She'd begun to write monologues when she was thirteen and tried throughout high school to get cast in a play. She always made stage crew. Later, while majoring in art at Kalamazoo College, she decided theater was a big bore. They kept doing Shaw. "Not really plays. They seemed more like blocking to me." Besides, she now hated theater people.

After graduating, after "flare-ups of lesbianism," she entered the wasteland of Michigan unemployment, landing a job at Burger King because she had connections. She worked the graveyard shift with outpatients from a nearby mental hospital. She was very fast with "the special orders that don't upset us." Soon the manager packed her off to Burger College in Chicago. She dropped out. "I took a step up. I was a waitress at Red Lobster for two years. I was on the fast track. I have a gold lobster pin. . . . I was trying to paint and trying to come out. Being really frustrated." In 1979, she moved to New York to attend the Feminist Art Institute. The years on hold in Michigan turned out to be good preparation for life in the East Village—with its post-television, junk-culture club spectacles by night, its crummy debilitating waitress jobs by day.

Like most outsiders, Hughes delights in the absurdity of what's passing for normal. Which is one way to describe both the "East Village aesthetic" and its most direct ancestor, "queer theater," as Stefan

Brecht describes it in his 1978 book of the same name. "Queer theater," Brecht writes, "is derisive low comedy or burlesque . . . yet with a core or nuance of despair or dejection as tho the universal comedy were tragic—portraying mankind [sic] as low, evil, and ridiculous . . . but aspiring to invest itself with beauty . . . the beauty of the low, the evil, and the ridiculous." Brecht chronicles the work of Jack Smith, John Waters, the Hot Peaches, Charles Ludlam and Ridiculous Theater in its preposterous, tacky, amateurish, vicious, sick, hermaphroditic, and transgressive glory, all suffused with "the sheer beauty of junk." Once a performance style practiced mostly by gay men, queerness crossed over in the East Village—influencing almost everyone.

Thanks to her dense visual language, Hughes's plays are more emotional, more abrasive, and more surreal than much of what started in the clubs. Yet she shares the same perverse sensibility that allows someone, for example, to be both a feminist and a Russ Meyer fan, as she is—to look at those bad girls in rocket bras driving through the desert and find them hilarious. Such politically incorrect irreverence fit right in at that "home for wayward girls," the WOW Cafe. Hughes began volunteering there shortly after it opened in 1982, and soon she was booking it, staffing it, making melted brie sandwiches (pretty much the only thing on the menu), and running the lights (such as they were). She'd given up any pretense of becoming a painter.

In its early days, WOW shared in the trash-and-vaudeville style, the postpunk anyone-can-do-it spirit that prevailed at other clubs in the neighborhood—the Pyramid, 8BC, the "old" Limbo, Club Chandalier, Darinka. Any club would book a gay show. It was just part of the scene. But WOW featured work—the first "queer" work—by gay women and their friends. Maybe it was a surge of that lesbian "community" thing from the seventies, some sweeping collaborative energy that extended into the audience—but there were nights at WOW when the boundaries between performer and audience disappeared. Resident old pros were the members of the Split Britches company—Peggy Shaw, Lois Weaver, and Deborah Margolin. WOW was also a safe place for beginners like Hughes to start out. Her first piece was the commentary to a WOW "fashion show" called *My Life as a Glamour Don't*.

"One day standing around in WOW with some girls, we started talking about how we should do a porn movie, and I was bragging about my porno-writing prowess, which was largely imaginary. So all of a sudden, this woman, who turned out to be a film producer said, 'Okay, we'll do it.'" Hughes came up with a script in a single afternoon, but it was more soap opera than pornography, and her collaborators did not want to film it. "They really wanted to sell a porn script to 42nd Street, and I had thought that wouldn't bother me, and then I realized it *did* bother me." Friends encouraged her to try staging the script she'd done—*The Well of Horniness.*

Over the next year, I saw *The Well* in five different clubs with five different casts. During the premiere at the tiny Limbo Lounge on Tompkins Square, a cast member ended up on an audience member's lap during one cramped scene. *The Well* never even had a run, except for four Mondays at the Pyramid. And the only review it ever got was in the Provincetown *Advocate*, which declared: "This is no *Iceman Cometh.*" Indeed.

The Well became something of a legend in its own backyard, though. Its heroine, a "would-be word processor," tries to outrun her lesbian past by getting married, only to discover that her future sister-in-law is also part of the "sisterhood of sin." The inevitable complications inspired two sequels, but *Victim/Victoria* and *In the Realm of the Senseless* were performed even less. Hughes remembers feeling shocked that people liked *The Well* and never tried very hard to get a booking. It's a campy play. It's also a *Blue Velvet* story, set in "a town like many others." Here beneath the placid surface—brays the narrator, a female Walter Winchell—"a whirlpool rages . . . sucking the weak, the infirm, the original, and all others who don't wear beige down . . . down, down, as carrots in the Cuisinart . . . so are souls in The Well [*scream*] of Horniness." Part One, in which there's a murder, ended dramatically that first night when the door to the Limbo banged open and a woman stepped in off 10th Street, announcing, "Stella Bruce. Lesbian detective."

For *Victim/Victoria* (Part Two), Hughes invented a detective named Garnet McClit, the tough cynical loner, "half Clint Eastwood and half Angela Davis." Later she became the title character in *The Lady Dick*, a play as grim as *The Well* was light. Set in a lesbian bar called The Pit, *Lady Dick* feels like a felony waiting to happen, its ambience both timeless and dangerous. Here both butch and femme fatales—in forties? fifties? sixties? clothing—threaten and insult and proposition one another. In this town (like many others), mean streets never bother to

Scenes from a quasi-marriage: Lois Weaver and Peggy Shaw in *Dress Suits to Hire*. (© Dona Ann McAdams.)

leave the room. Detectives never bother to detect. McClit likes a mystery much more than she likes solving it, after all. She's the heroic every-dyke, playing out a romanticized version of what it means to live on the fringes of society. To the tune of "The Lady Is a Tramp," she sings her outsider's anthem: "I won't take this show to The American Place/Rent an apartment and call it a space. . . . I never bother to pass for straight/That's why the lady is a dick."

In the even more claustrophobic world of *Dress Suits*, the two women act out their power struggles in poetic detective patter. They try on roles like so many tuxes-for-rent. Instead of a plot, they act out scenes from a quasi-marriage—seductions, break-ups, nostalgia, sexual fantasies, games—scenarios they can trigger with a word or a glance after so much shared history. "I never bought that stuff that all people didn't objectify the person they're in love with," Hughes said. "Of course, you objectify them. They become like a devotional object, or an idol to be smashed." What Hughes likes in the hard-boiled novels of James M. Cain and Jim Thompson is the way oppressed and oppressor link up, barely distinguishable, the way complicity and evil intertwine. Through most of *Dress Suits,* Deeluxe fights an inner battle with a character named Little Peter, embodied onstage by her right hand. He controls her whenever he appears, until she's able to admit that he's all in her mind.

Dress Suits is loosely based on an East Village myth about two sisters who lived together until one was murdered by an intruder. Lois Weaver and Peggy Shaw (Michigan and Deeluxe, respectively) asked Hughes to write a play for them and told her the story. As two-thirds of the Split Britches company, they were accustomed to making up their characters in rehearsal, starting with a certain physicality and attitude, which would eventually lead them to find words. In Hughes's play, they had to work backwards, giving a physical reality to highly stylized language—more fierce and more sexually explicit than anything Split Britches would do. And they haven't been able to use their "butch and femme thing," as they usually do. Shaw in particular has found that "it's tough doing drag." She hasn't performed in a dress since '77 when she toured with Hot Peaches, the only woman in the cast with eleven drag queens. And even then, she'd let *them* be the girls.

But Shaw and Weaver don't find themselves that far from the netherworld Hughes writes about. They just finished a long run of *Patience and Sarah,* a classic and romantic lesbian story. The *Times* review astonished them by referring to the characters as "wilderness women." Some new code word for "lesbian"? If you're the thing that can't be talked about, you are the netherworld. Weaver suggested that engaging the "dark side" could be liberating. Eight years ago while part of Spiderwoman Theater and their *Evening of Disgusting Songs and Pukey Images,* Weaver chose to create a sinister, slithery, vampirish character and now says, "That's what really enabled me to come out. It opened up a new life in me, and that's when my real life began."

Hughes points out that "women's sexuality is a tortured area. Whether it's gay or straight, it's always in the closet." But she claims that even if she fell in love with Don Johnson tomorrow, she'd still write about lesbians. She just finds them so entertaining.

May 1987

he woman in the blue wig and the dress cut full of revealing holes kissed every spectator who entered the basement of Franklin Furnace. "Wait for a midpriest to guide you to the world of dreams, to your own special place," she murmured, "and then to the cave of the shaman." I could hear the animal-like cries of the "shaman." Then, as a guide led a group of us through the low light and burning incense, I saw him up on the platform, in his "cave" hung with quilts, sheets, and strips of aluminum foil. He sat there naked in his wheelchair.

We were free to approach the shaman and ask any question, the guide told us after washing and kissing our feet. We were free to touch the shaman's body, but if we did so we were granting him the same permission. A naked man decorated in whorls of red body paint, his penis in green, danced by with a videocam. Musicians yelped and clicked and clucked to one side. Our guide, wearing a red gauze toga, poured us a drug (which tasted suspiciously like water) "to lower our inhibitions and fears." But no one had yet approached the shaman. Suddenly he lurched forward with a cry, flailing a stiff arm at one of the strips of foil hung along the front of his cave, knocking it down to see us better. And he howled.

Frank Moore, the self-described shaman, was born with cerebral palsy—99 percent physically disabled, spastic, unable to speak. "I am lucky I am an exhibitionist in this body," he once wrote in an essay about his work. "I have a body that is ideal for a performance artist." With his neck (the only muscles he can control) and a pointer attached to a leather headband, he can type on a word processor or spell out messages on a letter board strapped to his wheelchair. "People project onto me certain mystical powers," the essay continued. "They are reacting to some symbol of the deformed medicine man." And if people treat him like a baby—since he is physically helpless—that just allows him to get away with unsocialized behavior, like howling, staring, or inappropriate touching. In performance, Moore takes advantage of his disadvantage, becoming an unlikely guide into the pleasures of the body, taking audiences where they would probably never go without the example of his vulnerability and trust.

Maybe because I spent the sixties where there were no sixties, Moore's piece felt to me like five real hours from the Summer of Love, complete with group grope. Nothing nostalgic, parodic, or ironic about it either. To the first daring soul who ventured up to Moore's cave, he tapped out the lines: "They are afraid. They don't know what they are missing." The sixties is such an embarrassing era to reenter after twenty years of cooling off. But as the evening wore on, the room began to look like the photo of a Living Theater event—half-naked people walking through a mess.

Two of his gauze-clad helpers carried Moore out to a mat on the floor, and a woman read a text he'd composed about the "bony fingers" who cared for him. He lay there on his side, just as he'd been placed, his fingers twitching. "You may now explore Frank's body," the reader announced. One woman did. The story continued, as he and another performer acted out an apparent sexual fantasy about a new nurse (the "new prodder"). Total self-indulgence, I thought. But I realized later that this helped prepare the audience to join Moore in what he calls "eroplay." The nurse scene had been so real—the nudity, the obvious affection, the simulated lovemaking—that the embarrassment level in the room rose palpably. Theoretically, we would soon reach our embarrassment threshold and be able to do anything.

Helpers carried Moore back to his cave, where we could now "play" with him, those of us "willing to push beyond where it's comfortable and safe." The woman narrating began to explain eroplay—"an intense physical playing or touching of oneself and others"—as perhaps eight or ten people drifted into the cave. "Eroplay is innocent and childlike," read the woman with the blue wig, who turned out to be Moore's wife, Linda Mac. Eroplay would connect us with our own bodies and with other people. Eroplay was physical pleasure for its own sake, unconnected to sex or romance.

I didn't doubt that this was how Moore experienced it, but the next ritual certainly looked like a love-in. Over half the remaining audience of thirty chose to participate, seating themselves around Moore, who'd been carried to the center of the basement. Linda Mac paired the people off in same-sex as well as opposite-sex couples, and then read them instructions she picked randomly from a bowl. "Rub your genitals, not for sexual reasons but for body comfort." "Hug one another." "Rub one another's bare breasts." Clothes began coming off, and someone behind me muttered to a friend, "Things like this used to happen in the Village all the time. It's sick." They are among those who left before the conclusion, when the helpers wrapped everyone in a giant circle of cellophane, ribbon, toilet paper, and aluminum foil.

We live in a culture that is increasingly disembodied. Where William Burroughs argues that someday we may be "reduced to a magnetic field." Where the artist Stelarc suspends himself from hooks through his skin, stating that the body is obsolete. Where the computer-generated Max Headroom is a star. Where you don't need your own body to have a baby.

That Moore would be the one urging us to stay connected with our physical selves is both ironic and poetic, even if his performance didn't motivate me to explore the anonymous bodies at Franklin Furnace. After Moore's show, when he'd again been settled in his wheelchair with his pointer, I asked him how he'd decided he was a shaman. "A woman told me if I would stop hiding my body, it would be a tool," he spelled out methodically. The first thing I'd noticed about him close-up was the expression on his face. "You look happy," I said, and he tapped out, "Always."

May 1987

■ ■ ■ Lydia Lunch Faces the Void

She came to tell us that the end was near. But not near enough. From up in her black sarcophagus-shaped pulpit, Lydia Lunch spewed out her disgust for this horror called living. For this government of, by, and for a bunch of assholes. For a life that's "all about getting *fucked*"—as in *over, up,* and *with*. That forces you to "kill or be killed if ya ain't dead already." She, in fact, would kill herself if she only had the nerve.

"So *drop the fuckin' bomb!*" she shrieked. She said the concept of "mutually assured destruction" gave her something to believe in. She then announced that she was a candidate for president.

This relatively new incarnation of Lydia Lunch as enraged rhetorician or prophet of gloom doesn't really deviate from the baby-faced Fury she was in 1977. Anger has always been her business, and it's always been for real. Ten years ago she expressed it through the musical roach bomb that was No Wave. (Throw one on a turntable and watch 'em scatter.) Lunch became a punk icon as the seventeen-year-old leader of Teenage Jesus and the Jerks, keening lyrics of the "you are my razor" variety over a brutal cacophony. Now—four bands and countless films and records later—she practices a Theater of the Tirade. She has a message for us. It isn't a new one. And she doesn't care.

Her recent show at the Performing Garage, "The Gun Is Loaded," was a catalogue of bad moods. J. G. Thirwell's ten-minute industrial-music prelude created the appropriate foreboding—the sound of amplified construction sites and purring factories, the dull percussion of far-off machine guns. The din ended abruptly, and Lunch marched in and got right to the work of telling us how fucked we are—first, by government and the men, always men, who play at politics, "butt-fucking whoever gets in the way of their war games, their head trips, and their death trips."

I've heard routines like this from Lunch in the past, and I've criticized her in the past, wanting her to go further. Reagan is a cheap hatred. The real horror show is always closer to home. In "The Gun," Lunch eventually left her pulpit and spoke more personally than I've ever heard her do from the stage. Her stories are more effective than her messages. ("Daddy Dearest," on a cassette called *The Uncensored Lydia Lunch,* is probably the most honest, harrowing piece about incest I've ever heard.) At the Garage, she recalled her first memory—of "being rocked like a football" while her parents screamed at each other. Childhood seems to have been one long harangue, and she left home "at fourteen or sixteen before somebody got murdered." By then she was eating horse tranquilizers "twenty-four hours a day just to be able to stand myself"—and the world. "You *could* say I had an attitude," she remarked after this trip through the memory lane where she got it. The audience chuckled, almost too intimidated to laugh.

She was equal parts aggressive and vile, declaring "the plague" (AIDS, I assumed) nature's way of controlling the population and telling a couple of stories about "niggers." For a Performing Garage audience, such sentiments are probably more disturbing than any fuckoid expletive, and I speculated that that's what she wanted. Near the end of the show, she declared she was not racist, not sexist, not bigoted—"not more than the rest of you assholes." She is, in fact, an Equal Opportunity hater, lashing out at everyone as indiscriminately as a rotary blade slicing through a landscape. Inevitably she grabbed some sucker in the front row and shook him.

Lunch is a charismatic performer who has tapped into the concentrated energy of negativity, and I'm compelled by the emotional authority of her work. I even identify with her rage. But it's terribly limited as a world view—like breathing through a choke hold. In "The Gun," Lunch described the inherent sadness of nihilism: "Everywhere I've been—and by the looks of me you can tell I've been everywhere— it gives me that same empty feeling, that same old ugliness, that same old nothingness. . . ." And she screamed at the "fuckin' stinkin' world that TRICKS YOU INTO BEING BORN IN THE FIRST PLACE." This revulsion, cynicism, and despair outline what is, actually, a spiritual void in the culture. *That's* the hole that nothing ever fills. The stark and surreal black set by Izhar Patkin and Richard Phillips represented those institutions people run to for refuge. There was a small stage at center with its lectern/sarcophagus (though I saw it as a pulpit because steps up the back put the speaker at an even more exaggerated height). Then, to the left and right of the stage were a psychiatrist's couch and a white picket fence. Given the context, this was a map of the shaky ground where no one can believe in anything.

And once it was punk's job to be the ultimate earthquake. Funny how punk came along to destroy everything and then wouldn't die. But then, it *was* an ironic and parodic movement. Perhaps it couldn't die because it didn't believe in itself. Watching Lydia Lunch, I kept thinking of another misanthrope, Samuel Beckett. It isn't just Lunch but all the new fatalists who now seem to live inside one of his plays, telling whoever will listen, "I can't go on. I'll go on."

June 1987

■ ■ ■ Learning to Love the Monster

I t was the week Elvis spoke from the grave, his "ghost seen by dozens." (Quoth a tabloid.) Down at the abandoned gas station on Avenue B, the spectral image of The King flickered over a sheet tacked up on a board. Thirty people had gathered to watch a program of No Way Normal Films, the best and least normal of them breaking down the body politic of the fat ol' sex god from Memphis. Jon Moritsugu's *Der Elvis*, in fact, showed how He ain't nuthin' but a signifier.

Elvis represents the body primeval, just as Michael Jackson represents the body ethereal, the body as concept. But never had The King's insouciant sex appeal seemed so creepy, so nose-in-the-trough piggish as it did in the twenty-two-minute *Der Elvis* (also screened recently at the Downtown Film Festival). Moritsugu, too young (twenty-two) to have known The King as anything but a swollen image, taps into the same vein of All-American necrophilia that inspired Gary Panter's book, *Invasion of the Elvis Zombies*.

Der Elvis matches a furious hardcore pace to a structure like a term paper outline (complete with Roman numerals), placing the rock 'n' roll führer at the center of a culturewide vortex of addiction and greed. His lusts are legendary, while we're addicted/greedy for his image. Though not for those in this film: a bloated Presley impersonator, a female Presley impersonator, stoopid Presley flicks, needles injecting meat, food slopped onto a plate, data on The King's peculiar sex life, and lists of preferred drugs. Battered images of the young King (prearmy/pre-Germany/predrug) waver across television-set shrines, surrounded by candles.

Moritsugu calls one of his sections "Triumph of the Swill." *Jawohl.*

The junk (food-pills-Cadillacs) of life took him over, and Elvis turned, accidentally, into a monster, mutating uncontrollably till he died from it.

Johanna Went regards monstrosity with great tenderness, and makes use of its power. She pipes into the subconscious for material, then dresses the secret self in its rude and funny clothes.

On October 10, she brought *Twin Travel Terror* to Franklin Furnace in a rare New York appearance, and the basement had filled to the bricks with spectators. Two life-size and sick-green ghouls with clenched teeth stood center stage setting the mood, along with the snake head peeking from a long fabric pouch on the wall and the big mannequin stuck to it sideways, clad in a noticeably shit-stained jumpsuit. The red words painted on his chest read: "Did I Lie Again?" Went's piece would be gross, beautiful, and mesmerizing.

Went performs in a trance, with mask-a-minute intensity. Elaborate costumes for grotesque personas fly into the wings or get destroyed, sometimes before a human with one set of eyes can absorb all the details. This time she emerged first as a two-headed nun with a long green snake attached to her crotch. Behind her, two women in blue wigs, big dildos hanging from their jumpsuits, cavorted with a large satanic bunny. I guess there's never been a language that could tell *this* story. The "nun" had to keen and wail.

In each of ten bizarre incarnations, Went came eventually to the mike to twitch and shriek in a voice a reviewer once described as "a million Chatty Cathy dolls on acid." She was, for example, The World—her robe a large map, her head covered by a Kewpie-shaped globe. A snake seemed to crawl from her brain and slide over Europe, her forehead, as she tossed another heavy unbounceable globe in the air. Later, she wore a large fish mask and huge tent dress that held two life-size dummies. In this she walked laboriously, hilariously, chanting, "We are not alone," as her "twin" assistants pulled the dummies out, slapped and wrestled them, and knocked their heads off. The biggest crowd-pleaser, though, was Went's giant cunt headdress, which she squeezed as white liquid gushed from her mouth.

The visual/aural excess, "filthy" taboos made too big to ignore (a three-foot turd, a giant bloody tampon), and Went's uncontrolled un-

Johanna Went (right), twin assistants, and the giant mess ending *Twin Travel Terror*. (© Dona Ann McAdams.)

rehearsed stage manner generate an energy difficult to analyze. She wants a gut reaction, not analysis, though, and once told me that she uses props like dildos and turds because they're "funny" and "entertaining." Her pieces erase identity, embrace the unspeakable, and value the irrational. The key ingredient—her femaleness—makes them empowerment rituals, a way to experience the most primal (preverbal) human qualities, the ones women had too before they learned of their Otherness. Her willingness to be monstrous, outrageous, and transgressive onstage connects Went to performers like Karen Finley and Dancenoise (Lucy Sexton and Anne Iobst, who appeared in this show as the "twin assistants").

As it ended, the three performers collapsed into the giant mess they'd made of the stage, covered with fake blood and shit. They'd drunk "blood" or let it rain on them from the eyes of one of the green ghouls. They'd carried the big tampon and turd like ritual objects. They'd fought over a plucked chicken with a baby doll's head. And the friend with me, an intensive care nurse, announced that she'd gone into a trance. Experiences like this are what the witch trials once tried to burn away.

November 1987

■ ■ ■ The Kipper Kids in Middle Age

The Kipper Kids were singing music hall numbers in the Men's for a capacity crowd of cameras and mikes. Out in the hallway, I could hear a hearty chorus of "Roamin' in the Gloamin'." I could see the harlequin faces of Harry and Harry on two video monitors. As always, the two Kippers were dressed in shower caps and whiteface, huge noses and thrusting chins, painted stubble and raccoon eyes, but—here, for the first time—each wore a tire with rope suspenders over the usual jockstrap. This was for HBO, after all, not some downtown performance space. Perhaps it was a silly bid for decency. The Kipper Kid is now a character in transition—about to cross over. So hope the Harrys.

But these are still two giant, beefy, baby boys, two pubcrawlers from hell, two pugnacious blokes who combine the no-nos you learn not to do (like smearing food) with the manners that take their place ("nice cup o' tea"). So the Kids in the loo prepared for one of their ritual food fights, incorporating that tension—let's make a mess, but let's be precise about it. Wind the arm carefully to—splat!—smack an egg on the other's noggin. Circle slowly, menacingly—while singing. And dump flour on the geezer. Time that can of Spaghettios, the cranberry aspic, the Corona bottles full of blue or magenta paint.

"Well, it's not everybody's cuppa . . . raspberries," says a technician watching another monitor in the control room, where the film is rolling. The two Harrys were experiencing uniquely Kipperish difficulties with their finale: the firecrackers kept sinking before they could blow up in the shaving cream atop their shower caps. No doubt this had been the hardest food fight of their lives, full of interruptions. On stage they never stopped for anything.

For years, particularly in the late seventies, the Kipper Kids were plenty of people's "cuppa"—in the world of performance art, anyway. They were a legendary Punch and Punch show, gross, hilarious, dangerous, and bawdy. In early pieces done throughout Europe, they performed in a boxing ring, starting silly, taking foodstuffs from suitcases or rigging them up with pulleys, doing their ceremonies, drinking about a quart of whiskey per show, and building toward the violent climax when one Kipper would punch himself in the face till he bled. After they dropped the fight finale, later in the seventies, they maintained a certain threshold of outrage with scatological jokes (rubbing each other's asses with chocolate) and penis jokes (biting off a pickle as they exposed their cocks and sang "Diamonds Are a Girl's Best Friend"). They always managed to create an ambience of latent violence.

In a monograph published in 1979, David Ross, then a curator at the Berkeley Museum of Art, described their work as "actions that at times stress the visual, the visceral, and the violent aspects of social rituals. . . ." The Kipper Kids, whose real names are Martin von Haselberg and Brian Routh, say their work doesn't mean anything. They say they have no statement to make. In a way, the pieces are about the simple relationship between Harry and Harry, eggin' each other on, being bad to/for/with each other. "The Kipper Kid is the part of the personality that does away with all that conventionality," said Brian.

The Kippers-to-be met at East 15 Acting School in London in 1970—Brian, the working-class guy from Newcastle-upon-Tyne, and Martin, the aristocratic scion from Germany by way of Argentina. Quickly they became disruptive influences together, and the school ejected them. They went to Germany. "We know the exact moment in time when the Kipper Kid was born," Martin said. "It was about five o'clock in the morning in Frankfurt near the railway station, and we were just sort of fooling around in the street with these English working-class accents that we do, joking and pulling faces and posturing, when the Kipper Kid suddenly formed."

They couldn't remember which one of them spontaneously said, "We're our mum's best kipper kids." They couldn't describe how it felt when they realized they were inhabiting the same character. It's like being twins, they say. Twins joined at the name. For almost a year afterwards, they traveled around Germany and then to Paris, incessantly doing the character, *talking* about doing the character, and again doing the character—on the street or kippering down the autobahn "larger than life" and leaving a trail of in-jokes and snorts and pokes and farts behind them.

"We couldn't stop it," said Brian.

"It used to actually get on our nerves because anything would trigger it off," said Martin. "It was like being 'on' without particularly wanting to be 'on.'"

At first, they didn't realize they'd become Performance Artists. But when a friend invited them to play a festival, they decided to "just put the Kipper Kid into a situation." Soon after, they got themselves invited to the Olympic Arts Festival in Munich by submitting some fake press clips. And the rest is hysterie. From '71 to '75 they lived together. For a couple of those years, they were constantly on tour, driving around Europe in an old German post office van, often living daily life as a Kipper. "We wouldn't be where we are now if we hadn't done that then," Martin said. "We still have the momentum from that time."

> *In an age like ours, when people are assaulted daily by the most monstrous things without being able to keep account of their impressions . . . all living art will be irrational, primitive, complex; it will speak a secret language and leave behind documents not of edification but of paradox.*
>
> —Hugo Ball, Dada performer/provocateur, 1915

The Kippers performed together very little in the eighties. Martin, in Los Angeles, did the occasional "half a Kipper Kids show" and a couple of "Gong Show" appearances. Brian, in New York, did "verbal stuff" at clubs like 8BC and Chandalier, often sharing a bill with performance artist Karen Finley, to whom he was then married. Brian always billed himself "Harry Kipper." As did Martin. Martin says he finally felt "free of the yoke of the Kipper Kids" about a year and a half ago, just before he started working with Brian again. The Kipper Kids are bigger than both of them, not unlike other teams, from Laurel & Hardy to Gilbert & George, who became something more than the sum of their parts, as if the interaction itself were a third presence.

When I spoke to the Kipper Kids in September in their Los Angeles studio, they were weeks away from their first show in years. From a window they pointed to a former beauty-supply shop, now burned-out and roofless, which would be their performance site. They were planning to saw their way out of a box, emerge in silly costumes, sing

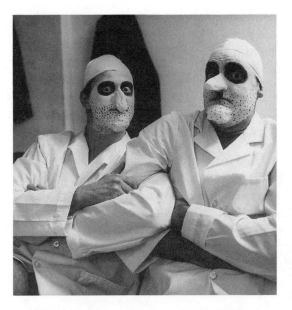

The Kipper Kids (Martin von Haselberg, Brian Routh) during a break in the filming of "Bette Midler's Mondo Beyondo." (Photograph by Sylvia Plachy © 1993.)

tunes with ukelele and soprano sax, and do some "messy and ener-gized" ceremony atop the box. Piled in their rehearsal area were suit-cases and the usual groceries. The crusty old Scout uniforms they wore back in the seventies for a three-month Munich gig decorated a wall, still stiff with food and blood.

"We're not out to be dangerous anymore," said Brian.

"We've become sort of middle-aged and sedentary," said Martin.

"We got as far as we could go at that level, and now it's time for us to go further," said Brian.

"Performance art is dead anyway," said Martin.

They want to make Kipper Kid movies and enter the mainstream. And that pressured trajectory was much on their minds as they planned the L.A. show. (Do you still rub chocolate pudding on each other's asses if a producer is coming?) "We don't want to ruin our po-tential careers, but on the other hand, we don't want to make any com-promises," said Martin. In the HBO special, now titled "Bette Midler's Mondo Beyondo," the Kippers are certainly the most beyondo in a cast that includes David Cale, Pat Oleszko, Paul Zaloom, Bill Irwin, Luke Craswell, La La La Human Steps, and Bette Midler. Martin is married to Bette Midler.

And because he's married to her, he figured, some people would be coming to see the Kipper Kids who would have never seen the like. "I think that a lot of them are going to be pretty horrified, and it's quite possible that my wife will also be . . . uh, hopefully, she won't feel disgraced when she really finds out what I do."

> *The Variety Theatre destroys the Solemn, the Sacred, the Serious, and the Sublime in Art with a capital A.*
>
> —F. T. Marinetti, Futurist performer/provocateur, 1913

What the Kippers do is related to a most ancient and popular form of theater—the carnival, the dizzying, vulgar, Rabelaisian "fayre," where every propriety went topsy-turvy. Reading a while back in a book called *The Politics and Poetics of Transgression,* I came upon a description of the "grotesque body" that carnival celebrates: a body defined by impurity, masking protruberant distension, disproportion, clamor, a focus upon gaps, orifices, and symbolic filth, physical needs and pleasures of the lower body, parody. . . . T'would seem to describe a Kipper Kid.

Since medieval carnivals grew out of earlier Dionysian rites, it isn't surprising that the Kippers feel an affinity for the performance artists of the Viennese *Aktionismus* group—notably Hermann Nitsch, who has consciously re-created such rites since the sixties. They've participated in at least one of his gory rituals, in which, typically, naked humans are covered with the blood and viscera of dead animals. Nitsch believes these performances result in catharsis for the spectators, an exorcism of repressed violence.

In comparison, the Kippers' work is a vaudeville act, if a perverse one. Vaudeville (in England, the music hall or "variety theater") is what carnival came to be in more prettified times, and they share some of the same bizarre acts—Armless Wonders, Human Blockheads, Singing Mice. Both Harry Kippers love music hall. And their character is certainly a clown, not of the benign floppy-shoed variety or the melancholy Chaplinesque, but a coarse and knowing clown, whose costume and affect give him permission to be rude, excessive, and unpredictable. His act might spill, literally, into our laps. Critic Kay Larson once observed that the Kippers perform an "exorcism by anger." Or perhaps by fear.

The Kippers say they don't feel influenced by anyone in the art world. (For example, they started kippering before they ever heard of

Nitsch.) "That's not to say we don't greatly appreciate the work," Martin said, "particularly, of Gilbert & George and all the Viennese people and Allen Kaprow. If anything, we're really much more theatrical and juicy, and just somehow strayed into the art world without any particular intention to do so."

There they found an appreciative and relatively unshockable audience. But then, carnival is the subtext to each new bohemia, which has to consort with the "low" almost on principle. In one of his umpteen manifestos, for example, F. T. Marinetti praised the Variety Theater as the "only theatrical entertainment worthy of the true Futurist spirit." Futurist productions often included clowns and acrobats.

A case can be made for dating the avant-garde from 1896, when the clownish and horrific Ubu character uttered the word "Merdre" ("shitr") and sparked a near riot. Today we say ho hum to that word, which only proves that it's possible to train an audience, even a mass audience. The Kippers had already dipped a toe in the mainstream during the seventies. Nearly got booked onto *Saturday Night Live*. They opened once for The Bay City Rollers, once for Public Image—the whole gamut of pop, right? But someone wasn't quite ready for crossover then. Maybe them. Maybe us.

The fact is that as the avant-garde disintegrated, the mainstream got quirkier. We now have a mass bohemia, antennae up for the Next Big Thing. The Kippers aren't the first, won't be the last, to slip over the now-fluid boundary between art and entertainment. But they're so much more outrageous than, say, Spalding Gray or Ann Magnuson or any of the New Vaudevillians, that I for one feel a twinge of anxiety—or loss—when I hear they've just signed a deal with Cinemax for a half-hour narrative film.

I think it's the anxiety you experience when the boundary breaks. More of that "center will not hold" business. What was once center floats to the edge, and vice versa. Everthing flattens. And the freaks aren't happy in the sideshow anymore.

February 1988

■ ■ ■ Life Is a Killer

A horror show is a glimpse of your own helpless guts.

I'd gone down the Lower Worst Side to Hotel Amazon (ex-public school). In what looked like a school auditorium gone creepy-crawly, one light burned at police interrogation intensity, and our master of ceremonies squirted pink gunk out the eyesockets of his oversized mask. It was horror show time, but it wouldn't be cute. And it wouldn't be a movie, where you know it won't leap off the screen. The three scheduled acts, short as adrenaline bursts, had the urgency of exorcism.

Kembra Pfahler inched down the aisle with a drawn knife, wearing a white dress and a dark, matted wig. I saw her as Lady Macbeth looking for a king to kill. Up on the stage ringed inexplicably with rocks, Samoa played a feedback solo. Pfahler stood on her head when she reached the stage. She was naked under her dress. This raised the clamor level in the scare-me-I-dare-ya crowd of bullies and brats. Samoa dropped the guitar and picked up an egg carton. One by one, he forcefully broke eggs full of red paint between Pfahler's legs. Some goddess offering of menstrual blood and womb? Punishment? Was it sacrifice? *Out damned spot.*

The ranting of Victor Poison-Tete, which followed, generated no real horror since it had no real target. "Get out of my head! Get out of my face! Get out of my shit! . . ." The free-floating aggression became a push-pull with the audience over who would control the room, but neither side intimidated the other. "I kill! I kill! I kill! . . ." yelled Poison-Tete, as he accidentally ripped down the dingy room's one decoration, a string of Christmas tree lights. "Am I changing?" he demanded. Assorted smark alecks yelled, "No!"

I suspect that most were there to see the infamous and frightening

Joe Coleman. (Though they would also taunt him. At first.) His would be a short and savage ritual. He would explode. He would kill. That's what he always does in his appearances as Professor Momboozoo: light firecrackers attached to his chest. Bite the heads off some rats or some mice.

In the recent "Pranks!" issue of Re/Search, Coleman says, "I was capable of becoming a Carl Panzram [a mass murderer], but luckily I was able to get my anger and frustration out through painting and performance . . ." Both have the corrosive power of spilled bile.

Apocalypse Culture, the paperback anthology with a Coleman on its cover, describes his paintings as "Thomas Hart Benton on bad acid." They're visions of a hellish, amoral, pox-encrusted world—landscapes awash in toxic waste, bodies rotting from the inside out. Coleman's work also has a subtext of perverse religious fanaticism: This world is a vale of tears; we are corrupted; the end is near. (Or let's hope that it is.) The Momboozoo character is a demented preacher. In the film Mondo New York, where Coleman does his rodents-and-explosives act, he tells these creatures who are about to die that they are going to a better place. And the show at Hotel Amazon had been advertised with quotes from the Book of Job: "Man that is born of woman is of few days, and full of trouble. He cometh forth like a flower and is cut down. . . .'"

It was around 1 A.M. when Coleman appeared with animal entrails draped over his suit, pig hooves tied to his arms, a white furpiece snaking down his back. Already onstage was a life-size bust of Coleman, wearing Momboozoo's preacher robe. Coleman began: "They cover the land like locusts. . . ." I caught some line about "cosmic retribution," and then a red flash of fireworks rocketed into the audience across the aisle. Coleman lit another match to the load of firecrackers strapped to his chest, filling the room with cacophony and smoke and the odor of gunpowder. He picked up a pitcher of what looked like blood and gulped at it as his wife, Nancy, entered in a white dress and fake pregnant belly. He spit the blood on her. Then he opened a little Chinese takeout container and began to scream, "It's my father!!!" as he pulled out the white mice. One crawled over his chest and he picked it up, screaming. He snapped off its head, flinging the carcass out into the crowd.

I'd felt the fear—as I anticipated, as I ducked, as I watched. I can't tell you how many mice he geeked. A couple. A few. And he was still screaming when he threw himself to the stage, writhing and twisting as though having a seizure. He was still screaming when he jumped up, ran down the aisle and out a back door.

The show had been disgusting and oddly affecting in its crude symbolism of "the beast within." Coleman seems to feel trapped by his own humanity. The blood, the bite, the bang: You're cursed before you're born; so bite back at what gnaws you; shatter your self and start over. "This is something we all want to do," a friend said to me. "Kill your parents." For Coleman, the act is obviously cathartic, but most of the audience responded as if they'd just seen a sideshow geek. As we filed out of the dark auditorium, I noticed a young dude spectator posing proudly onstage with one of the headless mice.

I flashed to Rachel Rosenthal's studio in Los Angeles last September, where she introduced me to her pet rats—some of the fat gray crawling-through-your-nightmare variety, all lounging in unlocked cages. As an animal rights activist, she purposely picked rats as pets because they're despised. As a performance artist, she's worked with them and with other animals onstage, believing them the equal of humans. I tend to agree. Coleman may even agree—that the human is vermin. But the relationship between human and animal is just one of the issues here.

Humans have a long tradition of watching all sorts of creatures die and calling it entertainment—from the days of the public execution and ye bear-baiting gig right up to the bullfight and a bat-geeking Ozzy Ozbourne. I'm both impressed and sickened by the infinite originality of human cruelty. And I didn't like watching the mice die, but I'm not sure I was appropriately offended either. Is this my thickening skin? Guess I was less tuned in to the one that had to die than to the one who had to kill. You rarely see anything this primal on a stage.

And a performer who transgresses one taboo might transgress another. A performer who's violent once might be violent again. Nobody rules. I felt, with those around me, the tension inherent in such a loss of control. So as Coleman fled the scene and a loud power tool suddenly roared up near the exit, we stood on our chairs, trying to see, expecting the worst. We'd entered the nightmare. It had to be a chainsaw.

Actually, it was an industrial vacuum cleaner, part of some other performer's piece, whose point seemed to be to blow strips of toilet paper into the audience.

Someone once asked me why I go to see such horrible things. Because. Watch a taboo break, and it speaks to the taboo events of your own life. Everybody has a couple. Or a few. Or more. I don't see the point in escapism when there's no escape. This is not to say that a moment of catharsis always comes. For the artist or the audience.

Often—I admit it—"transgressive" performances do nothing for me personally, and shock for the sake of shock does nothing at all. But I admire artists with the guts to address their own demons. There is no known way to talk to demons, however, and sometimes the artists get it wrong. Sometimes they just make bad art.

There's now a twenty-plus-year history in the art world of performances centered on taboo acts, and I've written or referred to many of them in the past: Paul McCarthy fucking a pile of raw meat, Gina Pane climbing a ladder of broken glass, Stelarc suspending himself by fishhooks embedded in his flesh, Carolee Schneemann and friends smearing themselves with blood and tearing dead chickens apart, Chris Burden having himself shot, Kim Jones rubbing himself with shit. (Why is it nearly always white people who do these things? And, in most cases, men? I suppose it has to do with who feels empowered to act out.)

". . . [T]hese artists have introduced into the art realm materials found elsewhere only in the psychiatric records of disturbed children and in the shamanic thread of the history of religion," writes Tom McEvilley in a definitive essay on this disturbing genre, reprinted in *Apocalypse Culture*.

A few months ago I saw some films made in the late sixties by Otto Mühl of the Viennese *Aktionismus* group. These "actions" once landed people in jail, and twenty years later they haven't lost their capacity to shock. Each film/"action" is an orgiastic mess of collapsed boundaries: food poured over a penis, a chain of assfuckers standing knee-deep in a pond, someone shitting on a guy's face, and other now art-historical acts between consenting adults. The "action" I found completely unwatchable was an orgy that included the slow slaughter of a swan. Guess I identified with the one that didn't consent.

People seem to confuse "transgression" with violence. Probably the worst act I've ever seen was a supposedly "transgressive" G. G. Allin show. He'd jam the mike up his ass and then try to club someone in a front row with it, while howling his wish to rape. (He's been known to jump women in the audience.) This "transgresses" nothing. Just reinforces the violence already sanctioned in the culture.

In a way, though, punk took up in the late seventies where most of the body artists left off, bringing deliberate ugliness, self-injury, and what McEvilley calls "the seeking of dishonor" into the mainstream. Apart from the few artists who still do ordeal or endurance pieces aimed at personal transformation or public symbolism (like Linda Montano and Tehching Hsieh tying themselves together with a rope for a year), the body art practice of the seventies is history.

Now the forbidden is connected much more to language. I don't mean obscenity, necessarily. A few years ago when I first saw Karen Finley perform—breaking rules so inherent in the landscape you don't even notice them till they collapse—I was astonished by her appropriation of male power and desire. Though I certainly didn't analyze it like that as I listened. I *felt* the monologue with a visceral sensation of empowerment.

Performers in this tradition appeal to a language in the subconscious which may never have words.

At Coleman's spectacle of rage, I only know I felt the pity and the terror of tragedy. I know I shared the pain of both mouse and man. It stayed with me for days.

May 1988

■ ■ ■ Is That You?

It was no dream. I'd simply entered a parallel universe that looked, shook, and smelled like Times Square. Suddenly I was meeting strangers on the street who seemed to know me quite intimately. They advised me in elevators, ran from me down dingy hotel hallways, and threatened me casually in the parkway at the Marriott Marquis. The man who put me into a passing car in front of St. Luke's told the driver, confidentially: "All she did was write some poetry." Who *were* these people? But, more important, who was "I"?

There was no escaping myself this time. I'd arrived for Fiona Templeton's *You—The City* at what certainly *seemed* to be an office. But my motives were already in question. A "secretary" asked me to fill out a questionnaire while I waited on a black leather couch. Dutifully I answered the cryptic queries. "Are you now or have you ever been?" "What is this making of you?" Meanwhile, a "businesswoman"—or god knows, some sort of "therapist"—opened her office door and asked the other "client" (Franklin Furnace's director, Martha Wilson) to come in. I could hear some sort of animated speech after they closed the door. Would I have to say something in there?! As they exited into the hall, I heard the "businesswoman" telling Martha to "laugh, if you are you. . . ."

You—The City is a play for an audience of one, taking you—the audience—through encounters with maybe a dozen performers. So I figured the "businesswoman" would return. For me. Yes, the office door was opening. But, no. It was some other "businesswoman" or "therapist." In any case, she was dressed for success. I took a seat in her "office." She sat behind the desk and began to speak as though we had an important deal to make. But she was saying things like, "Get your desire like you get a joke. . . . What you're not getting is in. . . ." Soon we, too, left the office to end up in the downpour outside, facing the novelty shops and the movie palaces. "Your new idea will get older," she said, taking my elbow. "I don't say your name to tell you it, but because it's not mine." The "businesswoman" jumped over a puddle into Seventh Avenue.

Was I supposed to talk back to her? If so, whadd-I-say? I didn't know my role. I had thought I'd do my usual: "professional spectator." But I couldn't take it all in. Couldn't write much of it down. I needed more distance for true spectating, and I'd been turned into a participant. I felt silly taking notes. I took a few anyway.

I had become what the piece was about.

Over at a theater showing *Midnight Crossing*, the "businesswoman" left me as a woman in a fake leopardskin coat rushed up. She and I, apparently, had known each other all our lives. Taking my arm, she guided me up the crowded sidewalk, her speech full of vague threats. I would have to "decide." My family would be "devastated." I seemed to be implicated in something.

This charade. My passivity. My voyeurism. Self-consciousness. The usual crises of perception and attention.

We'd arrived on 46th Street at a joint called the Harlequin. There a woman waited in the doorway. She started up the steps, then began to run. I followed, entering a shabby waiting room that seemed stuffed with soda machines. She'd disappeared. No. There she was in the corner being coy. She ran the minute I spotted her. As I followed, because I figured my role in this was to follow, she kept giving me just a glimpse, then running ahead through the brown hallways and up stairs until I found myself in a little room, where she closed the door, turned her back to me, and slowly dropped the raincoat from her shoulders. She was wearing an evening gown.

Directing me to sit on a chair behind a curtain, she took her place facing me through a window/mirror. I mean I saw both her and myself. Our faces merged as she confronted me: "Isn't that why you're here? Because you're terrified?" Should I answer? (What *was* the answer?) I tried to take notes on what she said to me. Was I supposed to? "You try to get it out of your mind by clasping your pen," she said. Was that in the script?

Finally, she told me to chase her from the room and down the steps. I did. There in the midtown rain was a sodden young man in a poncho and half-open shirt who began a one-sided lover's quarrel with me. "You're not really you, and yet you're here. . . ." We walked past *Fences* and the rest to Eighth Avenue, as he spoke passionately, insisting, "You choke me and I let you. . . ." He punctuated that by sloshing through a puddle. And then recalled singing the height and depth of me, and so on.

I was always about to be part of some plot. The next person I met was a confessor, who questioned me about "the affair I'd had" and then put me in the battered blue car, which, I suppose, I'd been expecting. It looked like a getaway car, with its fake leopardskin seatcovers, its broken pencils and empty beer bottles on the floor. The driver spoke surly poetry as we turned up Eighth Avenue to 51st Street. "Sophisticated audiences don't ask questions. You don't either, I see." I muttered replies to a few of his queries. But was I supposed to?

The driver choreographed me through rush hour to my next confidante, who walked me through a Hell's Kitchen playground in the rain. And that one, too, told me many things about me and my relationship to her. By the time I arrived dripping wet at the apartment on 49th Street with another performer—where I found Martha Wilson sitting on the couch—I had accepted my part in this mystery no one intended to solve. The performer who'd brought me there eventually changed his costume and his personality, and told me once we were back outside, "After what's happened between you and me, I think you can't expect to see me again."

He was gone. I had just experienced the drama of a relationship, without having to have one. Is that what they call acting? When I looked at these people who seemed to know me, who were inches away, I could see their "acting eyes," through which they'd pulled back a little bit, into another self. I could have been anyone. I wondered what they saw out there where the world was my stage.

May 1988

■ ■ ■ Deconstructing Dixie

I realized with horror that I knew those rubbery "Negro" humanoids on the screen. Those were my Saturday morning cartoons. As a kid, I'd watched all that jungle bunny stuff with unconscious, uncritical eyes. To see it again in Thought Music's deconstructed minstrel show at Franklin Furnace was to gag on that old racist muck. My legacy.

Laurie Carlos, Jessica Hagedorn, and Robbie McCauley—Thought Music—put on the minstrel masks just to stretch them out. They make two assumptions. That those images still inform everything. And that no one wants to talk about it.

America grew up on this shuck and jive. Minstrel shows began after the War of 1812 and by the 1840s were wildly popular. In *Blacking Up,* Robert C. Toll analyzes this "earliest uniquely American popular entertainment form" as a way for white audiences to work out their feelings about slavery. The caricatures onstage assured them that slaves were a peculiar, inferior, and happy lot. White performers in burnt-cork make-up had created a whole plantation mythology, featuring "empty-headed grinning darkies devoted to their masters." Real black people were allowed to join the shows just before the Civil War. But only if they, too, appeared in blackface and "acted the nigger."

Sure, the images got more refined. But I knew the dumb TV bumblings of *Amos 'n Andy* in my own childhood. And I loved the land of zip-a-dee-do-dah. That's still America's paradise fantasy. Songs like "Swanee River" and "Summertime" push some sort of nostalgia button. Thought Music's last show, *Teenytown,* began with Carlos, Hagedorn, and McCauley in polka dot dresses playing washboard and spoons, singing hell out of "Dixie" and the rest. In *Blacking Up,* Toll concludes: ". . . the minstrel show, long after it had disappeared, left its central image—the grinning black mask—lingering on, deeply embedded in American consciousness."

By the end of a Thought Music show, we get behind the grin. But on the journey there we've gone through uncomfortable territory, perhaps hitting nerves at the Dorothy Dandridge/Hazel Scott sketch. ("Hollywood is just too hard without a white man.") Or at the exotic emigrant "what-race-*are*-you?" number. ("The trouble with us is we aren't even niggers.") Or at the monologue conflating the millions of slaves pushed off the ships in midpassage with a little girl who won't be picked to dance on TV because she is too dark and her hair isn't "good."

Carlos and McCauley are black. Hagedorn is Filipino. They told me that after they performed at the Schomburg Center in Harlem, audience members questioned them: "How can you show this to white people?" McCauley said she thought the piece was hard for a new generation of black people who hadn't seen the really gross images, but could feel all the subtleties of racism in their lives. "Then when you present the strong images, they make a connection, and it's very sad." One older woman at the Schomburg was particularly upset about the cartoons. "Where did you find these. . . . I thought they were gone . . . our dignity. . . ." She felt ashamed. I had assumed that white people would feel ashamed. That black people would be angry. My misunderstanding made me feel more ashamed, made me feel like not discussing it. This is how these images do their dirty work. This is why racism is still a taboo topic. Once into the muck, it feels like quicksand.

Racism, like sexism, has a lot to do with role-playing.

Robbie McCauley grew up through the forties and fifties in Washington, D.C., and in Georgia. In the South, "you were clearly taught things to do in front of white people. And you accepted it as life or death. . . . Around white people, you really had to fix your face. . . . The smiling face. The serious face. But never the angry face. . . . It took me years to figure out how to look normal. I learned that from acting. How to be real."

She'd wanted to be a teacher or historian, but found "some fire connected to theater." It taught her self-knowledge and self-esteem, when all along she hadn't quite liked herself. And hadn't known that she hadn't quite liked herself. In the late sixties, after graduating from

Howard, McCauley studied with Lloyd Richards at the Negro Ensemble Company. There she met Laurie Carlos, "a kid." They did not then become friends, just admired each other's work.

Carlos and Hagedorn describe McCauley as the most political among them, while McCauley worries that she might not be political enough. She sees Assata Shakur, for example, as "doing something I didn't. . . . I'm only telling stories." But when other artists told her that her solo work was *too* political (rhetorical, didactic), she began to ask herself, "What's motivating this? And immediately I went to my father." McCauley's father, a career soldier, did hitches in the army, navy, air force, and national guard. He loved America. "But," says McCauley, "he was unspeakably angry with the white system. He would clench his teeth up and tighten his throat and get this sad angry look in his eyes. That's the look I couldn't look at when he was alive that I see very clearly now."

In 1985 she began a performance serial called *My Father & the Wars*, testifying to the everyday wars that don't make the evening news. Like her father fighting the white gas station attendant who calls him "nigger." Racism isn't really a rhetorical subject but a personal tragedy for everyone involved. The last installment, *Indian Blood*, focused on her grandfather, part of the all-black cavalry troop that took San Juan Hill before the Rough Riders did. Her grandfather also fought Indians, though his wife was part Indian and he was said to be as well.

McCauley is also collaborating currently with her husband, musician Ed Montgomery, on *Congo New York*. The piece will deal with Zaire as well as their personal struggles over gender, class, and race. (Montgomery is white.) McCauley says she is obsessed with bearing witness about racism, also with the possibility of connecting to white people. Which, she's decided, isn't easy. But, as she says in one of her pieces, "I was always a sucker for integration."

When she was fourteen, Laurie Carlos saw Gloria Foster perform in *White America* and "for the very first time I realized how much power the stage had politically, and I wanted that." Carlos grew up in the projects along Avenue D. She grew up around creative people—her father a musician, her mother a dancer, the Bobbettes and Shirelles and Chantels rehearsing in the living room because they had a piano, Jackie

Wilson buying her her first bicycle, Otis Blackwell playing stepfather
for a few months, and so on.

By the time she was nineteen, she was working for Harry Belafonte
and others as a casting director. This after graduating "an outcast"
from the High School of Performing Arts, where she was told that she
did not have what it took to be an actress. And she'd gotten into Performing Arts only to be told by her mother, "Actresses are pretty, and
you're not pretty."

Carlos was unconventional, rebellious, stubborn. She left the film
business, and, against everyone's advice, decided to have a baby.
Shortly afterwards, in addition to her chronic asthma, she developed
a form of muscular dystrophy known as myasthenia gravis. At one
point, her hands were paralyzed and her lungs collapsed. Shuttling in
and out of the hospital, she performed in *For Colored Girls Who Have
Considered Suicide/When the Rainbow Is Enuf* from the night it opened in
a Lower East Side bar to the end of its Broadway run. After one of her
sisters died of asthma, Carlos decided that "life and death are truly
choices," and, while she still takes medication every day, "I don't agree
to be ill."

This is another story of self-definition. Finding that she didn't have
the right "look" for commercial theater, and that she was not welcome
in the "patriarchal fortress" of black theater, Carlos decided to create
something for herself. Her performance art pieces like *Nonsectarian
Conversations with the Dead* and *Organdy Falsetto* are poetic, abstract, as-
sociative. Carlos has perhaps the opposite sensibility to McCauley's,
yet, McCauley points out, "She says she's not political, because she
doesn't have a 'line.' But the way she conducts her life, she does it with
great correctness. She'd hate me for saying that." In *Falsetto*, there's
the recurring refrain: "Is we still black? Still black." You can talk about
looks and money and smarts, but, Carlos says, that's the bottom line:
"Still black."

The original common ground for Carlos, Hagedorn, and McCauley was
actually Ntozake Shange's *For Colored Girls*. McCauley declined to join
the original cast, saying she had to earn some money. And who would
have guessed that something this black and this female would make it
to Broadway? (She did join it on Broadway.) And Hagedorn used to

perform with Shange in San Francisco, as she developed the piece in clubs.

Hagedorn had moved to California from the Philippines in the late sixties, and the artists around the Haight took her in, particularly Kenneth Rexroth. "I was this little 'exotic' in the hippy scene, and while those people were very good to me I felt like the Other constantly. I never could really articulate it." It became clear after she joined a group of Third World artists and realized she was "home."

Carlos says: "When Jessica's best work happens, you see Jessica in a new world, which is where she always is. That's when she's her most wonderful self onstage." Hagedorn often deals with that search for one's place in the world. It came up in her performance work with the Gangster Choir and in her last book, *Pet Food & Tropical Apparitions*. Where do you really come from when you've had a "very Western upbringing" in Manila? When *Ebony* picks you out as an up and coming black writer?

Hagedorn said she was very conscious of not being black and using the word "nigger" in performance, though some years ago when she was traveling a lot with Shange, people often assumed she *was* black. And it's all the same to some people. I discovered in my research that the soldiers who went to the Philippines to fight what Teddy Roosevelt called "a jumble of savage tribes" saw little difference between the American "savages" they'd just defeated at home and these Filipino "dogeaters," "tree-dwellers," "goo-goos"—or simply "niggers."

Currently Hagedorn is completing a novel about the Philippines— *Dogeaters*. She will visit her family there this summer, but admits, "When you go back, you can't find the answers to who you are."

One afternoon at a Thought Music rehearsal, Laurie Carlos mentioned that people sometimes ask her why Jessica is in the show. "People don't understand that Jessica's way of life has been determined by 'Swanee River,'" said Carlos. "So people will come up to you, especially black people, and say, 'Is she black? She's not black!'"

"It stops right there," said Hagedorn.

"You can stop the exploration of these images when you do that," McCauley added. And then—I see by my transcript—we went partway into the endless labyrinth: The way white liberals push the racist stuff away instead of dealing with feelings about it. The coincidence of Robbie doing *Indian Blood* last fall while Jessica was reading about Roosevelt in the Philippines. How black people don't want to discuss slavery. How Laurie's mother could sing "Dixie" with tears in her eyes. How black soldiers were willing to kill American Indians. And white people don't want to discuss any of it.

"So, yes," Carlos said, "that's what Jessica is doing singing 'Dixie,' because in the final analysis we're all singing 'Dixie.' If you think for one minute James Earl Jones ain't singing 'Dixie' . . . know what I mean? Not a damn thing has changed. Nothing. We wear more expensive chains. That's it."

That stopped us dead. No one knew what to say because we'd worked our way into unspeakable feelings. Our legacy. The muck. Was there any way out? None of us really wanted to be there in "Dixie." Finally, Hagedorn broke the silence by suggesting that we might need a drink, and we all laughed.

I remembered something McCauley had said earlier: "I think we're scared of the anger, because under the anger is sadness, and under the sadness is something impossible."

June 1988

■ ■ ■ A Crash of Symbols

Franklin Furnace reeked like a real-life furnace, the bite of something gaseous getting stronger as we entered the basement. Now we'd rub two performers together and—blow up the joint? Sherman Fleming and Kristine Stiles entered from behind a white screen, taking awkward baby steps because they were pressed up against each other, holding a board between their naked bodies. Once they were front and center, this black man and white woman began drumming their hands over each other's backs and buttocks, changing rhythms but slapping in unison. Intimate yet separated by that slash of plywood, they were a living hieroglyphic for "black/white" and "man/woman." At the Furnace, it looked more absurd than incendiary, but in other contexts (other states, other neighborhoods) such activity could start a fire and alarum. I'm speaking in metaphor, of course. But then, this was a piece about language, though no words were spoken.

Fleming and Stiles had separate manifestos in the program notes, outlining their mutual concern with issues of "logos and hysterias." Both are intellectuals who've obviously waded much further into the poststructuralist gobbledygook than I have, so I'm going to simplify them into the lowest common Derrida: Language doesn't just describe reality, it creates reality. If you're black or female (those proverbial Others), you're a born symbol. You're going to travel through life in a box that throws a shadow wherever you go. Walk onstage and that shadow goes with you. Only straight white men get to be the blank slates who can write anything on themselves, and that's probably how they become the "great artists" we've heard so much about.

After the drumming prologue, Fleming and Stiles put on shirts and jeans and began constructing *Western History as a Three-Story Building*. They'd been inspired by Ishmael Reed's metaphor in *Mumbo Jumbo*.

Reed described Western history as: a store dealing in religious articles; above that a gun store; above that an advertising firm specializing in soap accounts. That's capitalism, I guess: selling things to die for; selling things to die with; selling things to clean it up.

While Stiles set up rows of Coke bottles holding red candles across the back of the stage, Fleming placed silver bowls full of glowing charcoal across the front. Here was the source of the mysterious smell. She lit the candles, while he hung Coke bottles full of water over each silver bowl. Water splashed onto the embers. Now we had smoke in the front, fire in the back, grit on my notebook. The performers went backstage for big piles of onions and greens, which they diced with meat cleavers on two podiums, and then turned on the fans that had been sitting on the podiums. It smelled great, a ritual in Sensurround.

Fleming began to make an enormous cat's cradle of white ribbon, running the strands from wall to wall. Stiles stood at a blackboard with an armload of too many books, writing, "Ain [sic], end, drift, target, prey, quarry, game, view . . ." illustrating that words can only be defined by other words, creating a slippery unreliable trail. Then she made pictograms. She erased, wrote, erased. Meanwhile, Fleming attached flowers and bells to the white ribbons. The candles burned down. My eyes were smarting now from the onions and the smoke. And Stiles was writing, "Scars = certain elements of reality." So ended the religious section, with the space converted to a swamp of water puddles, onion bits, Coke bottles, and white lines.

The performers changed into formal wear and blindfolds. Precariously, the white woman wearing sequins and pearls carried the black man wearing a tux. They fumbled for the fans and the cleavers, placing these objects on the floor. They careened into the ribbons, made mush of some clutter. He, the taller and heavier, struggled to collapse himself into piggyback position. She struggled to hold him up. This was the moment with emotional impact, as they took their chances on the obstacle course, looking like unwanted guests at the prom. And so they did their damage as a unit, a bull deconstructing the china shop.

In the last section, they advanced slowly toward the audience while holding a pole between them. From it dangled shards of glass and mirror—blinding, jangling. Behind them, slick magazine ads flashed over the screen. I doubt if they intended this, but for me the piece evoked a funny suburban hell, from the odor of backyard barbecue to prom night to that monster version of a patio wind chime. Maybe even that makes sense if they're talking about "logos and hysteria," if you want to see everyday Americana as a good skin to peel, a good place to find something irrational and scary beneath the surface.

Back when Sherman Fleming performed solo, as RODFORCE, he might have been labeled an "ordeal" or "endurance" artist. In a piece called *Ax Vapor*, he wore shoes bolted to halves of bowling balls, round side down, and went spinning-falling repeatedly over an Oriental rug. In *Fault*, he swung in an arc while hanging from the ceiling by his feet. In *Something Akin to Living*, he stood at the center of two columns while an assistant fit some forty pieces of wood between the performer and the columns; the piece ended when he could no longer support the weight and everything collapsed. In 1987, Kristine Stiles wrote about Fleming for *High Performance*, comparing those columns to the Doric columns in Washington, D.C. (where he lives), and noting his "strong emphasis on the body as the material that bears the weight of such symbolic edifices."

I'm selecting that line because it carries over into the work Fleming and Stiles now collaborate on. Artists devise rituals and ordeals for themselves because these actions address either their own demons— or the demons imposed on them. When the body becomes a metaphor, its struggle is poetry.

April 1989

■ ■ ■ Two Birds with One Stone

I remember that night in '85 when I first stumbled into a Dancenoise show at 8BC and recognized the energy of some wild-in-the-streets girlhood: the black bras and combat boots; a deafening ugly sound-track; choreography built from the urge to brawl and make messes and put one's little baby dolls through certain ordeals. The act was . . . uncivilized. I knew I'd have to follow these girls to the ends of the earth if they ever got a gig there.

Anne Iobst and Lucy Sexton flaunt the aggression women learn to hide. In the next Dancenoise piece I saw, at Franklin Furnace, they fought each other with knives and finally "killed" the two mannequins they'd hung from the ceiling, leaving so much fake blood and real slime they could have skated over the stage. I watched with a guilty pleasure, unable to find words for what I loved. I suppose I saw it as a bracing new transgression. I suppose I had some predilection to champion anyone the tabloids would call a "terror gal."

But these are terrorists wielding a shtick, and with it they attack power in its many disguises. Their shows are always teeming with pop culture junk, since that's where power hides and where it emanates from—the evening sound bites, the advertising arias, the fashion fore-casts, the top forty wool-gatherers. The Dancenoise way of knowledge is to see life as one ungentrified unregenerate 14th Street, just a ram-shackle boulevard where everything from Shakespeare to the unwrit-ten law on how to wear a leotard can finally be destroyed and displayed in a bin. The performances level everything in their path, turning slo-gans into mantras, banality into ritual, pearls into swine. As a rule, they're a riot and a gas.

In *All the Rage*, Dancenoise used/abused the television conventions: short unconnected episodes, characters who banter, dreadful events

Near-stage-death experience: Anne Iobst kneels over Lucy Sexton in *All the Rage*. (©
Dona Ann McAdams.)

that never change the hero, and theme music telling you what to feel.
The show was not about television, of course, but about white noise,
the TV state of mind, and the possibilities of bursting out of the all-
around reduced personality in some startling, violent way.

In the show, Lucy and Anne go through near-stage-death experiences. In one of the episodes, nooses drop and the stagehands slide
in two sets of steps. Lucy and Anne, wearing teddies and combat boots
and red wigs with plastic apples embedded on top, pace the stage puff-
ing their last cigarettes. They don the nooses, climb the steps, and pick
up handguns they find there. They shoot at each other, then sit down
and begin a litany of wishes. They'd like, for example, to jump off the
George Washington Bridge—and then go shopping. From their bags
they pull the products they'd then like to buy—Lite this and Lite that.

Life is easy and answers simple in a world so coded and counter-
coded, where every possibility has been televised. It's enough to turn
a gal into a new generic human. "I get it," says Anne. "I quit drugs.
I get a job. . . . I master the possibilities. And [holding up a milk carton
decorated with a couple of Missing Children] if I feel like it, I save this

kid." Even the kidnapped sell commodities and are themselves consumable. And *Romeo and Juliet* is one more fake ridiculous symbol system. Lucy, alone on stage, calls, "Wherefore art thou, Romeo?" We hear the reply made offstage: "I'm changing, and my name is Anne."

The performers practice, and suffer through, unexplainable slapstick violence. A lion—perhaps hungry, perhaps lecherous—chases Lucy around a couch. Later, both Lucy and Anne (wearing bike helmets with toilet plungers stuck on top) cower behind the couch, as unseen forces in the wings pelt them with potatoes and onions. They decide it's a case of "female stress syndrome." They pick up the motorized Snugli bears careening over the stage and bite into their fluffy necks, looking sheepish as the "blood" drips down their chins. The dancing is intimate, playful, and fierce. They jump onto each other, take liberties, begin fights. They look like they're going by instinct, relying on their bodies to communicate and shake loose whatever sticks in the craw.

As with the Kipper Kids, their partnership is bigger than both of them. (*All the Rage* even featured an abbreviated Kipper-ish food fight.) But the Kipper Kid is a character, while Anne and Lucy aren't. They simply go through the motions of never-ending masquerade, always dressed alike and constantly changing their clothes. Often they peel off layer after layer—dresses, uniforms, underwear, wigs, some still dangling their price tags. But even as they dress for every feminine role from waitress to bored teenager to femme fatale to monster, they don't ever change in response to the symbols. Resolutely and forever, they remain "Lucy" and "Anne."

They concluded *All the Rage* by presenting their bodies, their selves, stripping naked to the tune of "you're just too good to be true/can't take my eyes off of you. . . ." Our voyeurism was schmaltz. Standing close to us, they then poured pots of "blood" over their heads. It dripped to their feet, and they danced a last duet. The blood de-eroticized them, made them terrible to behold. It was a last sacrament, not a striptease. They'd simply cut through the crap to the source of their power.

April 1989

■ ■ ■ A Public Cervix Announcement

Well before showtime, the little red Harmony Burlesque Theater was swarming and buzzing with sex radicals, sex buffs, camera buffs, and the plain old curious. "Feminist porn activist" Annie Sprinkle stood up front, near posters of the women who *usually* play the Harmony—the assorted "bombshells" and "exotics." Tonight the cast would be different, and the label would be "artists." Or, at least, "show people." Folks lined up to pose with Sprinkle. "Her tits on your head—three dollars," said the woman with the Polaroid camera. It was an act halfway between absurd and pornographic. It was tourists getting pictures taken with a native. It was Saturday night, and in theaters all over Manhattan, voyeurs consorted with exhibitionists. Here at the Smut Fest, the encounter was just a little more . . . in your face.

Just a little more . . . hairy. Our mistress of ceremonies, Jennifer Blowdryer, told us: "Take pictures. All kinds of exploitation are welcome." But can you be exploited if you *want* to be exploited? Does an act change when you redefine the context—when you call it "performance art" instead of "striptease," for example? I wasn't really having a philosophical evening—just making my first voyage to a new world. These burlesque joints aren't exactly female turf unless you're the fantasy object onstage, and even then, you're just passing through.

In a note, organizers Sprinkle and Blowdryer told me they wanted to "save sex" from the backlash triggered by AIDS hysteria and the new conservatism, "partly because sex is our favorite subject matter in our work." To the bordello-red decor, they'd added a giant drawing of a vagina by Rene, who bills himself as "the best artist." And they'd booked a wide range of talent and quasi-talent. There was a monologuist (male) who threw frankfurters at us to punctuate his tale of a six-year-old losing his virginity. There was an s&m comic (female) wearing corset, bridal veil, and dildo, who told us she performed because she hated it so; it was part of her masochism.

It was an evening for naked signs and signifiers. I've seldom been so aware of how much a message depends on the performer's gender. And how much we're still informed by mythologies of "good girls" and "bad."

Veronica Vera, self-described "sexual evolutionary," appeared in a crown and a black and gold dress, in the style of Snow White. She told a story about her "beautiful bondage" with Mistress Antoinette, a story lyrical in its perversity, in which she's forced to wear thigh-high boots polished by slaves' tongues—that sort of thing. Moving smoothly from eros to thanatos, she then talked about her testimony before a Senate committee investigating porn, later incorporated into the Meese Report. There in the Senate chambers, the lawmakers confronted her with their copies of *Veronica Vera in Tight Bondage*. They told her other women were afraid they too would have to do this sort of thing. Shouldn't the government ban such photos? "Ban the lives of the saints," Vera advised them. "That's what inspired me."

Sprinkle and Vera now work together running a Transformation Salon. They do makeovers, using their years of experience in the sex industry to "glamorize" other women. (That is, they make them look and feel sexy, then photograph them.) They also direct porn movies focused on women's pleasure. They refer to their work as "porn modernism" and see it as a tool for female self-empowerment. Not that someone who's been around the business wouldn't notice the . . . contradictions. Jennifer Blowdryer, for example, sang a couple of laments—as in "I bought some high heels/Now I'm not real/Now I'm a living doll. . ."

Annie Sprinkle appeared onstage wearing more clothes than she'd worn offstage. In her full flowery dress and sparkly Vanna White smile, she played it demure. But she *would* show her cervix. Sweetly, she announced that many people didn't know what (or where) a cervix was. I guess we needed some sex education. "This is the vaginal canal," she cooed, holding up a felt-tip sketch of the female reproductive system. "Let me hear you say, 'vaginal canal.'" And we said it.

A female assistant (dressed as a man) helped Sprinkle with the speculum. There Annie sat, legs spread, inviting the audience to peek

Annie Sprinkle solicits audience commentary on her cervix. (© C. M. Hardt.)

inside her with the aid of a flashlight. I recalled the old days of the women's movement, when looking at another woman's cervix—or one's own—was a political act (but never done as a performance, so far as I know). One female spectator came forward to look. "Amazing," she said. "I'm usually on the other end of this." And so the act became a little model of the world. Every other gawker who crushed onto the stage was male, and each contributed a dumb wisecrack after peering through the speculum on hands and knees. I guess they had to demonstrate that they were still on top of things, so to speak.

But to look inside someone's body is to see too much. Sprinkle had gone beyond nakedness to a supernakedness that transcends sexuality: body interiors aren't sexy. All that remained were questions of vulnerability and power. I've seen it happen before, though—that she with the most vulnerability onstage can end up wielding the most power.

Sprinkle noted, "My cervix is a hit." She ended her act before the gazers had tired of it. She stood up, and in a soft, hostess-with-the-mostest voice, said: "I'd like you all to go out and break a taboo tonight."

May 1989

■ ■ ■ Revisions of Excess

ometimes I love reading about "the loss of the Real" and other greatest hits of postmodern thought. But we're talking High Concept with most of this stuff, and the texts get ever more pre-, post-, and para-. Academic cultural critics have always invented their own little worlds and turgid new languages. But dip into some of this poststructuralist za-za, and you have to wonder if the alphabet itself isn't in deep trouble.

A performance group called the V-Girls recently launched a parody from within at CUNY Graduate Center with "The Question of Manet's *Olympia*: Posed and Skirted." This *faux*-panel discussion by five female *faux*-academics deconstructed Manet's painting in penetrating *October*-ese. That is, the discourse re-deconstructed what is already too-deconstructed. Seated at a long table (perhaps a telling reference to the Wooster Group?), the panelists (Martha Baer, Jessica Chalmers, Erin Cramer, Andrea Fraser, Marianne Weems) had a prim, suited, fresh-from-the-Sorbonne look. Haughty and deadpan, they delivered brief and ridiculous papers—"The Female Nude: The Beginning of the End of a Good Idea," "Semiotic Problems in Seeing and Spelling," "Olympia as Phallus: An Interrogation of the Horizontal." Etcetera. I particularly enjoyed "Manet's Best Friend" (illustrated with a slide of an imploring spaniel), which dissected "the gaze of the dog" in the usual opaque isms and wasms.

The V-Girls' last performance was a fake Lacanian analysis of *Heidi*. To find any of this funny, audience members probably had to know the basic po-mo buzzwords or buzzphrases—like "the gaze." Still, the panels are an anti-elitist project—they're about "foregrounding the privilege." (Or is that "privileging the foreground"?) When one panelist asked, rhetorically, "*Should* ideas be applied to art?" the audience applauded.

I'd like to send Lacan to see the Blue Man Group. In this show, the bodies kept oozing, and the byproducts became art.

With their blue bald heads, blue hands, identical clothing, and total silence, the group's members (Matt Goldman, Philip Stanton, Chris Wink) looked humanoid and anonymous. And the program at their recent Performing Garage show never called them Blue *Men*, but Blue *Man*—as if each were one piece of a single body.

This was a parasitic body. They sat down at a formal dining table and ate claylike pablum from their plates; more pablum immediately squeezed out of holes in their shirts and back onto their plates. They ate that. They were eating themselves. Their actions were comic, even gimmicky at times, but The Blue Man show had a subtext of profound alienation—discomfort with the self and with artmaking as a sign of individuality.

They are, in fact, generic performance artists, evoking images of Oskar Schlemmer, Yves Klein, and the Kipper Kids. They began the show by removing what appeared to be toothpaste caps protruding from their lab coats and, immediately, thick blue paint began to drip onto small canvases attached chest high. When all the gloop was gone, they hung their new abstract expressions from clamps. And as half the world once said of Jackson Pollock: "A monkey could have done it."

They made more trick art. Seated behind tubs of orange, pink, and chartreuse paint, the three splattered the liquid with plastic ladles, faster and faster, splashing it onto the audience. The front rows cowered, and for a moment, the air was a pixillated multicolor cloud. They then displayed the large sheet they'd been sitting on, which had become something of a Barnett Newman in pink and orange. Later, one performer threw ping-pong-sized balls into the mouths of the other two, who then broke the balls open in their mouths and spewed the contents—orange, blue, and purple paint—onto a canvas. The game was for each "artist" to catch the paint seal-style, no hands. The result was a bad Frankenthaler.

They also presented what they called a Poster Moment to illustrate how little a single human can do. Each held a stack of posterboards. Every board had a different message. Words flashed by so quickly that there was time to read perhaps half of one board and nothing from the others. And most of the messages were comments on the choice the reader had just made. For example: "This one isn't as deep as the other two."

Between each messy act, the three carefully touched up each other's make-up.

At last, a chance to join the biannual Biennial-bashing ritual.

The Whitney added performance art for the first time in years, and its choice of Eleanor Antin was truly a puzzle. She again played the black ballerina, Eleanora Antinova—a character she's been doing since the midseventies, and it certainly isn't getting less offensive as time goes by. As she recently told *The New York Times*, Antinova is "a survivor, a very positive and heroic image." Obviously, Antin can't see through the haze of her good intentions. A white person "blacking up" to create a "heroic image" for black people speaks of nothing but presumptuousness and naïveté. As the Whitney has to know—judging by the performers its been booking into its branch locations—the Antin/Antinova show is no indication of what's happening in performance art in 1989.

May 1989

■ ■ ■ An Artist Retreats from Rage

Readjust the knobs on the twentieth century, and you can re-tune history so the avant-gardists were headed toward "multiculturalism" all along. Rafael Montañez Ortiz sees the re-emergence of animism and ceremony and shamanism all down the great chain of isms. At least, that's his reading of Dada rituals, Duchampian found objects, and Cageian "chance operations." They may be highlights from the Western avant-garde, says Ortiz, but native cultures were using them thousands of years ago. Our art, their religion—or everyday life.

Ortiz has organized "Art and the Invisible Reality," an ambitious series of performances and panels convening next week at Franklin Furnace and at Rutgers University, where he teaches. The object is to bring native culture practitioners together with contemporary artists who, if not overtly "spiritual," use art to change their lives.

Back in the sixties, when he was known as Ralph Ortiz, he never used words like *shamanism* to describe his performances—in which he chopped up pianos or killed chickens and mice. Destruction Art was a bohemian companion to Minimalism and Conceptualism: all of them aimed at paring down if not eliminating the object. For Ortiz, it was something more. In 1962, he wrote an angry manifesto about transcendence through sacrifice, about destruction rituals connecting him to "deep unconscious life." Poor and Puerto Rican (Ortiz would later found El Museo del Barrio), he was an outsider struggling with "all the contradictions of my childhood, growing up in a patriarchal structure, within a racist society." The destruction events were cathartic.

In *The Life and Death of Henny Penny* (1967), Ortiz crawled out from beneath the voluminous dress of a woman collaborator, "newborn" and holding a live chicken. Snarling out "Daddy" over and over, he strung the chicken up by its feet, and swung it out over the audience. He stood ready with shears, and as it swung back, he snipped its head off. He then beat a flamenco guitar with the chicken carcass till he'd smashed it. In one other event that year, he destroyed both a chicken and a piano. During subsequent rituals, audience members intervened to rescue the chickens he intended to sacrifice—an act Ortiz accepted. "You have to understand my whole experience," he explains. "I grew up summers on farms and I used to help with catching the chickens and slaughtering. As an adolescent I worked in a chicken slaughter-house. For me, this is no awesome thing."

Nor was destruction uncommon in the art of the sixties. By the end of the decade, all such work was politically charged, half-lit with daily doses of Vietnam war footage. In one Ortiz performance, mice with number tags were drafted into a "war zone" full of mousetraps. Again, some spectators ran rescue missions. The killing had to do with facing reality, Ortiz says. He wanted to sensitize people.

As for the shattered pianos, Ortiz describes their demise in retro-spect as a "giving back to nature—releasing the spirits that were bound up in this logical rational construct called 'piano.'" Last spring, he recreated a Piano-Destruct "concert" at the Alternative Museum. The ruined upright then sat in the corner as an installation piece—strings propped against splintered keyboard. Musical instruments seem to have a life, because they play, and so they seem to have a death. It was a sad thing to see.

Ortiz did a piece called *Self-Destruction* at the 1966 Destruction in Art Symposium, in London. As critic Kristine Stiles described it: "Ortiz ripped his suit to reveal himself dressed in diapers. Whining, scream-ing, cajoling, and desperately calling, 'Mamma, Ma Ma Ma Ma' and 'Pappa, Pa Pa,' he banged a rubber duck and drank enormous quan-tities of milk from bottles until he vomited on the stage, bringing his psychic Oedipal drama to an end." While many in the audience were disgusted, Ortiz's piece wasn't unique in cultivating taboo material. At the same symposium, Yoko Ono did *Cut Piece*, sitting passively while audience members snipped her clothes off with a scissors. And Austrian artist Hermann Nitsch disemboweled the carcass of a lamb, scattered innards and gore around the room, and projected a film of male genitals onto the dead animal. Symposium organizers eventually went on trial at the Old Bailey for that one.

In the sixties and seventies, as artists claimed their own process or their own person to be the artwork, art's territory expanded into the unspeakable. And an art history of taboo acts emerged. [See "Life is a Killer," p. 157.] Artists were using their art to transform them-selves—with a thought toward transforming society. Spirituality had re-entered art through the most outrageous, least sanctimonious acts.

Now the edge has turned to mush.

Ortiz stopped doing destruction rituals by about 1970. "The whole idea of exploring Thanatos just didn't make any sense. There was no-where to go." For four years, he undertook a pilgrimage to study with healers, East and West (coast). He also dabbled in Buddhist medita-tion, dousing, yoga, psychic surgery—a trip through the New Age supermarket. He follows no particular dogma. Instead, he came to em-body what I think the New Age is all about—the creation of one's own personal religion. One can then make an artwork of practicing that religion. Artists scheduled to participate in the "Invisible Reality" sessions list activities like "trance inductions" and "bioplasmic field harmonizing."

What Ortiz came up with for himself is a form of meditation he calls "Physio-Psycho-Alchemy." Participants lie on their backs, squeezing a ball between their knees. The squeezing exhausts the legs, making them tremble, and Ortiz then directs the "initiates" in channeling that energy to the third eye. This dramatic change in his work, says Ortiz, is a shift from patriarchal to matriarchal shamanism. He also applies the shaman's language to his laser-video work, saying he taught the computer to dream. The cultural roots of all this—unlike the chicken rituals of yore—seem to be pure pastiche.

When discussing art, Ortiz constantly uses the words *authentic* (for native cultures) and *spurious* (for industrialized cultures). By this he means that we, the industrialized, have no relationship to nature, only to abstractions of nature and to machines. I asked him if the West isn't authentic in its own way, and he said, "No, it's authentically spu-rious," I don't agree. But Ortiz's point is that, surrounded by a coun-terfeit culture, we can't possibly perceive it, just as a fish doesn't understand it's in water. I guess the next question would be—who gets to describe what's authentic, anyway?

I can re-adjust the knobs on my twentieth century again, and say—yes, all down the great chain of isms, artists have stretched and discarded so many conventions they depleted the category of art. Now we have no traditions worth anything. We don't live in a culture of shamans, or know how to recognize or train them. We've had to go borrow from the Others.

Coming from us Westerners—the original one-and-only cultural imperialists—what is this multicultural craze? The chance to add those Others to our collection? Or are we talking about a whole new role for art and artists?

September 1989

S ome families get raised, and some get lowered. A deviant Dad stood in the air shaft outside Franklin Furnace's basement, leering through the window, snapping a handcuff around the wasp waist of his daughter, a Barbie doll. "You've just been waiting for your daddy, haven't you?" he smirked. He ogled. He oozed, because he was a slimeball.

Salley May's *Sinferno* cut the real horror in this scenario with simulated horror. The daughter's molested by Dad, unnurtured and unprotected by Mom. But the cheesy gothic ambience of the piece came straight from some plastic-bat-out-of-hell B movie. Cheap special effects seem appropriate to subliminal crud; they're two kinds of raw.

May sometimes played the father (in a mask). She played the daughter (as herself), or else Barbie did. There was also a surrogate Dad— a life-sized dummy in a wheelchair wearing a T-shirt emblazoned SUCK ME. EAT ME RAW. In his diapers and boots, with a Budweiser strapped to his chair, an anchor tattooed on his arm, the guy was a mess and a menace. Mom, that hollow figure, was a torso with prosthetic breasts. Late in the piece, May found Mom's head—the top end of a mannequin with raised brows and open mouth. "You look pretty surprised, Mom," said May. "Is that because you're finally getting the picture?"

The daughter's tone, though, was usually more ingenuous than angry. How come we only have sausage to eat? How come we never have milk? She would watch with incredulity as every treat became a trick, as the same people who put red roller skates on her feet also put bands around her arms stuck full of radiating needles. Maybe she could get something out of life's unpleasant surprises. Maybe she could use the rusty tools she finds under her pillow—to hack her arm off. That might get Mom's attention. *Sinferno* was a piece of antic invention, one of those shows where we don't know exactly why the plastic lobsters are dropping from the ceiling, but it works on some subconscious level. It's a dream world like childhood; things befall one.

The piece ended with the daughter getting what she wanted: milk (which she poured over her head) and a drum to play instead of the "dick bass." She un-haunted her house. A good thing, too. I figure she's the same girl who takes a gun down one day and says, "I don't like Mondays."

At Taller Latinoamericano, beauty contestants bustled in with their gowns and tuxes. Or pelts. Nine downtown theater venues had entered candidates, with proceeds to benefit the Bad Neighbors Company. And the Ms. Make-Believe Contest certainly had just the absurdity one could want from such an event: partisan judges, scowling beauties, and playful camaraderie between them.

MC Kimberly Flynn introduced "celebrity judges" Ellie Covan, John Kelly, and Carmelita Tropicana, who would choose "the woman or man who can really make people believe." Then the inevitable talent contest began, with a piercing scream. It was Judge Tropicana, shrieking and throwing herself at the first beauty, "Sonya" (Ms. wow Cafe). "Son-ya! Son-ya!" the audience chanted, as she began striding down the runway in beret and shades, toting a machine gun. Sonya then displayed her talent as best she could, given that the proletariat wouldn't have time to rise in the space of three minutes. "Talent is an instrument of the patriarchy!" she announced. Behind her on a little pink table sat the evening's grand prize: a lifetime supply of styling mousse.

The audience swooned for everyone. They loved the beauties with attitude—from Jennifer Blowdryer (Ms. Smutfest) to Matthew Courtney (Mr. ABC No Rio) to Jasmine (Ms. Dixon Place). But they *really* loved the sweetness personified by "Inga" (Ms. Atlantic Theatre Company), disarming charm dressed in a Brünhilde outfit. To make a long pageant short, Inga walked off with the crown, dangling it from one of the horns on her helmet, dabbing at her make-believe tears of joy.

Part of the round-robin evening at BAM that opened New Music America, *Industrial Symphony No. 1* had the precarious excitement of an evening at Franklin Furnace, despite a much larger budget. Film director

David Lynch (*Blue Velvet, Dune, Eraserhead*) created an industrial wasteland that gradually revealed its little secrets: airplanes above, a skinned
reindeer on stilts, our heroine in the trunk of a car. It began with an
unnecessary/uninteresting film clip, very different in tone from the
rest of the piece: Nicholas Cage and Laura Dern breaking up over the
phone. As soon as the curtain rose on the landscape of heartbreak, I
forgot about them.

Singer Julee Cruise, angelic in a white prom dress, spent a lot of
time floating over the stage on wires, moving slowly like a diver dropping into the deep. A midget came in and sawed at a log. The reindeer
rose from a gurney, staggered, and fell into the wings. The performance had moments of rock-vid surrealism with its obvious contrasts:
The beauty/the beast. The beast/the burden. But it kept surprising me.

The singer (her stuffed facsimile, anyway) crashed to the floor.
Fog-machine smoke rolled into the first rows. Bombers approached
through an air-raid warning and dozens of baby dolls floated down—
the bombs? The music by Angelo Badalamenti seemed to be one slen-
der tune, one languid torch song. It was pure ambience, a web holding
all the enigmas together.

November 1989

■ ■ ■ Radical Shriek

Diamanda Galas does not presume to speak for others. But people
with AIDS have occasionally told her that she speaks for them.
She is an instrument in tune with their rage and despair. And
she has a voice trained to explore the emotional extremes, to
approach the cultural alarm box and break glass.

Galas calls her music "interveinal song"—straight from the blood-
stream. She calls AIDS "homicide." Onstage, keening into two or more
microphones with her wild hair, dramatic makeup, and black clothes,
Galas is always a performer of febrile intensity. "I'm not singing about
the thing," she says. "I *am* the thing." But she's also someone who will
enter St. Patrick's Cathedral with ACT UP, knowing she's about to be
arrested, thinking: why don't PWAs have such a beautiful space? Why
don't they have a beautiful ritual? It's for them that she's written her
three-part plague mass, *Masque of the Red Death*.

Poe's story of the Red Death had haunted her since she was thirteen. She'd always known that she would create something related to
it. What Galas uses is Poe's central image—a pestilence both devastating and in disguise; it comes as a thief in the night. Her *Masque* has
no narrative. She has chosen to address the epidemic's most uncomfortable aspects—the stigma, the isolation, the grief.

Hers is a high mass for outcasts. Hers is also a mass confronting
"those who've twisted Christ's teaching into socially sanctioned con-
demnation of sexual difference" (as the program notes put it). That
makes her a target of the usual right-wing frothers. After a recent performance in Florence, Italy, for example, the Catholic church denounced her and the press labeled her an "evil singer." Currently, her
"Double-Barrel Prayer" video is in rotation on the Christian Broadcasting Network along with Slayer, enforcing the Pat Robertson idea

that music is the devil's plaything. Galas tends to shrug it off: "I've been called *witch* in every country I've performed in since 1980." She sees it as part of a timeless conflict: whenever there's an epidemic, the authorities look for a scapegoat. And the Cardinal O'Connor position is "obviously Inquisitional."

Still, Galas called her arrest at St. Patrick's last winter "pretty heavy for someone who's come up as a Greek Orthodox"—that is, with a background both circumscribed and patriarchal. A Greek American raised "somewhere between Tijuana and Sparta"—that's San Diego— she began to study piano at five and later played the Beethoven piano concertos with symphony orchestras. But she was forbidden to sing at home. "My father didn't like it. I think for him it was immoral. I trained myself to listen for his foot on the steps."

Though she also went on to play jazz piano with the likes of Butch Morris and David Murray, for Galas, voice was always "the most direct signal, the most visceral." While a college student in San Diego, she used to lock herself into an anechoic chamber—a padded cell—to do "vocal stuff." It was like getting permission to speak: "The singing is just an extension of that basic desire to break out of a limited communication structure." In college, by the way, she was majoring in biochemistry with a special interest in immunology and hematology.

While still a "misbegotten student" she saw Jimi Hendrix in *Monterey Pop*. "Hendrix I consider a divine inspiration," Galas says. "When I saw him, I just knew something—that I was going to have to do this shit myself." And that calling, as she once put it, is "burning the stage to the ground."

Now classically and rigorously trained, Galas's voice can only be called Herculean. She has a three-and-a-half-octave range but hates being described as an opera singer. "That's bullshit. My approach to the voice is like Mike Tyson when he goes into the ring. It's live or die."

Such talk is less hyperbole than urgency. "Half my friends are HIV-positive. Women, men, IV users—which I used to be myself, so it's not like an academic curiosity." Her brother, the playwright Philip-Dimitri Galas, died of AIDS in 1986. "When I think of my brother, I never think of him sleeping. I think of him as screaming, snarling, raising his fist. The murdered do not rest in peace."

As she began composing *Masque of the Red Death* in 1984, she was unaware that her brother—her "earthly twin"—had been diagnosed. She simply decided it was time to start when, one day at a friend's house in San Francisco, she opened the Bible at random to Psalm 88: "I am counted with them that go down into the pit. I am as a man that hath no strength. Free among the dead, like the slain that lie in the grave, whom thou rememberest no more." Shortly after, she visited a dying friend, Tom Hopkins, who told her—through an amplifier connected to his single remaining vocal chord—how his Southern Baptist family had disowned him when they learned of his diagnosis.

To Hopkins, then, Galas dedicated *The Divine Punishment*, first part in the *Masque* trilogy. It incorporates God's law on "the unclean" found in Leviticus and what Galas calls "cries to a God invented by despair," like the language of Psalm 88. The music, though, is far from liturgical. Chanted harangues, wordless croaks, eerie screeches and whispers— it sounds like the voice of one possessed. Galas stands in the fire and brimstone and outburns it.

The trilogy as a whole is about redemption. Most masses are, I suppose. But this one also questions traditional notions of sacred and profane. The first record Galas ever released was *The Litanies of Satan* (1982). Naturally, she's been called a satanist. But *Litanies*, based on the Baudelaire poem, is about alienation and oppression, not devil worship. Galas says, "I'm talking about people crucified by society, people considered outlaws who are really modern-day saints."

She will always see her brother that way, and it's him she's talking about in the second part of the trilogy, *Saint of the Pit*. She'd just begun working on it at the time of his death. "I didn't share my grief about my brother for about three or four years, because a Greek family is a very closed unit, and it's considered almost sacrilege to discuss the family. I'll be mourning my brother for the rest of my life, but at least I'm stronger now.

"My brother and I used to read—when we were young—de Sade and Nietzsche and Artaud, Poe, Nerval. This was more my climate for the beginning of a lot of my work." When she started working on *Saint of the Pit*, he gave her a favorite book of French poetry, and she read it by his bedside after he'd gone into a coma. There she found poems by Gerard Nerval and Tristan Corbière she turned into dirges for him.

Galas sees herself as part of the Greek tradition of ritual mourning specific to the Mani area of southern Greece. "The Maniots are always described as the women screaming and tearing their hair. That's a comfortably innocuous description meant to make them 'hysterical women.' It's a radical performance tradition." In Greece, says Galas, men never preside at funerals. It's a moment of female empowerment, and they use it to inspire revenge. The women sing directly to the dead. In a sense, they accompany the dead. That is the journey made in *Saint of the Pit*.

The last section of the trilogy recasts the Old Testament decrees of "divine punishment" into contemporary Bible Belt lingo. *You Must Be Certain of the Devil* ("because he's certain of you") is an attempt, again, to identify the enemy, and, says the program, "a call to the damned to arm themselves." These songs are built on the rhythms and themes of gospel, "the music of an oppressed people. It's military music."

Galas feels she's had little encouragement, except from her friends, to perform or even complete *Masque of the Red Death*. "People say, 'When is the funeral over, Galas? When are you going to do something else?' In Europe, it's too funny. They say, 'What are you going to do after the cure?' Well, the funeral *isn't* over. And I said I'd work from 1984 till the end of the epidemic. Anything else I do will have to transpire alongside it."

October 1990

■ ■ ■ Simulacra Stops Here

Standing in Tijuana on the invisible line dividing Mexico from the States, I felt viscerally what I'd once nodded at intellectually, an image from Guillermo Gómez-Peña's *Border Brujo*: the border as wound. After nightfall especially, the fracture is clearly visible. All light to the south. All dark to the north. All ramshackle houses and cacophony and food smells to the south. All silence to the north, punctuated by the occasional Border Patrol helicopter.

I'd arrived before dusk in Tijuana's oldest neighborhood with members of the Border Arts Workshop/*Taller de Arte Fronterizo*. Made up of Mexican, Chicano, and Anglo artists from the San Diego/Tijuana area, BAW/TAF has used the border as its stage, its think tank, its muse since 1984. As artist Robert Sanchez explained, "We want to participate in the history of the border instead of just being defined by it."

We parked next to the easily crossed wire fence marking it here and walked the rest of the rutted dirt road, down into Canyon Zapata. Here was an unofficial checkpoint on the road to *el norte*. No souvenir stand. No duty-free shop. People sat at several makeshift refreshment stalls with plastic tarp ceilings. They were drinking soda or beer, eating tacos—and waiting. Waiting for darkness and the chance to run for it, the chance to be undocumented in the U.S.A.

Technically, they were already sitting in California. The fence had been dismantled in Canyon Zapata. About a hundred yards into U.S. territory lay the flatland used by neighborhood residents as a soccer field, though the rusted husk of an auto sat nearly dead center. Beyond that field, perched on a mesa, were three Border Patrol trucks.

"It's not a war zone, even though the first thing you see is a helicopter," artist Berta Jottar told me. "That's the U.S. perspective, We sell tacos." She pointed out how the Border Patrol had "landscaped" the area, creating ruts and cliffs so no one could drive through. It was a no-man's land. And no-woman's land.

The artists, who've worked in the canyon a number of times, always begin by asking permission to do so at each of the stalls. Then they recruit performers from among those waiting to cross. Certainly this was a context for art guaranteed to overwhelm the art. A performance could be nothing but diversion before the larger drama ahead. As the border graffiti once quoted by Gómez-Peña puts it: "Simulacra stops here."

That day, the artists planned a simple tug-of-war across the border, which they'd marked with a broken line of chalk or corn starch. To six people, artist Richard Lou handed out silky wrestling masks which were half American flag, half Mexican flag, to represent the Border Artists. Then a dozen or so people got paper MIGRA masks, actual photocopies of the Border Patrol headgear that comes equipped with infrared lenses. At the center of the black rope they all began to pull was a round map of the Western hemisphere.

Like real life, the game was lopsided in favor of the *migra,* but nearly half of them were seven- or eight-year-old boys. And they were bare-foot. After five or ten minutes of struggle, four young men rushed out from the cheering crowd to help the Border Art side, these illegal entrants making them easy winners.

The sun was setting. Vendors began pulling their tarps down. Children romped into the soccer field, and people around me put jackets on, though it was still quite warm. No one had a bag or even a backpack. "They cannot. They have to run," said Berta. This crossing point was a dangerous one, someone explained to me later. There were vigilantes.

We made our way back up the hill and there, next to the wire fence, Berta found one of the "border sutures" the group planted in July. BAW/TAF had decided to stitch the border. For a month, they'd zigzagged over it in a bus, all the way from the Gulf to the Pacific. Traveling with a large Xerox machine, a dirt bike, and video equipment, they were constantly pulled over by the Border Patrol. What were they doing? Interviewing people on both sides of the line. Burying about twenty large steel staples, trying to make sure they got one prong in Mexico and one prong in the States, trying to bind the wound.

Back in Los Angeles a few days later, Guillermo Gómez-Peña premiered a new monologue, "1990," at the L.A. Festival. Gómez-Peña
was a founding member of BAW/TAF who has since left the group and
traveled, as he would put it, the "melancholy journey to the center of
the art world." There he's become a major voice in what he calls "the
multicultural craze." In an essay printed last year in *High Performance*,
Gómez-Peña wrote, "I am becoming exhausted repeating it: multiculturalism is not an art trend, a grant language, or a new investment
package for art *maquiladoras*. It is the very core of the new society we
are living in!"

Gómez-Peña is a linguist. By that I mean he is sensitive to the way
languages define, trap, elude. What do we mean, for example, when
we say Columbus "discovered" America? "Are you a citizen of this
time and place or are you still clinging to an order that began to die
five centuries ago?" he asked in "1990." "Are you Proto-American or
Post-Columbian? Are you a warrior of Gringostroika or a victim of political amnesia? Are you willing to cowrite with me the next chapter?"

As Gómez-Peña shifted from one character, one accent, one language to another, I reexperienced the vertigo of the border. In Tijuana,
I felt there was too much to take in, too much I didn't understand about
that tiny slice of risky life. Those who resist the multicultural reality
are really resisting the fact that they have a lot to learn.

October 1990

■ ■ ■ Rediscovering America

He's a citizen of everywhere and nowhere, a post-Mexican neo-Chicano trans-American. These transitional identities feed the work, become the work.

It's mid-August, one of the endlessly sweltering days. Up in the attic rehearsal space at the Brooklyn Academy of Music, Guillermo Gómez-Peña is pacing across his new performance continent—black oceans, Day-Glo orange terrain. It's cut into giant game-board squares "to give you the idea you can play with topography." Here, as the Warrior for Gringostroika, he'll rediscover America in *1991, a Performance Chronicle*. But the real collision of Worlds will be internal, within the characters: the Warrior, the Aztec High-Tech, the Tiger Knight, the Mariachi Liberachi. These hybrid figures plus odd syncretic props like the Pre-Columbian Robot, and the juxtaposition of, say, Spanish court music with art rock from the last years of Pinochet add up to an experience of the border, that place where cultures mutually invade each other and where Gómez-Peña feels most at home.

"I remember the cool waters of Veracruz, where Cortéz decided to burn his ships," he rehearses as the Tiger Knight. "His point being, there was no way back to the Old World. I remember the cold waters of California, where I decided to burn my tennis shoes, my point being, there was no way back to Mexico." Gómez-Peña explains that jaguar knights were elite Aztec warriors, misnamed by the Spanish who had never seen jaguars, and he'll play *El Caballero Tigre* as a "stylized *pachuco.*"

I've been to a couple rehearsals since late July, expecting to see "process," something less finished. But the artist has everything organized and nailed down, only needs . . . well, to rehearse. He wants me to understand his references, his inspirations—the Mexican street per-

Guillermo Gómez-Peña during rehearsal at the Brooklyn Academy of Music. (© Catherine McGann.)

formers ("chroniclers of urban tragedies") called *merolicos*, the Aztec dancers/musicians/activists called *concheros*, a pop singer named Tin-Tin, who was "the first to articulate the experience of the fruitpickers, the *pachucos*, the sadness of the departure." He gives me audiotapes and videotapes, explains the genesis of his characters. And I begin to understand that explaining this is part of the work for him. He is a bridge-builder. It's like the ongoing series of essays on inter/trans/multiculturalism he publishes in *High Performance*. It's like the concept for *1991*—do it in English (mostly), Spanish (partly), and an Indian dialect (just a tad), then divide the "English-only" part of the audience from those speaking "Spanish, Spanglish, Nahautl, and tongues" in the hope that, during intermission, they will be forced to communicate. Even the ongoing process of his self-definition is designed to instigate dialogue.

We leave the hot country of the BAM attic for a Cuban restaurant nearby.

A thumbnail bio: Gómez-Peña grew up in Mexico City, moved to California in 1978, attended Cal Arts, and ended up in San Diego/

Tijuana—San Diejuana—where he was one of the founders of the Border Arts Workshop. From there he began touring solo pieces like *Border Brujo*, while his essays, such as "Documented/Undocumented," helped to shape the art world's multicultural debates. This year he won a MacArthur Fellowship.

And he'll always be somebody's Other. "The Mexicans already consider me Chicano. My work has been Chicanized. My experience has been Chicanized. As for the Chicanos—the older nationalists still have problems. When the MacArthur was announced, [some of them] said the fellowship shouldn't have been given to me because I was Mexican. So that wound is still open in some sectors of the Chicano community, but for me it is no longer an issue. I believe in multiple identities. Depending on the context I am Chicano, Mexican, Latin American, or American in the wider sense of the term. The Mexican Other and the Chicano Other are constantly fighting to appropriate me or reject me. But I think my work might be useful to both sides because I'm an interpreter. An intercultural interpreter."

He has become an invaluable voice in the multiculti discussions for exactly that reason. Unaligned with a single nationality or ethnic identity, he is a "border citizen" and from that vantage can observe where everyone else is coming from. I remember an interview in *Third Text*, for example, in which he enumerated the many language-based misconceptions Mexicans and Chicanos have of each other. How the Chicanos have a culture of resistance and a confrontational way of relating intellectually. How the Mexicans saw the Chicanos as rude, too direct, while the Chicanos thought the Mexicans were flowery, too talkative. How irony is perceived differently in Mexico and California. And so on.

Now he has found "a very interesting pan-Latin Americanism in New York, very different from the Southwest where your cultural mechanisms are binary, where it's Chicano, Mexican, or Anglo. Here it's multi-hybrid." To foster "the Chica-Rican connection," he organized what he termed "a shy encounter" last year at the Yellow Springs Institute in Ohio, for artists from Latin America, Mexico, Puerto Rico, and both coasts. The two-week meeting showed them how much work would be needed to heal the schisms, which he declined to describe. "I would be scared of talking about them. I still don't know. Those are some of the things I want to discover by collaborating with Caribbeans on the East Coast." He's currently working with the Nuyorican artist Papo Colo on a book that will trace their biographies from Mexico City and San Juan to New York. "We see it as an act of cultural diplomacy."

Gómez-Peña lives and collaborates with the Cuban-American writer Coco Fusco, who plays Queen Isabella in 1991. She'll be circulating through the lobby before the performance, selling land titles to the New World. In 1992, they will collaborate on a project related to the "discovery" called "The Year of the White Bear." (They found a poem in an indigenous language referring to the Spaniards as white bears.) Among their many White Bear activities will be a book-burning in Madrid, like the one that destroyed the Mayan libraries. "We are selecting the Spanish books that were used to convert the native Mexicans, to oppress them, miseducate them, socialize them, deny their soul, and justify their slavery," says Gómez-Peña.

Now, constantly traveling his "personal Bermuda Triangle" between Brooklyn, Mexico City, and San Diejuana, he says, "I am replicating the migratory patterns of my people, trying to make art about that. About diaspora, acculturation, deterritorialization. About departure and return. About looking for yourself somewhere else. I don't even know where home is anymore. I feel more comfortable in the border zone."

Gómez-Peña wants me to meet Marco Vinicio Gonzalez, formerly a director at Tijuana's Casa de la Cultura. There Vinicio Gonzalez became the first to envision and support a border art milieu. "People on both sides considered the border the end of their country," Vinicio Gonzalez told me. "No one talked to the other side." In 1985, he and Gómez-Peña began publishing an experimental cross-cultural magazine called *The Broken Line/La Linea Quebrada*, which the Mexican cultural bureaucracy criticized as "integrationist" and "pro-American." Vinicio Gonzalez was eventually blacklisted. He now lives in New York where he's also working on 1991.

In 1985, Gómez-Peña became one of eight Mexican, Chicano, and Anglo artists to found the Border Arts Workshop/*Taller de Arte Fronterizo*. One characteristic project was carried out on Columbus Day, 1986: After notifying the U.S. and Mexican press that the continent had been turned upside down, and that Columbus would be arriving on the beach at Tijuana, the artists dressed as "border stereotypes" and took a large table to where the U.S. and Mexico meet at the Pacific Ocean. They positioned the table where the border would bisect it, Mexicans sitting on the south side, Chicanos and Anglos on the north. They then rotated the table in order to enter each other's countries illegally. Three sailing ship silhouettes positioned offshore were set ablaze, and artists and spectators shared a meal.

By the end of the eighties, border art was "hot." Now Gómez-Peña calls it "dead." The utopian idea of cross-cultural dialogue had become an exotic new fad.

"That is the kind of Faustian experience the Chicanos had in the past five years," he tells me. "We were quote unquote discovered by the Latino Boom in '87 and '88, and we began to have access to more funding, better spaces, more equipment, national magazines, Hollywood. But what the mainstream really wanted was the image, the accent, the Otherness—not the ideas." When Columbus returned to Spain with six Arawak Indians, one remained on permanent display at the Spanish court. Gómez-Peña says he sometimes feels like the Arawak.

Over the last couple of years, "multiculturalism went sour," says Gómez-Peña. "It coincided with the extreme right making multiculturalism into a bogeyman. This is a very delicate moment. Most of us involved in fine-tuning the debate were still finding its true shape. We hadn't even reached the point where we knew if we were talking about hybridization, interculturalism, syncretism, cross-culturalism, border culture, or using it as a euphemism for 'minority.' People were using this term in a very flexible way because we were in the process of reaching consensus, and suddenly we are forced to defend it. We don't know what we're defending, or what they're attacking."

Now he is looking toward the millennium. "We are all citizens of the end-of-the-century," as he puts it. "If we don't begin a dialogue across borders, races, genders, and generations, we are going to arrive at the 21st century in disastrous shape."

To stay grounded, to remember literally where he's coming from, Gómez-Peña continues to do a private ritual with each of his new personas, like the Warrior for Gringostroika. Every one must go to Tijuana and cross the border. Gómez-Peña knows that when he shows up in character, wearing the mariachi jacket or whatever, he's going to be sent to secondary inspection for questioning. Whatever character is rejected at the border will never appear on stage. (Some have died this way.) "It's a private thing I do, a reminder of a kind of political reality— that no matter what I do I am still fragile in the face of American law. And I might not be allowed to cross *this* time."

October 1991

■ ■ ■ **Talk Show**

I n the spring of 1990, I saw an early version of *Sally's Rape* at the Studio Museum in Harlem, in conjunction with "The Decade Show." Most spectators that evening had been bused uptown from Soho's New Museum. Most were white. I can't ignore that observation in the context of *Sally's Rape*, deconstructed as it is to bring racial subtext to the surface. So there we were. White people. In Harlem. Bused. Listening to Robbie McCauley talk about her great-great-grandmother Sally, who "had them chillun by the master like that's supposed to *been* something." Which is the kind of story most white people can handle. Horrific, but historic. Couldn't-happen-today. I-wasn't-there. Except that *Sally's Rape* is about the way we live now. It's about the way such stories continue to shape black/white relationships because the past has never been dealt with.

So, at the heart of *Sally's Rape* is the dialogue, the friendship, and the inexorable difference between McCauley and Jeannie Hutchins, "that white woman." In the words of a white spectator at the Harlem show: "I don't know what that white woman was doing on the stage."

Hutchins told me: "White people don't want me to be there. White people want to identify with Robbie."

Robbie McCauley is an analyzer who thrives on intense conversation. Dialogue isn't just the heart of her work but her life. When I first wrote something about her in 1986, she criticized me for "not saying how you felt"—which was a bit startling at the time but became an opening to conversation. Since then I've heard her talk about others' criticisms of her, always with the attitude—is there a lesson in it? "Bearing witness about racism informs everything I do," she once told me. And racism continues to thrive because people do not talk about it—across racial lines.

So she'll start the conversation. When the new full-length *Sally's Rape: The Whole Story* opens at the Kitchen this week, it becomes one of several current McCauley pieces about black/white dialogue.

In my experience, it is white folks who participate reluctantly and nervously in such discussions, afraid to say something wrong, afraid to feel guilty. McCauley and Hutchins both recalled the Guilt Response they got the first time they performed *Sally's Rape*, in Boston, because it certainly wasn't the response they wanted. As Hutchins remembers it, a white woman stood up and told McCauley she felt terrible about "what we did to you." McCauley remembers: "I told her guilt wasn't useful. That pain was useful but that you had to go really into the pain. And she said she didn't think that was fair. And I said, 'Well, if I can go into it, you can.'" For white people, guilt is often the first thing that comes up, and it often stops them from going further. That's why a Clarence Thomas can use the word *lynching* and watch all the white guys back off. That can only happen in a country where issues of race are so unexamined.

Plain speaking about race, between races, feels practically taboo. More familiar are platitudes from whites and rage from blacks. Most familiar of all is silence.

McCauley tells me, "When you bring up racism, the first thing everyone says is 'I'm not one.' And that's the end of the conversation."

After seeing *Sally's Rape* as a work-in-progress at three different venues, I began to develop a theory about how the piece gets around that defensiveness: What we first see of McCauley and Hutchins is their friendship, their easiness with each other. And because of this, I think, the white people in the audience drop their guard. So when McCauley suddenly steps back into moments from Sally's life, the don't-make-me-feel-guilty barriers are not in place. Then there's relief, as the piece moves back to the present, the equanimity of the friendship. Then the past intrudes again. White people always want these stories—please—to have some Hero Caucasians. But Hutchins is not a hero. Or a villain. She plays a regular white person. That's exactly what makes some white people uncomfortable.

There's a moment in the piece when McCauley gets up on an auction

Robbie McCauley stands on the auction block while Jeannie Hutchins directs the audience "bidding" in *Sally's Rape*. (Photo by Joyce George.)

block, naked, as both she and Hutchins direct the audience to chant. "Bid 'em in!" It's a kick in the gut, a glimpse at the unspeakableness that was slavery. And it's just there—shocking. No militance. No sentimentality. While we chant "Bid 'em in!"

I remember a white friend telling me after one show, "I just couldn't say those words." Slave buyer's words. Among the three performances I've seen, the whitest audience had the hardest time by far with getting words out. I recall Hutchins next to the auction block at that show, working hard: "Come on! You have to help her!" Black spectators always join in quite willingly. "They get it," says McCauley. The moment is a cleansing ritual. "White people have a problem because they don't want to be generalized as white. They don't understand that this is for all of us. We *all* participated."

McCauley had heard Sally's story from her mother, but "it's one of those stories we don't know the details of because it's shameful." Yet, she was fascinated. She identified with Sally: "It had to do with really being a slave woman. I felt that I was coming from that a lot. I would resonate it through everything without bringing it up."

McCauley wrote Hutchins's part. "I wasn't interested in doing my story and her story," she laughs. "I was interested in *my* story. And her being in it." Over the last year, however, they've opened the piece by using what comes up between them in rehearsals—questions or misunderstandings, for example. "The first one," says McCauley, "was that she thought she was supposed to be the weak one and I was the strong one. So we deal with that in the piece." Onstage, they talk about their feeling that McCauley's history is "heavy" and Hutchins's is "light." Hutchins says, "I can understand her story, but there's no way I'm going to have that experience. There's a certain bridge that can't be crossed. You have to accept that and go from there."

Early in 1990, McCauley began working in Buffalo, New York, to create a "performance dialogue" about the city's 1967 riots. But she and her cast of black and white actors first had to do some research. In Buffalo, no one talks about the riots.

They began breaking the "weird silence" in interviews with people who'd lived through the disturbances. McCauley found it much harder to get interviews from white people. White actors reported they were having a hard time getting interviews from black people. The performers ended up spending much of their rehearsal time talking to each other, a process they turned into part of the performance: "Black Confessions/White Confessions."

"We had these jokes," McCauley says. "Like black people figured that white people thought about them all the time. But white people never have to think about us. Just getting that out within the group—that was very hard to do. Then, the white actors found it so hard to confess anything in their backgrounds. I'd bring in texts I'd gotten from other white people in interviews, just to get the actors to a place where they could say, 'Oh, that's like my family.' My fantasy had been that the piece would be really hard-hitting, really radical. But I finally felt gratified to just get people to talk. Doing the project made me face my own unreality about how hard that is."

McCauley had done one of her solo pieces at Buffalo's Hallwalls in 1988 and was surprised to find very few blacks in the audience, very few downtown, very few anywhere. She finally asked, Where are they? And was told, "Across town." Buffalo is a very segregated city, with a long history of clearly demarcated turf for Germans, Poles, Irish,

Italians, and blacks. Both black and white people told her "This is the most racist town I've ever been in."

The Buffalo Project played to sold-out houses at Hallwalls Contemporary Arts Center, the Polish Community Center, and the Langston Hughes Institute. Performers told stories from the three-day riot: the white man hidden in a grease pit by his black coworkers; the black cop who quit the force; the one meat market that didn't burn. And these anecdotes were mixed with those of fear, shame, denial—about the blacks moving "too far," about the racial self-consciousness that has everyone obsessing and no one discussing. "We don't know enough about history," McCauley said in the piece. "That's why the rage lives in our bones."

After the show closed, she told a Buffalo newspaper, "I know that people who were closed up, opened up. That's what art can do . . . it can initiate a long-term process toward resolution."

With that ideal in mind, McCauley has begun working on new "performance dialogues" between black and white people in both Mississippi and Boston. The latter will address the early seventies turmoil over busing. In Mississippi, she's doing two pieces on the voting rights struggle. One's set for Holmes County, where it started; where local young people have already collected stories; where everyone's so accustomed to Hollywood folks taking their "stuff" that they accepted McCauley only gradually. A second Mississippi piece will originate with actors in Jackson, who will do interviews all over the state, drawing on the work of Fannie Lou Hamer.

With these pieces tailored to the needs and histories of specific communities, McCauley is developing a unique activist art. I went to see the Buffalo piece, and I didn't get some of it because I don't know the topography or local characters. But people in the audience, black and white both, were clearly moved that the silence around them had broken.

McCauley said someone told her: "I think you married Ed so you could have this dialogue." Not really. But Ed Montgomery, her husband of thirteen years, is a white man, and, she says, "one thing that makes it work is that we talk about it all the time. We share a lot in terms of class background, family conditions. The racial stuff is what we have in common politically. It's just that his experience is different from mine. We've considered that a problem to deal with. We confront it. So it's demystified for us."

She told me a story about their daughter, Jessie, who was once—to McCauley's horror—questioned by a cabdriver on whether she was "100 percent black." Jessie, who was four or five at the time, calmly replied, "My father is white but I'm 100 percent black."

Of course, said McCauley, "She'd been hearing that since she was born, because we talk black culture a lot."

Again the theme is talk. As Hutchins commented to me, "White people think they're supposed to have a sophistication or sensitivity addressing something they grew up not talking about at all."

Where things are stuck is with white people, because we can't admit to anything. I really believe this. So, while it feels a little strange to end this with something about myself "as if it was something," it also seems appropriate. At some point in our last interview, I told Mc-Cauley that, actually, my grandfather was in the Klan, though I hadn't known that till after he was dead. This is something I don't tell black people. But I also don't tell white people.

"For me as a black person, hearing that is a relief," she said. "Because I feel like I'm not making up something. The 'nice white people' I know all come from something. If we uncover and find the racists in our closets, then it's healing to bring that out."

I remembered finding a photograph of a lynching in my grandfather's hometown. I had searched through the grinning white faces to find his, but couldn't. I made some more inquiries to make sure that he wasn't there—and found out later that my sister had done the same thing.

"Those are the stories we need to hear, that white people aren't telling," McCauley said. "From my point of view, it's the only way. That's what standing on that auction block is for me. This all has to do with shame, and that's what makes it so hard."

November 1991

■ ■ ■ A Cinema Against the Vérités

On this day, Avenues C and D translate to avenues Cold and Debilitating, but the actors betray few signs of winter suffering. Sarita Choudhury stands next to the camera in a black cutaway coat that is surely more decorative than warm, her long hair twisted straight up with what seems to be wire. She's holding a television, and in this scene, she'll enter the shantytown to deposit it in a wall of twenty-two other televisions. In Shu Lea Cheang's *Waste Land* (working title), everyone's a media maven, whether homeless or at home. And so illusion meets disillusion. On this particular stretch of Loisaida's rubble-encrusted tundra, the homeless from Tompkins Square settled after they were evicted from the park. Some are still here. And making inquiries: "They gonna give away the TVs?" The thirteen shanties built by Cheang's crew are just stylized and less sturdy versions of the real thing, fashioned from found objects like traffic cones, a refrigerator door, a hunk of baby crib, rows of broken records nailed to sticks. A white turkey answers the cry for "Action!" with a gobble and a scene-stealing strut across the dolly tracks into the frame. No one stops the bird. It lives here too.

Cheang's film is about the waste afloat in ocean waves and on airwaves—pollution uncontrolled, media ultracontrolled. But that's clearly just part of this ambitious project's agenda. Sarita Choudhury—last seen opposite Denzel Washington in *Mississippi Masala*—plays Shareen, a salvager/recycler who tools around town in a graffitied pickup truck. Shareen lives in a Staten Island garage with her lover Claire (Erin McMurtry), and Claire's daughter. Who happens to be black though her mother is white and her mother's mother is black. But the movie is not "about" race or homosexuality. Set in a future that seems near-yet-so-far, *Waste Land* assumes a world of multi in the culti, a world of

Shu Lea Cheang directs Sarita Choudhury in a scene from *Waste Land*. (© C. M. Hardt.)

broken color barriers, where Lesbians may not need to be Avengers. The fire this time? Toxic waste. Everyone's food is beginning to glow.

This is Cheang's first feature, but it's informed by years of collaborative video projects like *Color Schemes*, for which she commissioned twelve monologues on racial assimilation from twelve Asian, Latino, black, and Native American performers. Born in Taiwan, Cheang moved to New York in 1977 to attend NYU film school, but she graduated thinking she'd never have enough money to make her own movies. She turned to video, working with Paper Tiger Television and editing other people's movies to earn a living. In 1989, she wrote the treatment for *Waste Land*, applied for grants, and solicited a script from one of the actors in *Color Schemes*, Jessica Hagedorn.

"I resisted the idea because it wasn't an original story by me," recalls Hagedorn, who's come to watch the shooting at the shantytown, "but when Shu Lea gave me total freedom and let me add characters. . . ." Hagedorn, of course, has since published an acclaimed novel about life in the Philippines, *Dogeaters*.

I listen to someone on the set joke that the film's been cast with

F.O.J.S—Friends of Jessica. Hagedorn thinks this is funny when I tell her. But no. It's only true for Laurie Carlos, who plays Mimi, Claire's mother and the renegade hostess of a public-access talk show. "I always had Laurie's voice in my head when I wrote that part," says Hagedorn. She did work with Cheang on the auditions, however, and admits, "I'm always casting, even when it isn't my job." For another role she envisioned Guillermo Gómez-Peña, who wasn't available. "You write with certain voices in mind, but the people you end up getting can surprise you and open things up in your head." Hagedorn and Carlos and Robbie McCauley perform together occasionally as Thought Music. McCauley has a cameo in the film, as do a number of other "downtown" performers: Karen Finley, Suzanne Jones, Greg Mehrten, Nicky Paraiso, Pedro Pietri, Alva Rogers, Ching Valdez, Kate Valk, Ron Vawter.

Their unique styles only add to an ambience, where there are no blandest common denominators. Most striking is the level of everyday surrealism, the level of odd detail. The incongruously dressed Shareen walks into the shantytown past "Reverend" Pietri and his trademark sign, POEMS AND CONDOMS FOR SALE, as he delivers a verse. The three cats who live with a homeless character all wear striped turtlenecks. And over at one side, Tim (Cochise Anderson, last seen in *Daughters of the Dust*) builds a rocket from scrap metal and plans to power it with a wheelbarrow full of onions. Cheang simply says she wanted the look of the film to have "a twist."

Later, the costume designer will describe the wardrobe as "off-kilter." The production designer says her sets are "anti-cinema-realism." And the cinematographer says her camera work's "not naturalistic."

Oddly enough, the scenes set in Claire and Shareen's Staten Island garage are actually being shot in a Staten Island garage, decorated to seem part boho pad, part carport; a *High Risk* anthology shares shelf space with the polishing compound, and Shareen's parked her pickup next to the kitchen. Claire's ten accordions sit on top of some tires. The actresses playing these lovers have now become friends. They approach me during lunch break at the Plumbers Local building. McMurtry: "Too bad you weren't here yesterday." Choudhury: "You missed our love scene."

The garage is near the waterfront, and freezing. Everyone in the crew keeps a coat on as they prepare today's "special effects"—a green filter over a bank of fluorescents. In this scene, Claire's daughter, Honey, will glow green and then disappear into a television during lunch with her grandma, Mimi.

Up a steep flight of steps at the back of the garage, in a cramped dressing/hair/makeup room, both McMurtry and Choudhury have rolled themselves into plaid blankets on the floor. McMurtry appears to be sleeping. Choudhury reads *The Picture of Dorian Gray.* Laurie Carlos, seated near the stairway, asks me if I've read the script yet. "It's vintage Hagedorn," she declares, while a stylist rolls pink curlers into the hair of the precocious five-year-old, Nelini Stamp, who plays Honey. A crew member who pops her head up through the floor observes that *these* two Mommies would never put curlers in their daughter's hair. "*I'm* putting 'em in," Carlos—or Mimi—assures her.

This casting decision—to give Claire, who is white, a black mother and a black daughter—seems central to both the style and the politics of the film. But maybe white people are more prone to reveries over "nontraditional casting." Here it's just "casting." As Hagedorn put it, "We don't have to explain. If the right person came along, we'd go with it, regardless of race." Choudhury is half Indian, half British, for example, and—as Cheang pointed out—they wanted to cast a black actor as her character's father but decided on a Native American.

Cheang explains that the lesbian characters "portray normal life. Lesbians with kids should be the most natural thing." The politics implicit in who's doing what, both in front of the camera and behind it, have been carefully considered, if not agonized over. Cheang made a particular effort to get women and people of color on the crew. "I tried very hard, but I wasn't quite happy." She did manage to get an all-woman camera crew led by Australian cinematographer Jane Castle (camera operator on *Sweetie*), and I noticed quite a few women of color in various production jobs, but not in technical jobs. All the grips and electrics were white men. "That is an area where I feel very vulnerable," said Cheang, "but in the end our principle is, let's get the film done." Choudhury told me that when she auditioned for *Mississippi Masala,* she was actually hoping for a job on the crew because she wants to write and direct. She'd never acted before.

One day I talked to makeup artist Marilyn Amaral, who's spent the last nine years in Los Angeles working in *the industry*—but happens to be an F.O.J. She told me that for the first couple years there, every job interview she went to began with someone telling her, "You didn't *sound* black." She'd left acting "because I didn't want to do black sitcoms or exploitation" and remembers the first professional makeup kit she got—all pink and porcelain. The one darker shade was called "Indian dirt." When she went to work on commercials, it was common to find two or three minorities on a crew of forty, and she was sometimes the only woman. Things have changed in the last five years because of black production companies, she says, but before *Waste Land* she had never worked with a female cinematographer and rarely with a female director because "even when it's diverse, the top never is." Nanxy Tong, the other makeup artist on the film, is based in New York, and said more women are now working behind the camera here but it's still hard to find people of color. "For years they would look at me and look at my portfolio and say, 'Are you familiar with non-Asian faces?'"

A couple nights after that conversation, I overheard a white crew member complaining: "I feel strange being straight and white around here. All the straight white people in this film are jerks!"

Cheang hasn't decided if she'll keep the name *Waste Land*. She worries that people will think of T. S. Eliot. "Someone said, 'Why do you have to use such a Western title for your film?' Everything becomes so political in our circle, it is unbearable."*

Politics made the film, and sometimes threatens to unmake it. Cheang chose the most expensive way to work—in 35mm—partly for political reasons. She thought about the framing and the color she could get with that film, but also about the fact that it's supposed to be out of her range. That if you're marginalized, you stick to 16mm. Or maybe go back to your camcorder. Cheang is working as if this were her one shot, and she's going for the best.

Back at the shantytown, they wanted to stage a quasi-Tompkins Square riot as a final scene. Cheang had two people in cop uniforms and a hose. She asked one of the residents of the lot to participate. He was the Vietnam vet who wore his Purple Heart every day and called

*The film was later retitled *Fresh Kill*.

himself Saigon. "I hope we can re-create something on our little budget here," Hagedorn said. "Shu Lea called me last night and said, 'We don't have a horse.' But I notice we do have a turkey." They made it work.

February 1993

■ ■ ■ Unplugged

■ ■ ■ Splendour in the Crass

"[The spectacle's] means are simultaneously its ends. It is the sun which never sets over the empire of modern passivity."

—Guy DeBord, *The Society of the Spectacle*

They were filling us up with their rules. No touching! No questions! Pack your ermines! But it was all for the sake of art. In their recent visit to the States—a four-day piece—the Royal Couple cleverly surrounded a traditionalist message with many references to vanguard performance art, a bold attempt to locate monarchy within the postmodern arena. Their "non-art" stance (they have never admitted to being artists) enables them to present this paradoxical banality—unreviewed—to a massive audience at quite literally the drop of a hat, as each performance turns into a media event.

The Royals follow the guidelines they've established for their work with great rigor. Their most recent piece became at times a subtle dance: Nancy Reagan "reaching out instinctively to touch the Princess" and the Princess "instinctively eluding the touch," as noted by ABC. Most important to the Royal Couple is their goal of breaking down the barrier between art and life. Their rules, for example, distance them from the audience (or "commoners"). And help make them works of "living art."

Certainly they've been influenced by another team of British artists, Gilbert & George, who designated themselves "living sculptures" in the early seventies. Always posed, proper, and smartly dressed, Gilbert & George took the cliché of English reserve as far as it could go— or so it seemed at the time. The Royal Couple's project goes even further by forcing a certain reserve—and often a dress code—on their audience. For example, near the end of the performance, the Couple

posed for photographs with spectators who had paid $50,000—a se-
quence so radical it outraged many in Palm Beach (a rigid community
ill-prepared for anything this "avant-garde"). As Gilbert & George
would explain it, "Make the world believe in you and pay heavily for
the privilege."

"It's all in the breeding," the Prince explained (after an inquiry
about jet lag). And certainly the performance could be interpreted as
a work of Endurance or Ordeal Art: a twelve-hour plane ride followed
by four days of "tasklike activities," each climaxing with a "black-tie
dinner" and requiring many changes of costume.

Viewed on the evening news, the Couple seemed to do little but
arrive and depart, pause and pose. They were appropriating the gestures of political power (both past and present, for the polo event near
the end of the piece must be read as a simulated joust).

Their collaborators at the White House reinforced the performance's
covert message ("monarchs know best") by coming out to greet them
in silly clothes. The President was dressed as a carpet (a huge green
and blue plaid) and the First Lady looked cadaverous (in beige). The
prince, turning away from them on-camera, seemed a bit embarrassed
at this lack of subtlety, appropriate though it may have been to the
Reagans' Hollywood classicism. The President contributed a second
blunder with his "Princess David" remark, obviously improvised.
Charles, unruffled, has always demonstrated as an artist his willingness to work in the spirit of John Cage and just incorporate whatever
happens into the piece.

"Royalty," after all, has been a conceptual project for some time,
though for the British Royals it was never an art of ideas, and they had
gone through the motions for years as affable ribbon-cutters. Nostalgia
fans were fond of these activities, but they'd grown frankly bathetic.
Then Charles met Diana, and they collaborated on their sensational
"Storybook Romance" project. In this successful early work, Diana appeared to be living out a fairy tale as the "shy schoolgirl from a broken
home" who had found the glass slipper and then some. This piece
made her a pop star and left many addicted to her image. Her charisma,
in fact, gave a new context to Royal work, rendering it a celebration of
privilege, and reinfusing it with myth.

Diana's particular genius is her apparent emptiness. The papers
constantly discuss her enigmatic smile, tucked chin, and upturned

eyes—"the look"—an obvious reference to Lacan. So the Princess has even the tabloids "rethinking representation," if only subconsciously. Meanwhile, her blankness compels audience members to project their fantasies onto her, thus involving them in the piece. In America, she was greeted everywhere like a Beatle. Hysteria! Screams! Queries about her favorite color! ("Royal" blue. No surprise there.) A woman waiting for her outside J. C. Penney's told a television reporter, "If I just get a glimpse I'll be happy for the rest of my life." Elsewhere, the members of her cult observed airport vigils in "Di" haircuts or trademark veiled hats. One disciple told the camera, in tears, "I've been waiting for so long to see her." The artists then incorporate these outbursts into the performance when, on cue from Diana, Charles announces that she has been "touched" or "moved." Her job is to stay silent, an eminently consumable image.

Diana, of course, is the world's foremost practitioner of Shopping Art. In a wry moment of self-parody, she and Charles "went shopping" at Penney's. There they found a work of late-Modern sculpture installed in their honor: a Rolls Royce balanced on teacups. Not about to be upstaged as a creator of incredulities, the Princess declared an interest in "novelty fleece tops." And even contributed a work of her own: the purchase of a polka-dot bow tie.

Central to their work is the Royal Couple's belief that they embody the masculine and feminine principles. Twice they went their separate ways, to act as "men" and "women" must. But the Nurturing sequence undertaken by the Princess was uncharacteristically surreal. On one afternoon, she shared with dying people her fear that the Prince would fall asleep during dinner. She spent a second afternoon "rapping" with drug addicts. (Under Nancy Reagan, this has become part of woman's role.)

Meanwhile, in solo appearances at the American Institute of Architects and the Library of Congress, Charles questioned the authorities who met with him, creating a theater of pseudocommand. He was seen on camera, gesturing at ceilings and walls as if giving direction. This Leadership sequence must be judged a success since it was everywhere announced in the media that Charles was no longer thought to be "thick."

Finally, their choice of the news as their sole artistic medium is the Couple's only display of real daring. They couldn't even be sure that the press would distribute their guidelines to the audience (saying that they were to be addressed as "Royal Highnesses," etc.). And how would the media edit each day's event? (The Palm Beach episode was not even adequately documented.) Obviously the Prince and Princess have been influenced by the sixties avant-garde and wish to make chance an element in their work. And chance it they must, since they are all image—meaningless without a mass audience. Recently they released their first video, the Wedding sequence of "Storybook Romance." But they are still looking for their first original thought, as they move among the ragtag and bobtail of their minds.

November 1985

■ ■ ■ Realms of the Unreal

ast week all the supermarket tabloids devoted their covers to a pseudo-event: the television wedding of "Jeff Colby" and "Fallon Carrington," complete with details on who "attended the ceremony." In a culture where media is primary experience, such events are quite real. Those hollow images surround us like extended family, emotionally resonant, part of everybody's autobiography. The French writer Jean Baudrillard even suggests that these representations are *more* real than reality. Certainly the "Colbys" are more real to us than the humans who play them.

It's common enough on what remains of the club scene to see a television format recreated on stage. (Childhood memories are made of this.) And when you're lucky, the simulation includes whatever stuck the original in your craw.

One small step for the sublime. If the moving pictures we grew up with haven't yet inspired someone toward a long day's journey into night, they still promise to. In recent work by John Kelly and John Jesurun, both moved beyond mere re-creation of media format to emotional confrontation with media imagery. In Kelly's *The Diary of a Somnambulist*, the performers were able to inhabit an old film. In Jesurun's *Deep Sleep*, the film struggled with those who refused to inhabit it.

Jesurun's play was the first I know of to address what Baudrillard would call "the loss of the real." Two movie screens and two projectors set in glass cases as if for museum display flank the stage area. The live actors and screen actors quarrel over which group is really alive. Those onscreen tell the actors onstage: "You can't stay down there. You'll run out!!" It's the youngest actor, a boy of perhaps twelve (Mi-

John Jesurun's *Deep Sleep*: actors onstage argue with actors onscreen over who is alive, who is projected, who will run out. (Photograph by Sylvia Plachy © 1993.)

chael Tighe), who responds with the most conviction. He is certain he's not a projection.

In fact, theirs is the great subconscious argument of the media age. We stare at movie stars because it's so shocking to find that they're real. We believe in their images. When they appear in human form, they're like people returned from the dead. Those performers in *Deep Sleep* who pass from the stage into the film find that they have become images who can't get back into "real life." The exception is Whitey (Steve Buscemi). After the projectors "run out," Whitey is alone onstage. He runs between the screens, repeating the words of the boy, who had screamed for help from the screen and bloodied himself trying to break out of its frame: "I will last forever because I am on film . . . over and over until I am shredded. . . ." Relating to images is the postmodern condition—becoming one its tragedy.

In *Diary of a Somnambulist*—a collaboration between Kelly and visual artist Huck Snyder—there's no struggle over which side of the movie screen to choose. No one is real. Again, a film character (*Dr. Caligari*'s Cesare) encounters a stage character (Lady Macbeth)—but without drama. Each sleepwalker seems trapped in his or her plot, as though on a film loop.

Snyder's set appropriates the look of *The Cabinet of Dr. Caligari*, everything in hallucinatory forced perspective, everything in black and white, like the original. In the diary of the title and on the clocks with three hands, all letters and numbers have been replaced with an eyechart "E," a sign used to judge but inherently unreadable. There are no words. Kelly plays the hypnotized, passive Cesare, a spectator to his own actions. His is a Chaplinesque presence, able to project menace and innocence almost in the same breath. The only sound from Kelly: a brief and startling mezzo aria.

There is no narrative. But the overwrought ambiance, the Verdi, the angled expressionist set—all imply a certain kind of narrative, an un-recoverable past. The piece suggests that once the "real" has been lost, an overwhelming nostalgia is the only mise-en-scène.

One giant leap for the ridiculous. I suppose this explains the current great nostalgia for every era. A seventies revival evening at Danceteria last weekend featured an obscene simulated *Match Game*, hosted by its original star, Gene Rayburn, but played by celebrity look-alikes, among them both "David Bowie" and "Ziggy Stardust" (Bowie's seventies alter ego). The unreal was out in force.

If consumerism is the American religion, the game show is its greed-crazed ritual. This copy was just as satisfying as the television original, if not more so, allowing the audience to chant and scream at each fa-miliar banality. Rayburn (to one contestant from the "studio audi-ence"): "Shithead Sheena is so chic. . . ." Audience: "How chic is she!?!" Rayburn: ". . . she put 'blank' in her hair." In *The Match Game*, as all of America knew in the seventies, the contestant wrote an answer he or she hoped the celebrity player would match. In this case, after shrieks of advice from the audience, the contestant—and three "ce-lebs"—wrote "sperm." Rayburn seemed delighted with the frenzy of audience participation from this crowd of imaginative haircuts, but I think it was aimed less at him than at the act of filling the familiar format with crude and naughty jokes.

The real king of untelevisable "TV," however, is the monthly "No Entiendes" cabaret at Danceteria, hosted by Haoui Montaug and Anita Sarko. Here the variety show returns to its roots in vaudeville, most of the acts either (1) too horrible, (2) too weird, or (3) too taboo ever to go nationwide. Last Sunday during the show's fourth birthday bash, we watched (1) an off-key affectless "blues" singer. Then (2) James

Sienna and Chaz Dean, in skirts, chanting lines about gay life, religion, and cartoons to choreographed body language ("It's kind of hi-tech! With art deco touches!" "I'm not allowed to tell you what my mantra is!" etc.) And (3) Karen Finley, who announced that she would talk about Germans scrubbing her butt, and venereal warts, then did so, and then some.

This was exactly what the audience came to see. Something that might put a Colby to flight.

March 1986

■ ■ ■ Nam June Paik's Global Groove

The "twain" was gonna meet in half an hour, but already East and West were watching each other—live via satellite—in the last-minute frenzy of preparation. A woman on 4D's dance floor practiced layering shiny strips of satin around herself in an Issey Miyake fashion statement, while on a nearby monitor her counterpart in Tokyo did the same. Later, on split screens, one would take it all off while the other would put it all on. "Look, there's a different dress in Tokyo," the American noted with some alarm.

She and her Asian "twin" were rehearsing for their couple of minutes in Nam June Paik's second piece of Satellite Art, the live intergalactic television extravaganza, *Bye Bye Kipling*. Ever the optimist, Paik had responded to the mixed success of his first satellite piece, *Good Morning, Mr. Orwell*, by planning something even more ambitious for this second one. *Orwell* had linked Paris, New York, and San Francisco—on the first day of 1984, naturally—and featured the varied talents of Joseph Beuys, Laurie Anderson, Allen Ginsberg, the Thompson Twins, and many others. Ironically, the program suffered sporadically from the occasional satellite glitch and/or banal performance. "Live TV is like life. You can't get everything done," Paik observed later. "You don't see what went well. You see only what went wrong." One thing that went well was the 34 rating *Orwell* scored in Paik's native Korea—despite the fact that it aired at 2 A.M. The duly impressed president of the Korean Broadcasting System suggested to Paik that his second satellite event include the Asian Games, scheduled for Seoul this year. KBS would help fund such a project, of course.

Bye Bye Kipling featured simultaneous live performances from 4D, from a new arts center in Tokyo, and from the last hour of the marathon run at the Asian Games in Seoul. Paik saw this configuration as a chance "to combine a kind of dialectic fugue of . . . live music and live sport." It would also address the Rudyard Kipling cliché that East was East et cetera and never the twain et cetera. Kipling, that old colonialist, hadn't foreseen interactive television or the global-village preoccupations of Paik, the man who invented video art and always insisted on thinking positively about the medium's possibilities.

Paik had purchased the first Sony Port-o-Pak sold in America, coinvented the video synthesizer, and became the first artist to use the TV set as an object. In 1964 he met cellist Charlotte Moorman, who became his constant collaborator. For her, he designed one of his most notorious pieces, the video bra, as well as a cello built from three TVs.

Moorman appeared for just moments in *Bye Bye Kipling*, playing under the credits at the very end. Obviously this show also suffered from being "like life" where "you can't get everything done." But, in television, more is more. *Kipling* was better than *Orwell* because there was more of everything: more events, more split screens, more prerecorded bits (some of it running in fast-forward). Paik apparently realized early in his career that the eye could consume much more than it's usually offered on TV, and his work has always been information-heavy.

Kipling also had at its heart a dramatic narrative—a marathon runner at the Asian Games hurtling toward a new world record. Paik had hoped that the Philip Glass ensemble playing at 4D and the frontrunner racing through the streets of Seoul would finish at the same time in "a kind of electronic orgasm." The Glass music was the perfect mirror to the concentrated struggle in the runner's face. Why didn't we see more of that face? Instead we kept seeing the musicians at 4D.

The show in general was just too New York. Hundreds of images from Korea whirled by, boiling hundreds of years of cultural history into minutes. (What other images of Korea have we ever seen? Reagan at the 38th Parallel?) Then the incredible Japanese troupe, Sankai Juku, got—what?—two minutes? Meanwhile, back in Western Civilization, we heard three complete songs from Lou Reed. This is cross-cultural balance?

Introducing cultures to each other actually worked much better than introducing culture heroes. Paik once wrote in a catalogue essay, "I feel it is a terrible shame that great geniuses may pass their prime without ever meeting. And even when such encounters have actually taken place (for example, Cage and McLuhan, Cage and Buckminster Fuller), no camera has recorded the event." *Kipling* recorded the embarrassing banality of genius well-met. Issey Miyake in Tokyo said to Keith Haring in New York: "I'll see you in Paris in two weeks." Replied Haring (let it be recorded for posterity): "I have an exhibition of paintings the same time your show is. Same day." Host Cavett quickly referred us to the Alvin Ailey dance troupe.

Then, when Cavett got his chance to interview the champion Sumo wrestler—who happens to be American—what did he ask? For a recipe. As host, Cavett outdid *Orwell*'s George Plimpton in the ad lib department so necessary on live television. He also knew some Japanese, but the script written for him was too cute in any language. At one point, he and the Japanese host, rock star Ryuichi Sakamoto (of *Merry Christmas, Mr. Lawrence*), clinked beer mugs together at the split in the screen—or tried to. Then, even less convincingly, they "exchanged gifts"—another television first.

Television news departments do "satellite events" regularly these days. And with fewer glitches. But in Paik's global projects, we see the triumph of the sixties avant-garde—a vision of art-induced global peace—now underwritten, ironically, by corporations. Remember when we thought the revolution was gonna happen in our heads?

October 1986

O ne eye is better than two," declares the sinister self-proclaimed "eye surgeon" whose face suddenly appears halfway through *Black Maria* on the giant screen hung above us like a ceiling. She reasons that two eyes in the same head will fight, since "one eye wants to see one thing and the other wants to see the other." We might be better off getting rid of an eye. She assures us that she sees more clearly since removing one of her own and replacing it with a patch. We can see, however, that she's wearing no patch.

With his usual contradictory contrariness, John Jesurun has made this scene in *Black Maria* the only one in which our eyes *aren't* fighting over where to look. The big face above us is the only image moving for the moment. The other four screens that wall us in have gone dark. We are an audience of tipped-back heads. We are, perhaps, anaestheticized upon a table? Sitting in the brain of the main character—a disembodied voice named X—and peering out through his eyes? "Think of me as a pinhole camera," he suggests.

Maybe we've found our way into Plato's cave at last. Turns out it's a box in the center of La Mama's Annex—walls and ceiling made of large squarish rear-projection screens—set up so that each of us will experience *Black Maria* differently. For we must choose to sit in one of two triangular wedges that face one another, the two screens behind each wedge most visible to those seated in the other. In this play, nobody struts and frets upon a stage. Everybody flickers and glows on five screens, half of them peripheral even as we swivel. Like the "surgeon," they're unreliable characters who lie to each other and to us. It's impossible to identify with them, to understand them, to enter their world even though it surrounds us.

Black Maria ends the cycle that began a year ago with Jesurun's *Deep*

Sleep, a play in which the actors onstage argued with actors on screens about which of them was alive and which projected—or fated to "run out." In last winter's *White Water,* three actors and twenty video monitors carried on an inquisition into truth and illusion triggered by a boy's tale of religious miracles. Now the "plot" of *Black Maria* has X (Larry Tighe) traveling to a leper colony to buy a horse. Kind of. A major "subplot" concerns a woman, Esther (Sanghi Wagner), who either has or hasn't been imprisoned, because she is or isn't a murderer. ("How many stories ya gonna believe?") In the second half of the piece, X doesn't want the horse the "lepers" try to make him take. And at the very end, he's looking for their colony again but can't find a trace of it.

In Jesurun's work, however, plot is often deliberately obscure. An issue of much more importance to him is how we can create a "truth" merely by believing, so that, for example, a media image and a religious icon have the same strange power. Often his pieces begin with characters asking "easy" questions—what did you see? what did it mean? These turn out to be veritable riddles of the sphinx, and they're compounded by the end, never answered. Jesurun is reconceiving the oldest philosophical problems in the light (literally) of new technologies.

When the first images in *Black Maria* come up on the screens, we see all the characters standing in front of stone walls. Later they seem to be at a "ranch." In the "West." (We're never going to be sure just what the hell is going on or why.) At the very beginning, though, they seem to have gathered in a small room. One woman announces, "I'm sorry that you're dead. . . . I was going to tell you about my unbelief in everything, but now I've changed my mind. . . . Don't you understand? You've been murdered." Does this mean that X has been murdered? That, like the characters in *Deep Sleep,* he has died by entering the screen world? Says Esther: "Nothing has a meaning. Meanings mean nothing." Even this nihilism is undermined when another character sarcastically replies, "How poetic."

Whatever his story, X's trip is no joyride for us. As a theatrical experience, *Black Maria* feels like an assault. In every Jesurun play I've ever seen, the audience is made to work to wrest some sort of order from the information overload. (And part of what's interesting is how our minds automatically start to do that.) Another commonplace in his work is rapid-fire and furious dialogue; the relationships among characters are a web of free-floating hostilities, accusations, and threats. *Black Maria* is his hardest piece yet to decipher because some of the audio is a strain to pick up, our eyes are "fighting," and the images are more muddy than engaging. I felt some relief that the whole barrage lasted just forty-five minutes.

For me the power of *Deep Sleep* was watching the actors "believe" in and relate emotionally to the filmed characters. In *Black Maria*, we spectators have that "live" role. But we aren't really drawn into the illusion of the film(s) which have done so much to distance us. I couldn't help but watch other watchers, for example. The piece is set up so that we're almost forced to do so. Yet even that brings a question to mind about how we watch movies—usually such a passive activity, usually a way to "lose" oneself. In *Black Maria*—neither a "real" play nor a "real" film—Jesurun wants us to look at how our minds have been conditioned, at how media have changed our perceptions of the world.

April 1987

■ ■ ■ Am I Living in a Box?

A s if expecting an audience of crazed Cardinal O'Connors, Ann Magnuson had thrown plastic gloves over the back of each seat in Alice Tully Hall. Near the end of her show, we all put them on, getting two or three send-ups for the price of one: AIDS panic meets Hands Across America with Magnuson and company onstage singing "Just Say Yes." We experienced the parody of joy.

Magnuson parodies everything she touches, as though her whole brain was in quotes. But that comes with her territory. Junk culture, especially the tube, infects her like a disease. Starring in her first feature film, *Making Mr. Right*, she mused (in *New York Talk*), "Do you think success might mean that I finally get my own TV show?" TV is the window into a land where cynicism, irony, and sarcasm rule. On every channel, a knowing gaze. And a fake one, but it still draws us in. Magnuson treats it as her love/hate thang.

She's become a star of post-television performance, the style once so familiar in all the East Village clubs. This is work that tries to beat the hell back into the lowest common denominator, while acknowledging how emotionally attached we've become to the unreal or the hyperreal—whatever you want to call those beloved beings made from dots and flickering light. Magnuson's comic characters exaggerate, vulgarize, and ridicule those images. For example, she's been on to Tammy Faye Bakker for years—speaking of media-made grotesques—with her character, "Tammy Jan." Magnuson doesn't *do* real people. Television has made it unclear what real is.

The tube's power is to absorb and flatten anything it transmits, giving equal weight to Ollie North, Bruce Willis, and the latest spokesmodel. It's impossible to know what, if anything, to believe. That theme shot through Magnuson's piece at Lincoln Center. Alice Tully

Hall, Magnuson's televangelist character, preached media omnipotence and no salvation ("You people think someone's gonna come save us, you got your head up your ass"). The entire Hall family emerged from a little shack to salaam and salute before a satellite dish. "Illiterate, but media-wise," Alice Tully declared her kin, all of them hillbillies with celebrated names—Jerry, Annie, Tajmah, Monte, Fawn, et al. Then, settling a colander with wires and bulbs onto her head, Alice began to channel-switch through her own brain (just like the bag lady character in Lily Tomlin and Jane Wagner's *Search for Signs of Intelligent Life in the Universe*). She was speaking in tongues. Television was the god, every channel a transchannel.

Suddenly "Alice" was gone. The channels began tangling themselves into a freak show, as Tammy Faye Bakker appeared at the Contra hearings to testify on Michael Jackson's bid for the Elephant Man's bones. With quick costume changes, Magnuson became newscaster Kimberly Crump, then a satanic teen who carved an "X" in her forehead, then a heavy-metal singer—female but just as sensitive as her male counterparts ("Get It Up or Get Out!"). As each character dissolved into the next, the transition altered the context for what we'd just seen, undermining the character's integrity. But this, I think, is Magnuson's point: any "conviction" they'd spouted was clearly an act. Crump, for example, read an editorial about a dangerous new trend— youth who don't believe in the work ethic, don't want platinum American Express cards, don't even want to visit Nell's. Suddenly she began pulling off her wig and her proper plaid suit to reveal exactly the bald, who-gives-a-fuck presence she'd been describing, a new character who wants to "rip off the trappings of capitalism" and, if possible, beat our brains out.

This hostility towards the audience leaks from other characters as well. It's one thing that makes Magnuson look too subversive for prime time.* (Television conspires to flatter or coddle us, never to attack.) For example, Fallopia, the Prince protégé character (not part of the Lincoln Center show), promises to be our "love slave" one minute, informs us that her act is a "witty send-up of sexuality" the next, and finally shrieks, "If you can't see the humor in me or my act THEN FUCK YOU!" Many of her characters are "media-wise"—aware that they're mere

*This remained true for her characters even after Magnuson herself got a part on the sitcom, *Anything But Love*.

images, captured by the audience. They wreak their revenge by refusing to meet expectations. Although some of Magnuson's alter ids and egos are televisable, the tube would censor her for "dirty" words. And I think the angry, foul-mouthed characters like Fallopia are her sharpest work.

Magnuson, however, gets a lot of attention as the downtown artist most likely to cross over. Her parodic style seems perfect—television *feeds* on parody, rendering real dissidence nearly impossible. (*Saturday Night Live* didn't look daring for long.) Sometimes I think this parodic ambience has poisoned the air, making it seem uncool to have a real feeling.

"It's cool to hate everything, but I'm sick of it," Magnuson said near the end of her show. "Who knows how much time is left for any of us. . . . I need something to believe in." She seemed serious. Said she was serious, then added, in a voice sounding close to tears: "This is not any cheap Carol Burnett skit-mongering." The audience roared.

It had to be a joke, right? There's no real "self" in Magnuson's show, so who was this person who wanted "to believe"? Yet I had a moment of wondering whether those feelings *had* been real. AIDS is obviously real to her, but it's impossible to address ironically once you get past the condom jokes. Maybe she just couldn't help getting cynical over wanting to be uncynical. She had come up against television's greatest failure. When parody and irony are used not to contain emotion but to replace it, they diminish whatever they touch. They allow for no sense of tragedy.

August 1987

■ ■ ■ I Am Not a Bimbo

O nce I knew iniquity and the God who could smite. But I came late to the Robo-god of television evangelism. Certainly, among all the harsh (mid)western Gods, this was the sexy One who could propel both Faithful and Un to thrash in the aisles. But the Robo-god, a postgod emptied of spirit, has to have a preacher—an Oz-figure—who can shout the fire and crank the brimstone. Jimmy Swaggart is the greatest of these.

Swaggart can pulsate with larger-than-life emotion, radiating through the throng before him and out into the tube. These televised religions are about nothing but that connection and that sweat-drenched Preacher-man image lifted from countless Southern melodramas.

Preaching before The Fall, he'd hold that giant limp Bible as he told of gnashing teeth, forbidden fruits, and abominations. He held that Bible open and aloft like this was the Word made flesh—the Word as an open cunt. Ready for thumping. Fulfillment to come in the here-after. Millions swooned.

But his passions were simulated. And when the Brother went looking for hookers, he wanted them to simulate, too. "The sex act itself, intercourse, was not achieved." Thus spake officials from the Assemblies of God when describing Swaggart's sin. No one will say just what was "achieved." Apparently the TV preacher was in the grip of a desperate voyeurism. Addicted to pornography. In thrall to The Gaze. Then nabbed by surveillance.

In the olden days, surveillance was done by God. But Robo-god does not watch. He *is* watched. Brother Swaggart thought it disguise enough to cast off the raiment of power. Lo, he cruised through the valley of the shadow of Hooker's Row in a sweatsuit and shades, a hat or a headband, his hair combed down over his forehead. Just another cowardly Dimmesdale.

Last week his transgressions got him the cover of *People*. He'd finessed the "sinner" image and made it work, as the Bakkers never could. They merely got mad. Swaggart surrendered. Swaggart said, "Judge me." Swaggart submitted to discipline, simulating masochism. His public confession, a riveting spectacle of degradation, both real and imagined, cuts right to the heart of Christianity. Christ himself was accused and sacrificed, 'buked and scorned, a man of sorrows and acquainted with grief, and with his stripes we are healed, et cetera.

Swaggart doesn't even need to articulate this for himself. He's a great performer, with that sixth sense for what the audience wants. He's poised for his comeback as a sleazeball redeemed.

A couple of weeks back at The Kitchen's "Carnival of Sleaze," sin was everywhere on parade—not a headband in sight. But was it sleazy? Or do you need something like religion to rub up against? "I still don't know what sleaze is," curator Carlo McCormick wrote in the program, "it's been so diluted in the general corruption of our culture." Karen Finley began the program by not performing, saying that was the sleaziest thing she could do.

"Carnival" was most interesting to me as an evening of unconnected bodies.

In Richard Kern's film, *Submit to Me Now,* characters in fetishized clothing create an expectation of sex. Instead, they run through a catalogue of self-inflicted violence: a woman masturbates with a stick, a man wraps a leather thong around his head till he bleeds (copiously), a woman cuts herself with a knife, a man hangs himself by his dick. Nearly every scene involves one person. Masturbation (the sex you do alone) gives way to suicide (the violence you do alone).

Two of the five "Carnival" performances committed simulated suicides. Kembra Pfahler, wearing prostheses of breasts and pregnant stomach, slit the blood bags on her wrists. Emilio Cubeiro undressed, stuck a revolver up his ass, pulled the trigger, slumped to the floor.

The show was depressing—one of those evenings when you think, "It signifies," but it hasn't been pleasurable.

Jimmy Swaggart's sackcloth-and-ashes routine, acted out for millions of viewers, was the most astonishing and deeply embarrassing performance I've seen in ages. With a sick fascination, I hunted for it on every channel, and watched the mouth contort, the cheeks glisten with tears, the eyes beseech the heavens. "I have siiiiiiined against you, my Lord," the preacher bleated—sniveling, voice breaking. After I saw it a couple of times, I noticed that all around him his congregation was crying.

Clearly Swaggart groveled for show, controlling it, pausing for cadence. "I would ask that Your precious blood [sob sob] would wash and cleanse [sniff] every stain" and so on. This was not real-life contrition; it was the made-for-TV movie of contrition.

Swaggart pushed public humiliation to new depths. He broke taboos, by bringing what is usually a private act into a very public arena. And I don't mean sex. He turned to his wife, who was seated in the audience, and said in a husky whisper, "I have siiiiiiined against you." Cameras caught the wife's tight little smile. Then because he'd siiiiiiined against his grown son, the cameras focused on the son, wide-eyed and fighting off tears, mouthing "I love you."

In some forthcoming episode, the hero will tell us that he wrestled with demons. Little tongues of hellfire will have nipped at his feet. He'll be bigger than ever.

True sleaze.

March 1988

■ ■ ■ Are You Now or Have You Ever Been?

Once upon a time, during the White House astrology crisis, the Reagan presidency looked quasi-Shakespearean. We had a Lady Macbeth figure, several Iagos, and a foolish king. Soon, however, this tragical comedy resolved itself as just another episode in "The Age of Reagan"—the eight-year not-so-mini-series. Reagan's fabled Teflon quality was really something more insidious. He was the first postmodern president, a "pure screen" and an "empty system of signs." Every event of his reign became just another show, with Reagan playing the role of the character who could triumph in the end—the Gipper or a television Dad or a Rambo. And America stayed tuned.

Now all the worst theories have come true.

The current presidential campaign seems to validate everything ever written by that poststructuralist webslinger, Jean Baudrillard. The poet/prophet of simulation and hyperreality, Baudrillard's been unfashionable of late (or was he too quoted two years ago?). Certainly he's negative, extreme, apocalyptic. But could George Bush have read him somewhere along the campaign trail? With typical hyperbole, Baudrillard writes in his essay *In the Shadow of the Silent Majorities*: "They [the masses] are given meaning; they want spectacle. No effort has been able to convert them to the seriousness of the content, nor even to the seriousness of the code. Messages are given to them, they only want some sign." Baudrillard's vision of a generally stupefied populace, unable to distinguish between real and "signs of the real," has become concrete with the success of the Bush/Flayle ticket and the ads that sell them like a couple of Michelobs.

Even this week's *Time* piece on "Myth, Memory, and the Politics of Personality" reads like the work of some Baudrillard disciple. Analyzing the collapse of the campaign into mere signs and symbols, Lance Morrow writes: "The candidates perform simulations of encounters with the real world, but the exercise is principally a series of television visuals, of staged events created for TV cameras. The issues have become as weightless as clouds of electrons, and the candidates mere actors in commercials."

We're talking demographics. The campaign became a contest to find the lowest common denominator. The Republicans established this discourse by choosing as veep (as future) the world's blandest whiteman, and by making the Pledge of Allegiance an issue. And it worked! Small wonder that Jesse Jackson disappeared. Small wonder that when I was asked to write about "images of women in the campaign" I found that, basically, there weren't any. Ferraro's gender and Jackson's race are more troubling to voters, apparently, than Quayle's incompetence. The polls indicate that people think he's unfit but will still vote for him. Quayle *looks* like a proper candidate. A Xerox of Bush who's a Xerox of Reagan who's a Xerox of fictional personalities, Quayle is the paradigm of "lowest common denominator," the ultimate in emptiness.

That works well on the screen, where gesture and image beat out content every time, and truth hardly matters. Authenticity and sincerity are not just rare to the tube, but difficult to distinguish from insincerity. Reagan, however, has been a master of "acting" sincere, employing what Garry Wills called "the choreography of candor": "'Well'—eyes down, eyes up, smile, slight dip of head to the right, and begin." It's subtle, but it works because television exaggerates. Michael Dukakis seems to plod—brows knit, hands pumping up and down. He seems heavy when what the medium translates better is lightness, and, best of all, emptiness.

This column began originally as a meditation on Patty Hearst—the media event that created her, the apparent emptiness that made it possible for her to change identities. Patty and Dan have so much in common—a coupla rich kids who inadvertently found work as professional symbols: the first Hostage Personality; the first Baby Boomer. They became, respectively, victim and victimizer of circumstance, the roles befitting their genders.

She's known adversity; he may have seen it on television. So, in Patty Hearst, emptiness reverberated, becoming *Patty Hearst* (the entertainment near you) and "Patty Hearst" (the representation by Natasha Richardson) and Patty Hearst (the signified) and, of course, Tania (the representation by Patty Hearst). And has anyone else noticed that Patricia Hearst Shaw doesn't look like any of them?

One of the first things "Patty Hearst" says in the film is: "I knew, or thought I knew, who I was."

Director Paul Schrader told *New York* magazine: "The answer to the question 'Did she convert or didn't she?' is 'Yes and no.'"

Patricia Hearst Shaw calls the film "accurate."

Patty always took the role assigned, whether it was student or guerrilla. Once captured, though, she no longer knew her part, her identity, and became confused. In the film, she tells the authorities in the end: "I want to tell the truth, but I don't know what it is." (Since she doesn't know who *she* is anymore.) In those innocent days when we were less acquainted with terrorists and their co-dependents, the hostages, Patty was treated quite badly for this. The prosecutor accused her of "acting"!

Terrorism is not violent in itself," writes Baudrillard, "only the spectacle it unleashes is truly violent. It is our Theater of Cruelty, the only one that remains to us."

When I saw the Hearst docudramas, I realized I'd forgotten all the particulars of the case but had total recall of its shocking images: Patty at the Hibernia Bank with a rifle sticking out of her pea jacket; Patty defiant, legs akimbo, in front of the SLA flag; and, of course, the televised inferno in which most of the SLA died.

The movie, unfortunately, is hopelessly dated, because it tries to show "what really happened" when the original media event wasn't real but hyperreal. It's impossible to make sense of it even now.

In the late seventies, however, one Cheryl Bernstein wrote an essay that exposed the Symbionese Liberation Army as a group of performance artists. Bernstein is a pseudonymn and the essay ironic (though its pompous language and academic style make it seem like "real" art writing). It explains the SLA "piece" in terms of art history—citing "the Duchampian gesture," Allan Kaprow's theory of the un-artist (who disguises any aesthetic intention), and the tradition of physical risk endured by body artists like Chris Burden.

"More than any other feature of the work, however, the use of the news media as framing underscores the issue that the work as a whole dramatizes: the inability of modern art to signify its given content as truth." Bernstein concludes that "political action itself can be no more than art performance."

In 1988, this parody rings too true. Faking it is everything.

The rise of Dan Quayle is so Hollywood—that is, scripted in the Hollywood of our collective nostalgia. He's the proverbial starlet plucked out of a soda shop.

In fact, right after the first Baby Boomer was nominated, a few in the no-doubt "liberal" press began comparing him to the empty shell who runs for office in *The Candidate*. Now, the latest Gail Sheehy psycho-bio in *Vanity Fair* reports that that film's take on political packaging actually inspired Quayle in his first congressional race. Maybe *The Candidate*'s irony passed him by, but it wouldn't have fooled George Bush.

Bush knows the value of the empty gesture.

November 1988

■ ■ ■ The Impact Addict's Last Crash

The guy dressed like Julie Andrews was gonna fall from five stories up. Five! I panicked as he wrapped himself around a fake tree near the roof of P.S. 122 wearing that ridiculous *Sound of Music* dress, because the stage down in the courtyard was awfully small, and the cushion was *really* small, and there, pressed up against a fiberglass rock in the front row with a horde of screaming thrill-seekers behind me, I calculated the arc-of-a-diver geometry, and . . . He'd fall on me! He'd die! I'd die?

Well, I thought I'd rush ahead to the Good Part there, because David Leslie's deconstructed re-creations of heroic moments in media always go right to the Good Part, with just enough buildup to crank hearts into throats where we want 'em. Because nothing else really matters. We know the heroes. We know the plots. Just give us the Good Parts—when the theme music kicks in and Rocky jogs through Philly, Popeye squeezes that spinach can, and we *know* what's going down next. The highlight footage.

Leslie calls himself an "impact addict," but his work is more than daredevilry. Media gives birth to each stunt, and to media each stunt returns. Larry Fessenden does the videos—typically, footage of a Leslie act intercut with slam-bang clips from Bruce Lee, Batman, the usual. Last week's event also began with a video, Leslie explaining how much he'd learned from the movies. More from *Bambi* and *Pinocchio* than from church, he said. "The Disney thing . . . I believed in that as real knowledge." Over clips from *Rocky, The Wizard of Oz, Born Free,* he spoke of the movies giving him something to aspire to.

I heard derisive laughter in the crowd as we watched Sentimentality's Greatest Hits—those legs pounding the beach in *Chariots of Fire,* for example. These were the people he wanted to emulate, Leslie told

In *Mismatch,* artist David Leslie
asked boxer Riddick Bowe (left) to
knock him out. Bowe declined.
(Photo by John Eder.)

us, and these people came with a soundtrack. He was not being ironic.
He *would* climb every mountain, and was about to risk his life to do it.

In his first stunt in 1986, Leslie propelled a little rocket off a forty-
foot ramp on Broome Street, trying to fly over a pile of 1,000 water-
melons and land in a net. But he was running inside the rocket—the
Flintstone version of Evel Knievel—so naturally he just crashed. Later
he said that that moment when he'd left the ramp had been the most
exciting of his life, the thing he'd been born to do. On Chinese New
Year 1987, he wore a tiger suit fashioned out of 10,000 firecrackers,
which exploded to reveal a rabbit suit underneath. In May 1987, he
jumped from two stories up *onto a steel plate* in the courtyard of Cafe
Bustelo, swathed in bubble wrap and white Christmas-tree lights. In
June 1987, he went three rounds on the Staten Island ferry with Olympic silver medalist Riddick Bowe, who declined to knock Leslie out
though the artist had asked him to. (Leslie called the piece *Mismatch.*)
Then, in October 1987, he donned the bubble wrap once more for a
Franklin Furnace benefit, dropped through the roof of a martial arts
school set, and had the school members kick-slam him around the
stage.

Now he was going to "retire," he said. In his commercial for this
"final act of excess and abandon"—because hype is inseparable from
such an act—Leslie promised that like a boxer going out for his last
fight, he'd "pull out a little something extra." For days he'd been installing cliffs, trees, and a plastic waterfall up the side of P.S. 122. Atop
one cliff sat a video screen, atop another sat a billboard for Extermi-

nator Chili. (Like network television, his events and videos have sponsors.) "I attempt to bounce male media's message off a fun house mirror," Leslie says at the beginning of *The Rocket Movie.* Yet that message obviously captured his imagination. He sees it manipulate him but can't resist.

"You don't want to be in a wreck and have somebody get hurt, but you wouldn't mind a little fender bender just to get that jolt," he says on another video, over clips from *Jaws, Raging Bull,* the usual violence. "In the movies, it's just depicted pain, beautiful image."

I think of J. G. Ballard, whose characters read primordial messages in the technology that surrounds them, whose "heroes" crack through the veneer of official reality with the aid of some violent act. In Ballard's world, images are more real than real life. Someone in *Crash* collects footage of automobile collisions and dreams of dying in one himself— an act finally so real that he won't be able to watch the replay.

Leslie's work is a pure response to growing up in hyperreality, where we respond to images with our most powerful emotions. This creates a crisis of the real, a crisis of authenticity related to a crisis of the body, to needing what artist/writer Mary Kelly has called "the authenticating imprint of pain."

This makes Leslie's work poignant to me, even and maybe especially when it's a bit silly, as the final stunt was. Silly, earnest, and spectacularly exciting. Four people in bubble wrap and Christmas lights danced first—the warm-up act. Leslie's heroes—Evel Knievel, Bruce Lee, and James Brown—hopped onstage for cameos. And then who should appear but Maria von Trapp (Lucy Sexton), who disappeared behind a "rock" at the first strains of "Climb Every Mountain." Moments later the impact addict emerged in von Trapp clothing, like the stunt artist who comes in to take the hit for the star.

Leslie struggled up the cliffs as the song soared, his boots cracking into the fiberglass as he strained, heaving himself up, knocking off part of a rock, jumping a chasm, working without a net. Four stories up, he began to climb that last tree. The music changed to a stately rendition of "How Do You Solve a Problem Like Maria," and suddenly three nuns were standing below him on the fire escape, two with giant red axes. "Maria's not an asset to the abbey," the chorus warbled as the nuns chopped.

He fell with no grace. Thunked into the cushion, and just barely, it seemed. It had happened too fast to be visible to these naked eyes.

But now he belongs to the videotape, and there I can watch it in slo-mo.

December 1988

■ ■ ■ Fin-de-Millennium

The 80's Are Over
—*Newsweek* cover, January 4, 1988

T he young "urpin" professionals were out prowling the shops for fake Etruscan bits, plunking down their hundreds for, say, a cement bowl with simulated broken rim. I got these facts straight from the Home Section. "To be desirable, objects have to look as though they were found in an archaeological dig" (*New York Times*, January 14, 1988). Every home a museum.

The past has flattened out behind us, making every decade and epoch of equal weight like so many television channels. Flip from the fifties to the twenties to the Etruscans or revive 'em all simultaneously. I think the world's life is flashing before its eyes. Certainly this sense of apocalypse will dog us till millennium time.

Jean Baudrillard, that signature philosopher of the eighties and one I appreciated for hovering right on the border between plausibility and fantasy, writes in his essay "The Year 2000 Has Already Happened": "They can already smell the terror of the year 2000. Our societies instinctively adopt the solution of those cryogenics that preserve things in liquid nitrogen while waiting for the discovery of a mode of survival." There's that museum thing again.

We want damage!

The eighties may well be over, but they were never about the stock market. That was just one manifestation of the real themes: speed, panic, transgression, the hyperreal, a fascination with images.

My eighties began in '77 with Johnny Rotten, and I think it makes a neat arc to finish them off with another extreme and self-created media personality, Michael Jackson. But while Rotten thought he could become the black hole at pop's core and force it to implode, Jackson seems to know that that's no role for a mythological being. And stars (even antistars) are always mythological now.

Here's my theory of Michael Jackson: As a media creature since childhood, he thinks he's all image. He has, in fact, abandoned his body, in order to inhabit its simulacrum. I think of him as a sort of radical "body artist." He doesn't want to be black, yet I don't think he wants to be white. And I don't think he wants to have a gender. He's so ethereal he can hardly believe he has a body. Those dance steps are his human part. But the rest of him died in some head-on collision between illusion and reality. The videos, in particular, reveal how much of him passed away. They're pure nostalgia. They celebrate a life he's never lived, and feelings he's never had.

He has mutilated himself, still projecting what I can only call innocence. And this struggle to so literally control his image, this endless submission to the knife, has a certain pathos. As John Merrick, The Elephant Man, once wrote: "'Tis true my form is something odd/But blaming me is blaming God/Could I create myself anew/I would not fail in pleasing you" (from *The True History of the Elephant Man*).

It's been the function of this column to rub up against the exploratory and experimental, the sort of work that doesn't quite have a context yet. And every once in a while I encounter something I don't know what to do with. One night last November, for example, I went out late to one of those batcaves I'll frequent, in my Search, and walked by the sign about entering at your own risk, and sidestepped the guys rolling and punching their way across the floor to the tune of Metallica. I felt more than usually like a visiting anthropologist. Especially since I'd just come from Anna de Keersmaeker's show at BAM, which featured five women in tight dresses and high heels clinging to and flinging themselves around chairs, and was all about femininity and containment and tedium.

So here I was a couple hours later, watching G. G. Allin in a jockstrap and matted hair and scrawlish tattoos, who began by socking himself in the nose with the mike, drawing blood, and rasping out lyrics of a pathological misogyny. See—he likes to pick up where Sid and Iggy left off, then start abusing the audience. He clocked one guy with the mike stand, then whipped it around like a billy club as the panicked crowd fell back in a rats-off-a-ship movement. The true fans (young, white, and male) always regrouped—to chant something like "Shit! Shit! Shit!" The performer jammed the mike up his ass, drew more blood, then charged the audience again—this time swinging the mike over his head. I'd moved to the back. I watched him yank exposed wires down from the ceiling while a big glob of blood ran down his chest.

This was a performer I didn't want to publicize with so much as a Bad Review. But I felt the "show" raised crucial questions. Like: If we're going to destroy taboos, and call that good, does that mean we shouldn't have *any* taboos at all? And how come the "avant-garde" is so centered on taboo, anyway? (Is there unknown territory that isn't forbidden?) And was there anything about this show that we haven't seen a million times since the cave? Was it a performance at all? I mean—was it an act? While there, I took it for the real thing—an assault. I don't just mean the bruises I got.

I forget to tell you that the guy's fans were enraged by this show. Betrayed! *There'd been no real damage!* "Last time," snarled one, "he left on a stretcher."

February 1988

■ ■ ■ War on Art

■ ■ ■ The Sexual Politics of Censorship

We're not talking about artistic nudes.
—press secretary to Representative Dana Rohrabacher

Martha Wilson, director of Franklin Furnace, a major downtown venue for experimental art, came to work on May 21 to find large white stickers fixed to the front door: "VACATE—DO NOT ENTER. THE DEPARTMENT OF BUILDINGS HAS DETERMINED THAT CONDITIONS IN THIS PREMISES ARE IMMINENTLY PERILOUS TO LIFE."
After fifteen years as an archive and performance showcase, the Furnace has been charged with not having an illuminated exit sign or emergency lighting, and with keeping the front door locked during a show. The action, however, had been prompted by another kind of emergency.
It started the day Karen Finley's installation opened, one week after syndicated columnists Evans and Novak ridiculed the performance artist as "a chocolate-smeared woman." Wilson says: "Karen's show triggered it. I don't think there's any doubt about it. People for the American Way told us we could expect something from the religious right because this has been going on all over the country."
According to Franklin Furnace, a man who'd attended Finley's opening got into an argument with staff members later that evening, when he wanted to leave and couldn't figure out how to buzz himself out. "He's not a performance goer," says Wilson. "He was there for another purpose." The man decided to report the Furnace. As spokeswoman Barbara Pollack put it, "We're operating in an atmosphere where people feel if they don't like art, they can call in the authorities."*

*On the day this article appeared in the *Voice*, a man phoned me to say that he was

Franklin Furnace is open again, but the basement performance space remains closed. Of course, it was the fire department, not the vice squad, that shut them down. But when people send the law after art, there's always some hidden agenda. That's true from here to Sincinnati.

I grew up in Fundamentalist Land, that theme park of guilt and transgression. I knew little of art, but lots about the God who could smite. Lately, I've wondered whether the National Endowment for the Arts didn't fund the experience that helped to open some door—no, some fire exit—in *me*. I was stuck in the glue of depression out in the heart of Illinois when I happened to see the Bread and Puppet Theater on cable television. In this play of shrouded, masked characters, all moving at a foghorn's pace, a dead man rises. A river is a very tall character. The narrator whispers. I still can't quite articulate what moved me, but the piece said: "Possibility." Eighteen years later, I can still remember nearly every line and image.

So, as the zealots force their scarlet letters on the art world, I know they're desperate to hold the fire exits shut. They see boundaries breaking. They see libidos play prime time. Porn walks in and out of the video store. Abortions are still legal, women who want sex aren't necessarily "bad," and gay people keep popping out of their closets. "Secular" can't even describe such humanism.

The Saved are always a minority among the Damned. Practicing zealots don't feel powerful, but beleaguered. That's why they're obsessed with policing the boundaries of the permissible. For a while in the eighties, it looked as if the right might sell their moral majority idea and transform the culture into some Heritage Park version of *The Handmaid's Tale*. But the Saved lost their Ronnie; their grip on prime time,

the one who'd called the Fire Department—not because of the Karen Finley installation but because of Diane Torr's performance, *Crossing the River Styx*, staged in the basement. Torr had been working with a live band and the man said he wanted to leave because he could not take the high-decibel music. The upstairs door was locked, however. Though the man refused to identify himself, this version of events was later confirmed by Torr. But for the Furnace staff to have assumed what they assumed was completely logical in the repressive atmosphere of summer 1990. On June 29, just weeks after this article appeared, NEA Chair John Frohnmayer defunded Finley and three openly gay performance artists—John Fleck, Holly Hughes, and Tim Miller. Then in July, the General Accounting Office called the Furnace's Martha Wilson (and Kitchen director Barbara Tsumagari) at the request of Senator Jesse Helms, seeking information about performances by Finley, Cheri Gaulke, Frank Moore, and Johanna Went.

if not Congress; even their moral high ground. How will they erase those sex-crazed Jimmies (Bakker/Swaggart) from our minds? Regroup around some unseen enemy. That's how. And wouldn't ya know, fresh outta godless Communists, they've discovered the art world—a rich new motherlode of sinners.

And deconstructionists. Jesse Helms hasn't lashed out at artists "deconstructing representation," but that's how a lot of this "pornography" got into the museums to begin with. Artists were pulling labels apart, questioning the God-given basics, like what it means to be a "man" or a "woman." They defiled the sacred barriers around "high art," and soon the "low"—from carnival to rock—rushed in. They acknowledged the Other and soon a few "others" dared to intrude. Isn't that what the postmodern lingo boils down to in the end: loss of authority for all powers-that-be?

In the good old days of modernism, the boundaries artists attacked were formal. Riots broke out when *Nude Descending a Staircase* was first exhibited, and *The Rite of Spring* was first performed, and *L'Age d'Or* was first screened. These works opened doors by expanding the parameters of perception. Now, there's all this *content* in art, all these dangerous messages—that you can become a *different* sort of man, a *different* sort of woman.

When Jesse Helms brought those "disgusting" Mapplethorpe photos to the Senate chamber, he asked the women and adolescent pages to leave. Representing sexuality: that's for grown men to decide, to judge, to control. That's why they're waging this war on difference. At stake is the sexual order.

Every artist attacked so far has challenged that hierarchy. (In Andres Serrano's case, it's the patriarchy implicit in church hierarchy.) And each is guilty of working with primal imagery, trafficking in the unclean, forcing contact with the body as it is: the coolly unregenerate s&m images in Robert Mapplethorpe's *XYZ Portfolios*; urine, semen, and menstrual blood in Serrano's photographs; the demystified female body in Annie Sprinkle's performances; the frankly homosexual body in David Wojnarowicz's paintings/writings; the documented "body modifications" in *ReSearch* magazine's "Modern Primitives" issue; and the exteriorized female body in the work of Karen Finley.

The far right often discusses this work in metaphors of chaos, dissolution, sewage, engulfment: "the river of swill" (representative Dana

Rohrabacher); "stinking foul-smelling garbage" (an American Family Association coordinator); "a polluted culture, left to fester and stink" (Patrick Buchanan). The heightened emotions and uncontrolled sexuality of the Other threatens each of these wrathful Dads. It threatens their identity, their separateness from women and gays, their very sense of self.

There's an apocalyptic quiver at the heart of the religious right's anti-NEA campaign. For in this art, they see the decline of civilization. It's an old story. "Theater, art, literature, cinema, press, posters, and window displays must be cleansed of all manifestations of our rotting world. . . . Public life must be freed from the stifling perfume of our modern eroticism. . . . The right of personal freedom recedes before the duty to preserve the race." The author of these words: Adolf Hitler. And though the jackboot will not be televised, its imprint is evident in the current rhetoric of reaction. As Pat Robertson decried "tax-supported trash" on his *700 Club* one day, his co-host Sheila Walsh gravely concluded, "It's just a hellish plot to destroy this nation."

The American Family Association, the 700 Club, the Eagle Forum, and so on: let's call them the Gang of Fear. They'll pounce on Pepsi, circle the cineplex, picket 7-Eleven—wherever the obscene and the blasphemous show their faces. But when "art" is at stake, the gang grows larger and more genteel, as blue-chip conservatives enter the fray. Too highfalutin to be bothered with pop culture imagery, these critics and columnists *do* care about canon, about intrusions of the Other into their hallowed halls. The difference between these groups is one of class: neocons *do* hate to dirty their hands among the "yahoos" (as William Safire has called them)—and they're no less condescending to transgressive artists. The artist they've chosen to attack is Karen Finley, known henceforth in the ivory tower as "a chocolate-besmeared nude live performer."

Safire claims he isn't for censorship but wants the NEA abolished because "Federal support ultimately conflicts with freedom of expression." This is exactly the point made by the Reverend Donald Wildmon of the AFA, who calls the Endowment a censor because it determines what art the government should fund. And they don't fund Christian art, do they? Rohrabacher told the *New Art Examiner* that most art "produced by the NEA [is] ugly and grotesque." Phyllis Schlafly, former ERA opponent turned NEA opponent, makes an inevitable connection between sexual hierarchy and the right kind of art: "Why didn't they give a grant to have a statue of Rocky on the steps of the museum in Philadelphia?"

The NEA isn't even the issue, just the first target. Ultimately, the Gang of Fear wants to control what's presented. Destroying the Endowment would cripple much that's marginal and developing, while helping to keep the Other confined to large cities. Barry Blinderman, who curated Wojnarowicz's retrospective in Normal, Illinois, told me, "The NEA made the difference between us being an outpost and us being connected to all the major art institutions. People in Normal are proud of that." NEA grants are the most prestigious available, emblems of an artist's worth or a venue's seriousness, and they attract corporate funding.

Tim McClimon, vice-president of the AT&T Foundation, a major corporate arts funder, points out that an "arts ecology" has developed among corporations, private foundations, and the government over the last twenty-five years. "We're partners. Restrictions on the NEA have a ripple effect. [The private sector] starts looking at the same issues. You can't view parts of an ecology in isolation." If the NEA collapsed, he says, "we might continue to support the arts, but we can't pick up where the government leaves off."

The war's already spread beyond the Endowment. Thanks to AFA pressure (55,000 letters), the Southeastern Center for Contemporary Art (SECCA) lost their funding from Equitable after exhibiting Serrano's *Piss Christ*. Corporations have become nervous. One New York presenter heard from a private funder: "The arts used to be safe, used to be good PR. They aren't safe now."

"The change in the atmosphere in the last few months is striking," says Laura Trippi, a curator at the New Museum who worked on "The Decade Show," consponsored by the Studio Museum of Harlem and the Museum of Contemporary Hispanic Art. "A year ago, 'The Decade Show' was extremely popular with corporate and private funders, because of the cachet around multiculturalism," she said. "Now, even with funders still committed to the project, we're finding a lot of caution and concern. We've had to give a lot more detailed information about any political or sexual content. Everything's been scrutinized to an extent that's unprecedented."

The Gang of Fear smells blood. When *New York*'s John Simon speared the Mabou Mines version of *Lear*, he listed all their funders and asked: "Jesse Helms, where are you when we need you?" Could it be a coincidence that this was a gender-reversed production, with a drag queen for a Fool? They were "raping Shakespeare," Simon wrote.

Mississippi senator Trent Lott will reportedly seek "disciplinary action" against the Kitchen for presenting Annie Sprinkle. Says Barbara Tsumagari, the Kitchen's executive director: "All we can do is to continue to honor the mission of this institution. If that means that the environment can't support a place like the Kitchen—better to close than to compromise."

You'd think the Helms Amendment had passed. One Helmsman (Senator Warren Rudman) gloated in defeat: "We have fired a warning shot across their bow." I don't think the military metaphor is accidental. The right has designated art as an area to be patrolled, even pacified. As John Killacky of Minneapolis's Walker Art Center told me, after two members of the vice squad came to monitor a performance there by Karen Finley last January, "People on the right now feel empowered to stop art. They don't just want to disagree with it. They want to stop it."

The impulse has filtered down to the streets. Last month, a pack of roving art critics appeared at Max Fish, a bar on the Lower East Side, to "review" Allen Frame's double image of men touching, *Boys on the Couch*. While one connoisseur distracted the bartender, the others took the offending picture from the wall, went outside, and smashed it. One of them explained, "This isn't art."

Suddenly we're a nation of critics-at-large. (Some very much at-large, since they haven't even seen the work that so offends them.) We're caught up in a struggle between two sensibilities, two moralities, two kinds of critique—one that separates good art from bad, another that separates good from "evil."

The Gang of Fear has found an ideal transgressor in Annie Sprinkle, the ex-porn star. She goes to the very crotch of the matter for them. Of course, Sprinkle has never received government funding, nor has she applied for any, but it isn't like the Gang to let a fact stand in its way.

The religious right feasted on Sprinkle's piece, *Post Porn Modernist*.

They repeatedly described it as a live sex show. In fact, the performance was about Sprinkle coming to terms with her years of work in the sex industry. Porn, after all, has its own conventions about what should and shouldn't be seen in order to arouse the audience. In one segment, "Bosom Ballet," she manipulated her large breasts in time to music, subverting any turn-on with silliness. The point for Sprinkle is to do a show *she* enjoys, something sex-positive for grim times, something . . . well, educational. One bit that roused ire and umbrage in the Gang (only one of whom actually saw the show) featured Sprinkle inserting a speculum and inviting people to look at her cervix. "Demystifying the female body," she called it. This action also impressed me as the moment when a woman who's been ogled all her life says, in effect: You wanna look at me? Go ahead and look—all the way inside.

It nearly landed Sprinkle in jail on Easter weekend. She'd opened the Cleveland Performance Art Festival with the vice squad in attendance at both shows. Sprinkle changed her act when police implied that the cervix piece would be grounds for arrest. The irony is that Sprinkle used to perform in Cleveland during her porn-star days, at a burlesque theater she describes as the "wildest" place she's ever worked. She actual *did* live sex shows then, and the vice squad never even showed up. "As long as it was in the porn ghetto. As long as it was *their* pleasure arena. But now that it's something for me. . . ."

Sprinkle onstage is sweet, sometimes coy. There's a part of her porn persona she can't or won't drop—the part there for men. She who drops it, after all, risks monstrosity by embodying a female energy that men fear or hate. During the eighties, however, a sort of rude-girl network developed in the downtown clubs. Performers like Lydia Lunch, Dancenoise, and Karen Finley had edges instead of softness. They allowed themselves to be monsters. Finley can be disturbingly confrontational in subverting images of the female body, as defined by male desire.

A few years ago, I wrote a *Voice* cover story praising Finley's work and Pete Hamill denounced her in the next week's paper, after days of interoffice uproar and graffiti sprayed across men's rooms. Like Evans/Novak and Safire, Hamill mocked Finley by focusing on food. He said her work was all about stuffing yams, just as the others say it's all about smeared chocolate. None of these Wrathful Dads has ever seen her. They write in that vacuum called male entitlement.

Obscenity is Finley's subject—not four-letter words but the emotion propelling them. Her monologues expose unspeakable acts and unforgivable feelings, deconstructing relationships into the most primal urges. She holds the mirror to what people try to hide, and for those things there are no polite words: rape, AIDS, incest, abandonment, brutality, emotional damage. She transforms food into an emblem of catharsis. It's where the boundary breaks, the boundary of the body. Inside goes outside. No doubt the reaction to that moment, and to her work in general, has to do with male terror when "primal" meets "female." Herstory is the history of such instincts kept under control.

We Keep Our Victims Ready, the show criticized by Evans/Novak and Safire, is more straightforwardly political than anything Finley has done. Here, she uses food ritualistically, smearing on chocolate as she talks about female victimization. Because women are treated like shit. Slowly, she recreates herself, applying sprouts, red candy, and tinsel. By the end, she seems to be wearing a strange and beautiful costume. That is the heart of her work: to take some horror on, then turn it over. This show moved people to tears.

To those fretting over the social/sexual order, gender traitors take on this quality of monstrosity. So, it's a short step from rude girl to rude queer.

The Gang plays steadily and lucratively on the fact that homos are asserting themselves. Jesse Helms, who augments his NEA attacks with fulminations against *any* spending for AIDS, informed his Senate colleagues last fall that "Mapplethorpe's obscene photographs were an effort to gain wider exposure of, and acceptance for, homosexuality." The American Family Association, which has consistently attacked any television program with a positive take on homosexuals, runs anti-NEA newspaper ads that rail about such innocuous-sounding exhibits as "At Home with Themselves: Gay and Lesbian Couples"—confident that any tax money going to queers will trigger outrage.

The Corcoran Gallery's decision to drop "Robert Mapplethorpe: The Perfect Moment" sanctioned homophobia. And other artists have been encountering the fallout ever since. During a gig in Philadelphia, "I felt like people were gonna jump up on the stage and lynch me," says Holly Hughes, an openly gay playwright/performer. Recently, she says, presenters at venues that might ordinarily book her have been saying,

"There's a problem with you coming, because it's lesbian material."
Hughes feels the homophobia has "mushroom-clouded."

Last summer, Creative Time distributed an AIDS education card by
Gran Fury, "Kissing Doesn't Kill: Greed and Indifference Do," and as
director Cee Brown told me, "We got three complaints following the
Corcoran thing. One artist from Boston called and said, 'My daughter
could pick this up and it's promoting homosexuality. I want to talk to
every one of your funders.'"

Performance artists Anne Iobst and Lucy Sexton (Dancenoise)
appeared at the University of Massachusetts, and had their own problems when the young Puritans there complained about a sneak preview they did, because *these two women appeared in their underwear!* But
in describing the campus mood, Sexton told me that the university's
gallery had recently been vandalized (smashed windows, shaving
cream) because an exhibit there included gay images. In the school
newspaper, she says, young Helmsmen-in-training were declaring
that their tuition money shouldn't have to pay for such art.

Obviously the NEA-bashers are horrified to discover that grants actually go to gay artists who make gay art. No wonder the Gang of Fear
targeted David Wojnarowicz. A "Dear Colleague" letter from Representative Rohrabacher described the artist's NEA-funded retrospective
at Illinois State University as "sickeningly violent, sexually explicit,
homoerotic, anti-religious and nihilistic." The Gang just doesn't want
to see the body through gay eyes. The AFA's Reverend Wildmon, master of the mail-order Judgment Day, went on a penis-hunt through
Wojnarowicz's catalogue and diligently sent the xeroxed results to
every member of Congress, 3,200 Christian leaders, 1,000 Christian
radio stations, 100 Christian TV stations, and 178,000 pastors.

Wojnarowicz's work—political, emotional—is quite a contrast to
Mapplethorpe's formal, depersonalized studies. But both insist on
homoeroticism as a valid subject of art. It so obviously informs Wojnarowicz's worldview that deleting it would leave a shell, while Mapplethorpe's work is either hardcore transgression or lilies—art that could
"pass." The antiporn diehards in Cincinnati kept proposing something
to the tune of: *just take out those bad pictures; the other ones are nice.*

The Mapplethorpe pictures for which museum director Dennis Barrie will stand trial include five from the *XYZ Portfolios* plus two showing
children with their genitals exposed. The work may not be benign, but

neither is it pornographic. The stark images of sexual extremes in the *Portfolio* (fistfucking, water sports, rubber fetishists) don't reinforce fantasy, which is porn's job. They confront fantasy, which is art's job. They admit to the multiplicity of sexual experience, and pass no judgment on it.

What happened in Sincinnati is the culture war in microcosm: Your Patriarchy at Work. It had nothing to do with the NEA, everything to do with Dads who claim to know best.

The rest of the country may get to read *Hustler*, or hear N.W.A., or see . . . *Equus*. But the town fathers in Cincinnati like to think this smut won't get past *them*. Since 1974, the city's had no adult bookstores, no X-rated videos or cable, no massage parlors, and no strip joints. *The Last Temptation of Christ* didn't play there either. (And don't try renting the video.)

"There's always a posse here to protect people from what we artists might perpetrate on the public," says Worth Gardener, artistic director of Cincinnati's Playhouse in the Park. Last year, the vice squad requested a police preview of *Equus*, because it includes a brief nude scene. "I've never lost my amazement at gestures like this. The banners are in the basement ready to come out."

There are gay people in Cincinnati, and I found them the old-fashioned way. Surreptitiously. At least, that's what it felt like when someone handed me a name written on a napkin: "He'll be able to tell you things." Once I got to that name, though, I plugged into a huge phone-tree of people offering to help—most of them closeted.

Others I met talked about the local chapter of Planned Parenthood: "a fort," constantly besieged by pickets. National Right to Life president and "founding father," Dr. John Willke, lives in Cincinnati. So does the Reverend Jerry Kirk, founder or chairman of the National Coalition Against Pornography, STOP (Stand Together Opposing Pornography), and the National Consultation on Pornography. (The AFA's Donald Wildmon was part of the latter group's "leadership team.") The group that went after Mapplethorpe, Citizens for Community Values, is another creation of the ubiquitous Reverend Kirk.

Cincinnati's antiporn ardor was born in the mind of a single fearless crusader for morality: Charles Keating. He is better known today as the symbol of the savings and loan crisis; the man who sold uninsured and now worthless bonds to 23,000 Californians, most of them elderly and investing their life savings; the man who forked over generous campaign contributions to several U.S. senators with the power to influence banking examiners; the man who will eventually cost taxpayers an estimated two to three *billion* dollars.

Charles Keating lived in Cincinnati for fifty-five years, and there began his war against "diabolical and evil" pornography. One local woman, who did not wish to be named, recalled going to a meeting for teens at a friend's house in the early sixties. Keating arrived, she told me, with a briefcase full of *Playboys*, much to the chagrin of her friend's father. She herself had never before seen a *Playboy*.

Far from Sincinnati, but all too near—Karen Finley recently dedicated another project made possible by government funding, an outdoor sculpture with a monologue from her recent show cast in bronze, *The Black Sheep*. It sits at the corner of First Avenue and Houston, across the street from a small park filled with the homeless.

The day she installed it, someone from the Parks Department worried that people would tip the work over, hit it with sledgehammers, throw paint on it. But as one sallow, sunken-cheeked local said, "You'd have to be a lowlife to do that." He said he'd help her plant flowers in the few remaining patches of dirt in what could only pass in New York City for a park. And the next day, when it rained, someone came out and draped a coat over the sculpture.

"I just know all these people are black sheep," said Finley, as scores stopped to read her text. *We are sheep with no shepherd/we are sheep with no straight and narrow/we are sheep with no meadow. . . .* These were the homeless, and people in ties, workers leaving the subway, and one guy who lived *in* the subway, "under the rock," as he put it.

Finley's piece for the black sheep of the family describes everyone the American Family Association will always hate and fear. The people who see things differently because they honor the reality of their own identities. As she says: *Black sheep's destinies are not in necessarily having families/having prescribed existences like the American Dream/Black Sheep destinies are to give meaning in life—to be angels, to be conscience, to be nightmares, to be actors in dreams.*

June 1990

ast April in Tupelo, Mississippi, the Reverend Donald Wildmon of the American Family Association got his hands on a copy of David Wojnarowicz's exhibition catalogue *Tongues of Flame*. Here was something the preacher could use: raw material to further the Lord's work of killing the National Endowment for the Arts. He would testify later that the catalogue made him "kind of sick at [his] stomach." Still, Wildmon doggedly went on looking for the naughty bits. These assorted homo- and heterosexual images were fragments of much larger pieces, but the heck with the larger pieces; the heck with what the work *meant*. Tax dollars had paid for a catalogue with fourteen depictions of sex! And the artist was an admitted homosexual! Now Wildmon had proof of an NEA transgression to mail to Congress, and the media. Carefully he labeled the envelope "Warning! Extremely Offensive Material Enclosed."

On June 25, in a U.S. District Court, Reverend Wildmon and his American Family Association stood accused of deliberately misrepresenting the work of David Wojnarowicz and defaming his character.

Well, to be precise, the reverend first stood accused out in the hallway or somewhere, because he wasn't present as the artist began to testify. It must have galled him to be there: his lawyers had filed several motions to dismiss the case and a couple more for change of venue (to Mississippi), and it hadn't worked and he'd had to come all the way to New York to face "Mr. Wojnarowicz, a homosexual." (So Wildmon had referred to him in a follow-up letter to those "Christian leaders.")

Donald Wildmon is a major player these days in cultural politics, the guy fanning the flames of hellfire right behind Jesse Helms. He's a master of direct-mail pressure. For years, the AFA's major targets have been television networks. Each issue of the *AFA Journal* lists offending programs, from *Golden Girls* (an "illicit sex show with anti-Christian humor") to *Alf* ("complete with child sex and incest") to *L.A. Law* ("pro-homosexual"). Comments conclude with a hit list of advertisers' names and addresses. In 1988, Wildmon and the AFA helped lead the attack on Martin Scorsese's movie *The Last Temptation of Christ*. In 1989, they frightened Pepsi into dropping its Madonna commercials. The whole NEA controversy started when an AFA member last year alerted Wildmon to Andres Serrano's *Piss Christ* (1987), an "NEA-funded blasphemy." Wildmon organized a massive letter-writing campaign directed at Congress. And recent issues of the *AFA Journal* concentrate almost exclusively on the Endowment.

Wildmon is a moral terrorist of legendary proportions. Before him, mighty Congressmen cower. Yet he rarely leaves Mississippi and no longer gives interviews. So some in the courtroom crowd had come just to hear him testify, just to see what it would feel like to be in the presence of his tunnelvision.

Well, he's . . . Fudd with a hank o' hair. As extremists go, he's a banal one. His lawyers even tried to keep him off the stand. First they announced that they'd call him as a witness, so Wojnarowicz's lawyers declared that they'd wait to question him until cross-examination. Then, as soon as the artist's side rested, Wildmon's lawyers announced that they would call no witnesses at all. Theoretically, the plaintiff couldn't call the reverend now either, but Wojnarowicz's lawyers put the matter to the judge. "They did not list him as a witness," argued Benjamin Bull, who presented most of Wildmon's case that day. Judge William C. Conner didn't buy it. The gray-haired preacher walked to the stand.

Perhaps an anticlimax was appropriate, even inevitable—all this material was well chewed, the issues clear. David Cole of the Center for Constitutional Rights, representing the artist, asked the reverend why he'd chosen particular images to excise. The judge interrupted, "Isn't that obvious? He picked what he thought was offensive." As Cole questioned the reverend further—on a falsehood in his letter, on whether he'd published anything to correct a misleading statement, on whether he had ever said that the images were details—the judge interrupted again: "You know, this is all very obvious." But then the whole one-day trial was rather cut 'n' dried. Wildmon never denied that he had taken the images out of context. Or that he'd chosen what was most likely to offend. Basically, his lawyers argued that the preacher had merely been exercising his First Amendment rights, and that Wojnarowicz was trying to censor him. Wojnarowicz's lawyers replied that they were not challenging Wildmon's right to criticize but his right to distort, "falseley representing that [the artist's] work consists of nothing but banal sexual images." Wildmon had nowhere indicated that the bits he'd excised were details of Wojnarowicz's densely layered and very political pictures.

When Bull questioned Wildmon, he tried to make the point that the preacher was no art critic but a concerned citizen. "Would you know the difference between a collage and a portrait?" he asked Wildmon. The reverend said "No." Would he object—as a taxpayer—to any sexually explicit images, even if done by, say, Rembrandt? Said the reverend: "Sure." And why had he excised these images and mailed them to key leaders? "One of the problems you have with pornography," declared Wildmon, "is that in some cases you cannot adequately describe it. Sometimes you have to do what John Frohnmayer said: confront the art."

Wojnarowicz first became a far-right target last fall, when he wrote a catalogue essay for an NEA-funded show about AIDS at Artists Space in New York. The artist's angry and almost surreal denunciations of assorted right-wingers prompted NEA chairman John Frohnmayer to order that no grant money be designated for the catalogue. Wojnarowicz then drew the attention of another anti-NEA zealot, Representative Dana Rohrabacher, who denounced him in a "Dear Colleague" letter sent to every member of the House of Representatives.

Given this history, argued Wildmon's lawyers, the artist was a public figure in the NEA controversy. (A public figure has restricted redress under current libel law.) A rage leaked through their legalese. One pretrial brief even compared the artist to Hitler, by way of arguing that not all of a work need be shown: "One may criticize Hitler for the gas chambers without being required to compliment him on the trains running on time, even if it is argued that the failure to so compliment him gives a distorted view of his regime. So one may criticize an artistic creation for the moral repugnance of a part of it without being required to evaluate the rest as to its artistic merit." They also argued that the artist's reputation had not been damaged but enhanced. That the artwork itself had not been mutilated, only the reproductions. That Reverend Wildmon's description of the pictures as "part of" the exhibition catalogue had indicated that they were details. That criticism of art can't be defamation, and that this in any case was not art criticism but political criticism and therefore "protected" speech. And the most startling assertion of all, considering the source: "even assuming *arguendo* that the defendants really intended to label the plaintiff as a pornographer, this is not defamatory . . . pornography can in many instances exist as a protected art form."

Again, Judge Conner didn't seem to be buying it. At the trial's end, in a move that surprised even Wojnarowicz's lawyers, he enjoined the AFA from any further publication of the pamphlet, saying "the balance of potential injury weighs strongly in favor of the plaintiff." As the judge finished, Bull leaped to the podium to state that the injunction violated First Amendment rights and would have a "chilling effect" on the American Family Association. Judge Conner, who characterized himself as "not entirely unacquainted with the First Amendment," assured Bull that the AFA could publish anything it wanted about Mr. Wojnarowicz's work—as long as it was true.

The religious right is so postmodern. They've appropriated all the arguments used against them: First Amendment rights, the specter of fascism, even the dread "chilling effect." But whose interpretation will prevail? Whose voice will be heard? As evidenced in this courtroom skirmish, the battle over the NEA is really a battle between two irreconcilable ways of looking at the world. And compromise is out of the question because these twain just ain't gonna meet.

September 1990

■ ■ ■ With Mapplethorpe in Cincinnati

The night "Robert Mapplethorpe: The Perfect Moment" opened in Cincinnati last April, more than 4,000 people crowded into the Contemporary Arts Center (CAC), filing through a space built to accommodate 450. They weren't there to schmooze. They concentrated on the pictures as if they expected them to be snatched away at any moment. As if that were inevitable. They waited for up to an hour to get in, then for another hour to view the infamous *X, Y,* and *Z Portfolios*. "I know you all want to see at least one nasty one," joked curator Jack Sawyer at one point as he tried to keep the line moving. "The photos will be there 'til May 26. You'll have another opportunity." Almost instantly the line grew longer, as if people didn't believe him.

This, after all, was Cincinnati. Where you can't find an X-rated anything. Where *Hustler* publisher Larry Flynt got a sentence of seven to twenty-five years for pandering obscenity. Where—weeks before Mapplethorpe's photographs arrived—the county sheriff declared several of them "criminally obscene." The whole town knew that meant police action. It was only a question of *what* action: Arresting museum director Dennis Barrie? Shutting down the exhibit? Confiscating the pictures? Throwing a sheet over the *X, Y,* and *Z Portfolios'* display case? I heard all these possibilities discussed in April. And I realized, as the trial began September 24, that most Cincinnatians thought something else was inevitable as well—that the museum and its director would be convicted.

Dennis Barrie, however, entered the courtroom that first day of trial declaring his "faith in the system." Local reporters rolled their eyes. Museum supporters smiled politely. Over the next two weeks, I heard Cincinnatians giving their hometown such unflattering labels as "a feudal society" and "Albania." They were already tallying up Barrie's grounds for appeal.

Such fatalism was born out of a long history of moral crusades. Part of that history, county Sheriff Simon Leis, stood outside the courthouse on day one of the trial, staring grimly down at protesters from Gay and Lesbian March Activists (GLMA), ACT UP, and Voice Against Censorship. A square-jawed ex-Marine, Leis was ready for them. Facing the 150 demonstrators with their anti-Helms, anti-Leis placards were barricades, paddy wagons, 30 sheriff's deputies in yellow latex gloves, the mounted police, and a SWAT team.

"I believe that there are certain moral standards not protected by law but which have been established through the ages, that all of us are required to adhere to. Homosexuality is one of the immoral acts," Leis once declared. While county prosecutor in the seventies, Leis routed every adult bookstore, massage parlor, and X-rated movie theater out of his jurisdiction, though he was unsuccessful in shutting down *Hair*, *Oh, Calcutta!* and *Last Tango in Paris*. In 1977, he won the conviction against Flynt, and, though that decision was reversed on appeal, it is still impossible to buy *Hustler* in Cincinnati. Elected judge in 1982, Leis left the bench after several years to run for the lower-paying job of sheriff. "He couldn't stand being a judge, because he had to obey the law," quipped one lifelong Cincinnatian.

Hamilton County's obscenity laws are no different from anyone else's. It's just that Leis has been so aggressive for so long at finding "probable cause" for arrest. The scenario usually goes like this (and it's what everyone predicted for the Contemporary Arts Center): the accused hires a lawyer, stands trial, gets convicted and ends up in appeals court, where the conviction is eventually overturned. But few can afford to go through this process. The result is self-censorship. Residents know they can cross the river to Kentucky to buy what Hamilton County store owners are too intimidated to sell.

Meanwhile, the vice squad—what with *real* vice in short supply—has become a cultural arbiter, investigating the possible lewd play (*Equus*), tracking down the errant 2 Live Crew record, attending a photo exhibit of male nudes at the one alternative art space. Last May, four sheriff's officers apprehended a model at a nightclub fashion show for wearing a "see-through" lace bra. Three days after the courthouse demonstration, they arrested a gay couple for holding hands—as they sat in their own car. And both times I've visited, I've met people who insist that the Hostess product called "Ding Dongs" has been relabeled "King Dons" in Cincinnati because Leis thinks the first name is obscene. Hostess says it was a trademark issue. ("What's obscene about Ding Dongs?" asked an incredulous spokesman at the company's St. Louis headquarters.) The story only illustrates how sensitized Cincinnatians have become to what might pass for sex crimes in the judgment of Simon Leis.

"What you have in Cincinnati is not virtue. It's purity by blackmail," says Allen Brown, a defense attorney and cooperating counsel with the ACLU, who fought Leis in court many times over a forty-three-year career. "It's a very corrupt town. Cronyism corrupt. People who are part of an inner circle cut each other breaks."

And Leis was just the front man for an anti-Mapplethorpe cabal that included some of the most powerful businessmen in Cincinnati. Leis did not invent the town's anti-porn fervor either. Charles Keating did. For fifty-five years, the indicted S&L king lived in Cincinnati, where he began Citizens for Decent Literature (later Citizens for Decency Through Law) in 1957. Under Keating—nicknamed "Mr. Clean"—CDL declared "holy war" on such threats to morality as *Playboy*, phone sex, and the Ramada Inn chain, which offered adult cable programming to guests. According to *The Cincinnati Post*, "[Keating] fought showings of the X-rated *Vixen* and *Oh, Calcutta!* in Cincinnati and said homosexuals should be prosecuted and put in jail." Allen Brown, who also faced Keating many times, says, "He pushed the prosecutor's office to adopt the Leis-like approach."

Keating left Cincinnati during his *first* brush with federal regulators. In 1976, the Securities and Exchange Commission began investigating him and his business partner at American Financial Corporation, Carl Lindner, Jr. Keating and Lindner were accused of "illegally profiting at the expense of shareholders and receiving preferential treatment as insiders." In 1979, the SEC filed charges against Keating, Lindner, and Keating's former law partner, Donald P. Klekamp—all of whom settled out of court.

The major behind-the-scenes power attacking the Mapplethorpe show was Keating's old mentor, Carl Lindner, Jr. Lindner's son, a fundamentalist Christian known locally as Young Carl or Carl Three, probably played an even bigger role. Cincinnati business people, even museum supporters, tend to blanch at questions about the Lindners. The family controls American Financial Corporation, Penn Central, the United Dairy Farmers chain, Great American Communications Corporation, Great American Insurance, Thriftway, Chiquita Banana, Provident Bank, one Cincinnati television station and two radio stations. According to *The Cincinnati Post*, Carl Three spoke out against the Mapplethorpe exhibit in March at a local businessmen's club. Lindner and others (including George Baillou, the city's biggest developer) then began applying pressure to Central Trust Co., N.A., whose executive vice president was chairman of the museum's board. Central Trust was told that it could lose three hundred accounts if the exhibit opened. The vice president resigned his museum post. Such tactics, reported in *The Cincinnati Post*, never made the pages of the city's other (and larger) daily paper, *The Cincinnati Enquirer*. Charles Keating's brother, William, is the publisher of *The Enquirer*, a paper once owned by the Lindners.

Keating's shadow fell over the Mapplethorpe show in one other way. Before moving to Phoenix in 1978, he'd entrusted the local smut wars to the Reverend Jerry Kirk, who went on to found the National Coalition Against Pornography and other anti-porn groups, including Citizens for Community Values (ccv). The ccv's advisory board includes Carl Three, Donald P. Klekamp, two local judges, and Cincinnati Bengals coach Sam Wyche. Weeks before the Mapplethorpe photographs arrived in Cincinnati, the ccv began clamoring for "public debate" about them, though Dennis Barrie told me the ccvers never returned his phone calls. They demanded the removal of seven pictures: five from the *X Portfolio* plus the two photographs of children with their genitals exposed.

A month before "The Perfect Moment" opened, this group had mapped out a "Mapplethorpe strategy" aimed at "turning public sentiment against the exhibit" (as a March 15 memo to board members put it). They planned to have two or three doctors write an article for *The Cincinnati Enquirer* to "specifically relate the worst material." (Such a piece appeared on March 24.) They also organized a highly sophisticated letter-writing campaign, targeting the museum's board members. But otherwise, they decided, they would maintain a low profile. After all, as ccv president Monty Lobb Jr. declared in his memo:

"*. . . prosecution of the most objectionable and possibly obscene photographs will occur*" [my italics].

What most characterized the Mapplethorpe adventure in Cincinnati was a constant intimation of conspiracy, a sense of events controlled from behind the scenes. The Citizens for Community Values knew by mid-March that the exhibit would be prosecuted. And while the museum didn't know that, it could guess. Leis had declared the photographs "criminally obscene" on March 23, even though they hadn't arrived in Cincinnati yet. In what defense attorneys Lou Sirkin and Marc Mezibov called a "pre-emptive strike," the museum filed a lawsuit on March 27 against Leis, the county prosecutor, and the Cincinnati police chief, aimed at preventing them from seizing photographs or closing the show. Sirkin and Mezibov asked that a jury trial decide immediately whether or not the work was obscene.

With the exhibition scheduled to open the next day, all the parties met in court on April 6, Leis and company unhappily present under subpoena. Through their lawyers, they declared there was "no threat" to the museum. As Leis's attorney told the judge: "We're not sure what this so-called Mapplethorpe exhibit consists of." The judge dismissed the museum's suit without comment or explanation. In chambers beforehand, however, the judge had suggested to Sirkin that the museum could easily work things out by removing pictures.

During the trial this fall, a police officer admitted under cross-examination that city and county officials *had* met to discuss the exhibit on both March 21 and April 5. "You knew on the 5th that the county prosecutor intended to take legal action?" Mezibov asked him. The officer was not allowed to answer.

At 10 A.M. on April 7, the day after declaring in court that the police would only investigate the show, sheriff's deputies did exactly that, but they brought a grand jury right along with them. By midafternoon, officers had warrants.

Dennis Barrie and the Contemporary Arts Center were charged with "pandering obscenity" for displaying pictures that document gay male sadomasochism, part of the *X Portfolio*: one man urinating into the mouth of another man; a self-portrait of Mapplethorpe with a whip inserted in his rectum; a man's hand and forearm inserted into the rectum of another man; a man inserting a finger into his penis; a man inserting a cylindrical object into his rectum. Barrie and the museum were also charged with "illegal use of a child in nudity-oriented material"—for two portraits of children, *Jesse McBride* and *Honey*. If convicted, Barrie faced up to a year in jail and a $2,000 fine; the Contemporary Arts Center faced a $10,000 fine.

"As responsible citizens," Leis announced at a press conference, "the CAC board now has an obligation to remove those pictures."

The next morning—Sunday, April 8, at 10 A.M.—everyone convened again, this time in a courtroom at the University of Cincinnati law school. Sirkin and Mezibov had gone to a federal judge for a temporary restraining order. Stating, "There is no evidence these photos are obscene," U.S. District Judge Carl Ruben ordered police not to close or otherwise interfere with "The Perfect Moment."

No one in town seemed particularly shocked about the judge assigned to the trial. "That's Cincinnati," as so many told me. Chosen by computer lottery, he was Municipal Judge David J. Albanese, a close friend of Simon Leis. Albanese was first hired as a prosecutor years ago by Simon Leis. His last election campaign consisted of television endorsements by Simon Leis. In Allen Brown's words: "The judge is practically his vassal."

The judge's decisions in two pretrial hearings over the summer seemed to follow no precedent set in the wider world, and both went against the museum. Judge Albanese, in fact, had ruled that the Arts Center was not a museum. It was now a gallery (because it had no permanent collection) and as such had less protection under the law. ("Ruling that CAC is not a museum jolts [the] art world," reported *The Enquirer*.) Even more damaging, however, was the judge's ruling that the Supreme Court requirement that the work be "taken as a whole" did not mean the whole exhibit but each picture. The defense wouldn't be allowed to present or discuss the context for the seven pictures— the figure studies, the still lifes, the portraits, the rest of the *X, Y,* and *Z Portfolio*s. To this news, even the main architect of the Meese Commission Report on pornography, Frederick Schauer, had reacted with astonishment, calling it "not plausible."

But the trial was a feast of implausibles. On the fourth and final day of jury selection, for example, a prospective juror named Carol Murphy admitted that she had known the Reverend Jerry Kirk for twenty years,

agreed with his opinions, was employed by his church, had once attended a National Coalition Against Pornography convention, sub-
scribed to the ccv newsletter, saw xeroxes of the Mapplethorpe photos
in March, formed an opinion about them then, thought they should
never be displayed any time, anywhere, for any reason—but yes, she
insisted, she could be a fair and impartial juror.

Defense attorneys Lou Sirkin and Marc Mezibov pleaded that the
judge dismiss her for cause. Prosecutor Frank Prouty argued, "Just
because she has some opinions isn't grounds for dismissal. She's indicated that she can be fair." The judge agreed with Prouty, telling
Sirkin and Mezibov: "I'll grant you she's opinionated."

This meant the defense had to use a "peremptory challenge" to get
rid of her. (Each side had six of these—six jurors they could dismiss
for any reason at all.) In general, Prouty seemed to be culling the jury
of anyone who knew too much (two people who'd seen the exhibit, a
guy who'd read a *Playboy* article on Mapplethorpe.) And the defense
was trying to cull the jury pool of those who knew too little (a man
who hadn't seen a movie in ten years, a woman who said God's law
was higher than the state's law).

Prosecutor Prouty, bald on top with a fringe of white hair, looked
about ten years older than his forty-five years. He was the city's most
experienced obscenity prosecutor. Working with him was a young assistant prosecutor named Melanie Reising, who was silent throughout
the trial but for the occasional, disgusted "*Objection.*"

Sirkin was a familiar First Amendment gadfly, a Cincinnati native
and protégé of Allen Brown, who has defended video and bookstore
owners all over the country. Following his usual custom, Sirkin would
not cut his hair during the course of the trial, and asked Mezibov to
refrain as well. Mezibov, Sirkin's law partner and general counsel for
the local chapter of the ACLU, was representing the museum. Or
gallery.

Though the judge almost didn't let them get away with it, the defense introduced the content of the five *X Portfolio* pictures during jury
selection—"one man urinating into the mouth of another man," etc.
That way the defense could measure reactions. Most of the jury pool
claimed to know practically nothing about the case. Many said they
didn't read newspapers. Most could count their visits to any kind

of museum on a single hand. Nearly all of them belonged to a church. And only a quarter of them lived in Cincinnati, the rest residing in the even more conservative suburbs.

"Do you subscribe to any magazine that deals with obscenity or art news?" Prouty asked one. Every potential juror who'd ever visited a museum was asked why he or she had "had cause" to go there. "Do you think a museum is above the law? Think the CAC should have the right to show anything it wants? Think you need someone to tell you what art is?"

The defense was also establishing its argument: "Could a photograph of a nude child be morally innocent? Do you realize that art doesn't have to be pretty? Should there be laws restricting what adults can see and hear?" They were also trying to gauge attitudes about gay people, though the judge never allowed anyone to answer the question: "Do you believe there should be laws prohibiting homosexuality?" They asked the question anyway—twenty-five times.

"A majestic system has been put into motion," droned a TV talking head in the basement of a gay bar called the Pipeline. ACT UP and members of the Gay and Lesbian March Activists were celebrating their demonstration on the first day of trial. They played and replayed the news coverage—the march down Main Street from the courthouse to the Contemporary Arts Center, the clogged traffic arteries, the anti-Leis slogans, and a little bit of dry-humping on the pavement. They'd been a sensation. Such demos don't happen here. Nothing like it since Kent State. As the week went on, though, even some who agreed with the protesters called the demonstration "embarrassing" or "in bad taste." Scott MacLarty, GLMA facilitator, told me, "Most people here are conservative, even gay people. They don't want to see things change too fast. The activists tend to come from out of town."

Kimberly Henson of Voice Against Censorship told me: "This covert repression has gone on for so long people are deadened to it."

"It's corrosive," said Hendrik Gideonse, a professor of education and policy science at the University of Cincinnati. He noted that many artists and art supporters like himself had sort of left it up to the gay groups that day. "You're constantly worried about who's looking over your shoulder. You don't go out and demonstrate for the First Amendment. You let someone else do it. Controversy is not appreciated in this city." But another part of his "laziness," he said, was the unshakable feeling that the museum couldn't win.

The protest would not go unpunished. Eight days after it happened, the police issued thirty-five arrest warrants for people who'd been "running amuck." Able to identify only two after studying their videotapes, the police issued thirty-three warrants for either "Jane Doe" or "John Doe," each one attached to a photo of the perpetrator. MacLarty reported that the vice squad had stepped up its surveillance of Burnet Woods park, a gay cruising area, immediately after the demo, and he was afraid they'd start going to bars now with those pictures. The police did bring the photos to a Voice Against Censorship rally the second week of trial and arrested six more people.

I recalled one of the demonstrators telling me that, sure, he could always move to the East or West Coast. But gay people who were tough would stick it out in Cincinnati, and fight.

All over town, in fact, I found people in the trenches, fighting. But they were all in separate trenches. There were the women at Planned Parenthood, for example, who just a couple years ago faced up to two hundred Right-to-Lifers a day jammed into the forty-eight feet in front of the clinic. Planned Parenthood finally got a court injunction to limit the number. And they got a new clinic after the last one was firebombed. But the pressure never lets up. This is the city, after all, where Right to Life's founder, John Willke, lives.

Then there was the young woman from the University of Cincinnati Film Society, who believed the county prosecutor when he said he'd throw her in jail for showing *Vixen*. Who was better prepared, though, for *Hail Mary,* which became a mini-Mapplethorpe, what with the letter of protest from the mayor, the debate in the city council, the daily outcry in the media, the death threats on her answering machine. The Film Society was also the only venue in town that screened *The Last Temptation of Christ*. "I'm moving to Minneapolis," she told me. "I've done all I can to change Cincinnati."

But in Cincinnati there's yet another world of art patrons—one of "old money" that prides itself on its gentility and sophistication. The night the Mapplethorpe show opened, numbered among the 4,000 was a veritable Who's Who of that community—the Tafts (heirs to William Howard Taft), the Reeds (from the Whitney Museum board), the Scripps (of Scripps-Howard), and so on. "All the old families were there, as a show of support," former museum board member Daniel Brown told me. "And as you saw, there was no raid that night." Brown, who is also an arts adviser, a guest lecturer at the Art Academy of Cincinnati and a major collector, thinks the controversy was, to some extent, an "old money/new money" split. The Lindners are definitely "new money."

"It's not in Cincinnati's nature or definition of itself to break heads publicly. Things happen behind closed doors here. The old families kicked in to support the CAC behind the scenes. They didn't agree with the censorship. It was considered crude and uncultured," he said. "And I don't think anyone, pro or con, expected this to go beyond the region."

Last April, after Barrie and the museum were indicted, *The Cincinnati Post* (a Scripps-Howard newspaper) commissioned the University of Cincinnati's Institute for Policy Research to conduct a poll asking, What *are* the community values? Should the Contemporary Art Center be allowed to display these photos? Nearly 59 percent said yes. About 38 percent said no. Three percent had no opinion.

"I recognize that we've been inundated with aliens," said an annoyed Judge Albanese on the first day of testimony. "Some of you are strangers to Cincinnati, and a few comments are in order on how to conduct yourselves." He meant us—the national press corps. He and his bailiff had personally picked up candy wrappers the day before. And we weren't to conduct our interviews in his courtroom anymore.

Judge Albanese's courtroom was the smallest in the building, and it was wise to claim one of the twenty-six seats early. There, for an hour and a half before the Mapplethorpe trial each day, the judge took care of his docket—the man accused of swiping two cans of tuna, the guy who'd smashed into the side of a bus.

And here a jury of eight ordinary citizens—a secretary, a sales clerk, a warehouse manager, a telephone repairman, an electrical engineer, a data-processing manager, a medical technician, and an export co-ordinator—would finally get to make the decision on freedom of expression for which the far right had clamored.

Organized in 1988 at the Philadelphia Institute of Contemporary Art (ICA) with a $30,000 grant from the National Endowment for the Arts, "The Perfect Moment" had become a symbol of everything the far right found wrong with public-arts funding—and with art. Senator Jesse Helms declared that Mapplethorpe's work "deliberately promoted homosexuality and child molestation," and many of the artist's new critics invariably mentioned that he had died of AIDS. The Corcoran Gallery of Art in Washington, D.C., dropped the show in the summer of 1989, afraid of the political fallout, an action that sparked the firestorm around the NEA. In October of that year, Helms complained on the Senate floor about the perverse and tax-wasting "arty crowd." He was certain that "if the test for obscenity in the Miller [vs. California] case were left to the average person to determine whether the Mapplethorpe exhibit or similar works contained some serious literary, artistic, political or scientific value, I would not worry, not one bit." This Cincinnati jury could fulfill the far-right fantasy: the average person sticking it to the arty crowd.

As Frank Prouty put it in his opening statement, "You people have a unique circumstance. There has never been a museum or art gallery charged with obscenity before, and you have the chance to decide on your own—where do you draw the line? Are these the kinds of pictures that should be permitted in a museum?"

Since work with "artistic value" is not obscene under the Supreme Court's Miller vs. California ruling, the jury would really be deciding whether the Contemporary Arts Center had the right to exhibit work like this and call it art. Or should that decision be left to the jury? Or to Sheriff Simon Leis?

Observers speculated that the state might call one of the doctors who'd written the Enquirer article, which denounced the "exploitative" pictures of children and the depiction of "dangerous sex acts." Or maybe they'd call neo-con art critic Hilton Kramer. But Prouty put just three witnesses on the stand—all of them police officers who testified that they had indeed seen the photos in question at the Contemporary Arts Center. As if the museum had ever tried to deny that. Prouty finished presenting his case in less than a day and a half. "Arts Case Strategy Perplexes Experts," read a headline in the next day's Post.

Sirkin and Mezibov moved for acquittal as soon as the state rested. Where was the evidence about community standards? Where was the evidence that the pictures were obscene? That they had no artistic value? "The state must prove this through experts," declared Mezibov. "It's wrong for lay people to guess."

"The bottom line is the pictures," Prouty countered. "Once the pictures are in evidence, it can be determined whether they follow community standards. The court is the community standard."

Allen Brown told me at one point during the trial: "The whole secret around here is to make the jurors think they're the protectors of Aunt Nellie." Apparently, Prouty expected that he could just hand those photos to the jury and their knees would jerk the way his did—call it a "getta-load-of-this" strategy. He was presenting the ideology of the far right, straight from the mouth of Pat Robertson or Donald Wildmon: This isn't art, and it isn't for regular people. And don't let some "expert" tell you otherwise.

Prouty began to salt these notions into his cross-examinations of the art experts, adding a local spin that came from Citizens for Community Values: "Cincinnati has higher standards." To the museum directors who testified that the work of Robert Mapplethorpe was indeed art, Prouty would invariably say something like, "Is it fair to say you've never lived in Cincinnati?"

He asked Janet Kardon, who'd curated "The Perfect Moment" at the ICA in Philadelphia, "Do you have to be responsible to your local community? Don't public values ever come into play? So the values of the local community are secondary to the artist's?" To her, these were clearly questions from another planet. "I don't know what you mean by the local community," she replied. "It was our job to present the best art we could."

Kardon, the first defense witness, had worked closely with Mapplethorpe in putting the show together. Mezibov asked her about that process, with Prouty objecting to every question. ("Irrelevant.") The judge decided—at some point when Prouty hadn't even objected to anything—that Mezibov could ask her no questions about "retrospectives" or "thematic shows." Kardon was not allowed to discuss the show's theme or to explain what was meant by its title, "The Perfect Moment." Nor could Mezibov ask her anything specifically about the seven pictures (though Prouty could during cross-examination). She was not allowed to discuss the sequencing of the pictures or to say why they were the only photographs presented in a case, not hung on a wall, or to say why she thought they had serious artistic value.

Mapplethorpe himself had designed the case for the X, Y, and Z Portfolios, which displayed thirty-nine photographs in three rows.

Along the top were the "X" pictures (gay s&m), then the "Y" (flowers) and "Z" (figure studies of black men). Seen together, the pictures inform each other. All of them seem sexual. But all of them can be read, horizontally or vertically, for their compositional elements. Mapplethorpe wanted to see if he could turn pornographic subject matter into art, and most people probably find the "X" pictures far from titillating. Many of them isolate body parts, where pornography tends to show more of the body, if not a whole scenario. Pornography is an aid to sexual fantasy, while the "X" pictures confront the viewer with dispassionate documentation of sexual extremes.

Prouty asked Kardon, now the director of the American Craft Museum in New York, to look at each of the five s&m pictures and tell him why it was art. She talked about the horizontal lines, lighting, the way a figure had been centered. Looking at a picture of a finger sticking in a penis, she commented, "Robert said he thought those hand gestures were beautiful."

As Prouty told Kardon: "You call them figure studies. I call them sexual. The jurors here can call them whatever they want."

Dennis Barrie had decided to bring "The Perfect Moment" to Cincinnati in the fall of 1988, before the art wars began. He had no reason to expect trouble. The Arts Center had exhibited work with sexual content in the past, and the city's moral guardians—ardent though they were—had left the museum alone.

No one on the jury had ever been to the Contemporary Arts Center, and—over Prouty's objections, for a change—Judge Albanese allowed them a short visit. It lasted all of twenty seconds. They caught a glimpse of the current show by Mike and Doug Starn, but were not allowed to walk past the reception desk. The CAC—located in a downtown mall above a Walgreen's, with the usual pristine walls and polished floors—was obviously not a porn shop.

And Janet Kardon, who'd wanted to work with this "criminally obscene" artist, was a conservatively dressed middle-age woman with a professional air. The defense pointed out that no one under eighteen had been admitted to the show. They emphasized the respectability of the people involved, their professionalism, their doctorates. During jury selection, either Sirkin or Mezibov had asked every prospective panelist whether they'd be willing to listen to expert witnesses who came from out of town. Testifying to the work's artistic value were Jacqueline Baas, director of the University of California Art Museum (Berkeley); John Walsh, director of the J. Paul Getty Museum (Malibu); and Robert Sobieszek, former curator at the International Museum of Photography at the George Eastman House (Rochester, New York). Sirkin said he figured Rochester was as close to New York City as they dared to get. He and Mezibov made a point of calling the critics from *The Cincinnati Post* and *The Cincinnati Enquirer*. Both had praised "The Perfect Moment" when it opened. (*The Enquirer*, however, tried to quash the subpoena to *its* critic.)

Prouty struggled to get these witnesses away from the abstractions they saw and into the sleaze that he saw. He asked Janet Kardon to define pornography, and had she ever seen any? To Sobieszek, he put the question, "What is 'fisting'?" He asked Baas (whose museum had shown "The Perfect Moment" just before it came to Cincinnati) whether she wasn't advocating homosexuality by showing such photographs.

The defense had introduced the idea, beginning with jury selection, that art did not have to be pretty. In his closing remarks, Sirkin referred to the s&m photos as ugly and possibly offensive. Sobieszek had described them as "a search for understanding, like van Gogh painting himself with his ear cut off." Dennis Barrie, who spent less time on the witness stand than one might expect of a defendant, went through each photo when Prouty cross-examined him. "This is difficult subject matter," Barrie said, "and I don't dismiss the difficulty." He described several as beautifully composed but "not titillating." The Mapplethorpe self-portrait with a bullwhip in his rectum he called "tortured."

Prouty had tried to make much of the fact that the museum did not have formal written permission from the mothers of the children who'd been photographed—Jessie and Rosie (aka Honey)—when the show arrived. And could such pictures possibly be "morally innocent," he asked Barrie.

"As a father and a museum professional—yes."

Sirkin and Mezibov presented depositions from the mothers of both Jesse and Rosie. Both women were friends of Mapplethorpe who testified that they'd consented and, in fact, wanted him to photograph their children and were present when he did so. In both these portraits, Mapplethorpe has captured the children's un-self-consciousness about their bodies. They are pictures of innocence, the opposite to the photos in the *X Portfolio*.

Coaching the prosecution throughout the trial had been a short, animated woman, who, Prouty announced, would now be the prosecution's rebuttal witness. She was Dr. Judith Reisman, a former research director for the American Family Association (AFA). Led by the Reverend Donald Wildmon, the AFA had led the far right's attack on artists.

Reisman had once written a piece on Mapplethorpe called "Promoting Child Abuse as Art" for *The Washington Times* (Washington, D.C.'s far-right Moonie-owned daily). The article compared his work with fascist art and labeled the *Honey* picture "child pornography." Sirkin and Mezibov argued strenuously that Reisman should not be allowed to take the stand. That she could not qualify as an art expert, based on her years as a songwriter for Captain Kangaroo. That "she serves no purpose other than to pollute the jury with unqualified testimony."

"The court has been liberal in admitting experts," said the judge.

She sat on the witness stand, referring to a detailed résumé as Prouty questioned her on her qualifications. "Ever done expert testimony before?" he asked. "Is that like Janet Kardon?" But Reisman did not have Kardon's self-assured cool. She fidgeted and worked her hands through the air as she analyzed the five s&m photos, concluding that they were not art. Of the fisting picture, she said, for example, "There is no face. There are no eyes. There is no aspect of the human body that would tell us anything about human emotion or feeling. This is an anonymous image." Of Mapplethorpe's self-portrait with a bullwhip in his rectum, she said, "This would be one of the only photos that might offer emotion, but the face is blank. It says, 'I am here.'"

In the pictures of the children, she found "a triangulation focusing on the genitals." The little girl, she said, was not centered over the vaginal area, and, "This indicates some degree of real strain." In the picture of the little boy, his legs—"bracketing the triangle"—lead to his genitals. She described a refrigerator cord, visible at one side, as "very disturbing." She then implied the worst about the mothers of these children: "Unless you have children who are runaways, the use of children in pornography comes with consent." Placing such photos in a museum legitimized them, she said, and put additional children at risk.

"We've arrived at Scopes," muttered one of the reporters.

At the very beginning of *Inherit the Wind*, the play based on the Scopes "Monkey Trial," the stage direction indicates, "The town is visible always, as much on trial as the individual defendant."

In Mezibov's closing remarks to the jury, he invoked the image of the Cincinnati skyline he'd seen on national television the night before. The Reds were in the National League play-offs, and he said he was proud. "That light will be nothing compared to the light you will shed on us if you find the defendants not guilty. You have a chance to show the country that this is a community of tolerant and sensitive people."

Frank Prouty had made a case for Cincinnati as a city different from other cities. He reminded the jury that Jacqueline Baas, for example, said art's subject could be anything—"*she's* from California." He suggested that the outsiders wanted to put one over on them. "The art world is trying to tell you these are art," he said, comparing Mapplethorpe's work to the emperor's new clothes. "You're the audience. *You* tell them what is or isn't art." Prouty even suggested to the jury that the 81,000 people who saw "The Perfect Moment" at the CAC may have come from out of town. "Were they from Cleveland? Columbus? Los Angeles? New York?" he asked. "You have no idea who they were."

He said the art world—these defendants in particular—had put itself above the law. "They're saying they're better than us." But just the opposite was true. The art world had come forward to explain itself, while—the jurors complained later—the prosecution hadn't given them a single credible witness. They found the defendants not guilty on both counts after two hours of deliberation.

The verdict was a big defeat for the far right. On October 11, several congressmen stood up in the House of Representatives to defend the National Endowment for the Arts, invoking the decision made by the jury in Cincinnati. Now they could safely say, as one did, "The far-right agenda has been rejected by the American people."

The far right seeks to appeal to the worst side of the American character—its fear of difference, its know-nothing provincialism. It's a very cynical view which doesn't give "the average person" much credit.

That's why the sheriff's deputies were in that museum in the first place, determined that they would decide *for* their community just what that community ought to look at.

Cincinnati is a tightly buttoned town, but the attack on "Robert Mapplethorpe: The Perfect Moment" may have catalyzed something. I'm always going to remember that moment when the police came bursting into the Contemporary Art Center last April, pushing away the artgoers and knocking down the velvet ropes as if chasing some deadly criminal. And then, Dennis Barrie going out to address the crowd gathered in the mall, covering his face with his hands: "It's a very dark day." I remember the hundreds and hundreds of people down there, those who'd been waiting to get in, and those the police had thrown out when they'd evacuated the museum—which had been full to capacity. I remember them roaring their outrage. And I took it as a good sign—a sign that Cincinnati, for all its conservatism, could be the turning point in the war on culture, when they all began chanting at a surprised-looking police force: "*We're* the community standard. *We're* the community standard. *We're* the community standard."

October 1990

■ ■ ■ The Adventures of Andres Serrano in Pursuit of the White Supremacists

The night Andres Serrano arrived to photograph the Imperial Wizards, he found both men sitting in the kitchen at James Venable's house near Atlanta. Venable, the retired Wizard, was eighty-three years old, senile, and poor. He'd loaned his robe out the year before and never gotten it back, so the new Wizard was going to let him borrow his. Serrano wanted them hooded and masked and in the green robes designating their Ku Klux Klan rank. It was all agreed. Everyone who'd told him that he'd never get to these people, that he shouldn't even try because he was a person of color and infamous for all the wrong reasons, would soon be proved wrong.

But no one said "hello" to the artist when he entered the house. The old Wizard's caretaker was there and someone in a military uniform and a man he'd never seen before. Serrano went into another room and set up. He was photographing Venable in full KKK regalia when the stranger sidled in: "So your PR man, Jesse Helms, is coming to town tomorrow."

Now Serrano knew that *all* of them knew. That he was *that* artist. The one who'd done *Piss Christ*.

"Oh, yeah," the artist replied. "I'm gonna go see him. I bought a ticket."

The young Wizard, David Holland, walked in. "You know," he told the others, "Brother Serrano won't take no for an answer. You tell him no, no, no, and he goes to your lawyer, who puts the screws to you." Holland had been particularly tough to convince, but that night he, too, sat down to pose.

Andres Serrano had spent the last year trying not to be distracted by his sudden and unwanted notoriety. It was *Piss Christ*, his Ciba-chrome print of a crucifix immersed in his own urine, that had triggered the far-right war on art in 1989. Vowing to continue the fluid pieces "as they move me," Serrano had undertaken a new project. He wanted to photograph the marginal, the invisible. He wanted to pair these Klan pictures with his studio portraits of homeless New Yorkers, "The Nomads." Serrano says the work is about "extreme poverty and extreme prejudice." It's a vision of America's wounds, an intimation of genocide—those who would suffer it, those who would carry it out. And the artist is shocking all over again, because he regards these people with a certain tenderness. *All* of them.

He set out to photograph the homeless last winter, inspired by Edward Curtis's classic, turn-of-the-century pictures of Native Americans. Four Curtises hang in his dining room. "I was interested in what he saw as portrayals of a vanishing race," says Serrano. "Also a certain historical moment which would be lost forever unless he captured it. So I decided I wanted to photograph not a race, but a class of people on the verge of displacement. As far as I'm concerned, the displacement of a people is the first step in their genocide." Curtis's work is now thought to be romanticized and inauthentic, but Serrano isn't bothered by that. "If they're not strictly documentary, doesn't that make them more artlike? It's true—they're fabricated reality, but that's what a tableau photographer does."

Carrying lights, a backdrop, and a stool, Serrano went looking for the "hard-core homeless" between midnight and five in the morning, setting up his ministudio in subway stations. Occasionally, Transit Authority inspectors stopped him midsitting because he didn't have a permit. He didn't want a permit. He'd decided that his subjects operated outside the system, so he should do the same. He just had to work quickly. "I paid these people a flat fee and they signed model's releases. We entered into a relationship. Essentially they posed for me the way they wanted to."

Wrapped in their layers or blankets or scarves, these are the people it is so hard to look at when they actually appear on the doorstep or subway bench. But as long as they remain "the homeless," they are easy to dismiss. Serrano's formal portraits give them individuality and dignity. "How can they be thrown away?" he says. "What does it mean for the rest of us if we allow that to happen?"

Serrano is careful to insist that he is not a political artist. Taking on

Andres Serrano
photographing a Klan
member, somewhere
in Georgia. (Courtesy
of the Fay Gold
Gallery, Atlanta,
Georgia.)

the Klan project was a "formal decision." He just wanted to do portraits
of masked people. But the first place he made inquiries was North
Carolina, home of Jesse Helms, who has so often excoriated him on
the floor of the Senate. Who has called him "a jerk." Called him "a yo-
yo." Serrano admits that "if I could bring a small measure of embarrassment to Jesse Helms, it would make my day." But he had no leads
in North Carolina.

Someone in Georgia got him James Venable's phone number last
summer, and he spoke to the old man's caretaker, a woman named
Bobbie, who promised to introduce him to people. "I said, 'OK Bobbie,

I gotta tell you one thing though. I'm not white. I'm Hispanic. Does that make a difference?" And she said, 'Don't make no difference at all, babe. Don't worry about it.'"

To some, of course, it did make a difference. Serrano went to Georgia over Labor Day weekend for the big Klan rally at Stone Mountain. He never got in. The skinhead security force stopped him some thirty yards into the park. "You're not white," they told him. "We can't guarantee your safety." Serrano spent the rest of the evening near the park entrance, talking to some black people who lived nearby.

The adventures of Andres Serrano in pursuit of the white supremacists is as surreal and unlikely a story as anything to emerge from the art wars. He discovered that the Klan was in the middle of a Supreme Court battle over the right to wear their masks and hoods in public. So he went to the hearing in Washington. He met their lawyer, Michael Hauptmann—a Jew, as it turns out. Hauptmann gave him some leads. He began to meet Klanspeople in Georgia—in the dead of night, in the middle of nowhere. Wasn't he ever afraid? "Only that I'd come back empty-handed." He realized, for one thing, that these people were dirt poor. "My understanding of it is that even scapegoats need scapegoats." Many didn't have phones. He'd have to just show up at someone's house and make his case.

Five days after the big rally at Stone Mountain, Serrano went there after dark to meet the young Wizard, David Holland. The forty-foot-tall burnt crosses were still stuck in the ground. Holland drove up in a Jeep with a friend. "This is the notorious Andres Serrano," he told the friend. Serrano was pleased. "I felt—here's a Klansperson who knows who I am. I didn't want them to feel tricked. The fact that they knew made it better."

Serrano had not made announcements about who he was, however. And some did not know. One Klansman who posed asked him: "You get any of that government money?" Serrano replied truthfully: "Not anymore."

At another Klan home, he took the adults out back in their robes to photograph them, while their children ridiculed them as "dunces" and "nerds."

Some told him they would not pose, because he was not white. "The ones who *were* nice to me were genuinely nice," says Serrano. "I can't make judgments about these people." And that, probably, is why they agreed to pose for him.

These pictures of "wizards" and "titans" and "dragons" are as sad, in their own way, as the pictures of the homeless. It's a different brand of horror, but you're left with the same question—who *is* this person? Serrano's far-right critics will now be able to denounce him as a humanist.

Shortly after he finished the Klan pictures, Serrano found a copy of the first letter protesting *Piss Christ*, printed in *The Richmond News-Leader* back in March 1989. He'd forgotten about this. "The Virginia Museum should not be in the business of promoting and subsidizing hatred and intolerance," said the letter. "Would they pay the KKK to do work defaming blacks? Would they display a Jewish symbol under urine? Has Christianity become fair game in our society for any kind of blasphemy and slander?"

"I've always had trouble seeing things black or white," Serrano told *The New York Times* at the height of the *Piss Christ* controversy. "I'm of mixed blood. I have an African-Cuban mother and a Spanish white father. My great-grandfather was Chinese. I've always accepted that duality in myself. My work is a reflection of it."

Serrano's fluid pieces—particularly those made with piss, semen, or menstrual blood—created something beautiful from the hidden or repellent. They challenged the meaning of "loaded" symbols. Had the crucifix in *Piss Christ* really been defiled? Or had the urine been sanctified?

The new portraits also see the beauty of the damned. It's easy to accept that in the photos of the homeless. But in a way, the Klan pictures are even more extraordinary, especially given what Serrano has been through for the past year. The far right made him a pariah, ridiculed him, reduced him to a symbol—The Blasphemer. He got death threats. And his response was to go to the most despised group of them—people Jesse Helms wouldn't even want to be associated with—and approach them with compassion.

The irony is that this is what, in the best sense of the word, you call "Christian."

November 1990

■ ■ ■ Portrait in Life and Death

Each day I sounded with new afflictions
which you, insatiate one, devised,
and they could not kill my mouth;
look to see how you can quiet it,

when those we devastate and crush
are finally lost and driven far away
and are perished in the danger:
for then I want in the rubble-heaps
at last to hear my voice again,
which was a howling from the very first.

—Rilke

■ ■ ■ Portrait of an Artist in the Age of AIDS

This kid ran down the block, at age six or seven, giddy with what he'd just learned: "We all die! One day we're all going to be dead!" As he told his little friends, they burst into tears, and parents rushed out of their houses, and David Wojnarowicz was seen as a very sick little kid for exposing the Real Deal. Recalling that moment, David smiles: "That's a metaphor for the rest of my life."

Last November, David Wojnarowicz (pronounced Wanna-row-vich) was the catalyst of a row between the National Endowment for the Arts and a major downtown institution, Artists Space. His catalogue essay for a publicly funded show about AIDS made front page news. The dailies seized on David's description of Cardinal O'Connor: "this fat cannibal from that house of walking swastikas" and "this creep in black skirts." But the real subject of David's essay was the less noteworthy topic of mortality—and not just his own. "When I was told that I'd contracted this virus," he wrote, "it didn't take me long to realize that I'd contracted a diseased society as well."

Last December, in the wake of that uproar, David agreed to appear on a local television talk show, *The Eleventh Hour*, on the condition that no one see his face. He wore a Reagan mask throughout the interview, and hit 'em with lots of statistics (edited to a few voiceover sentences). Then he read, his back to the camera, from the text of his painting on the gallery wall: ". . . and I'm carrying this rage like a blood filled egg. . . ."

His rage was explained away by the director of Artists Space, attributed to what he calls "my diagnosis." Critic Grace Glueck, who'd reviewed his work early on, now rendered him a nameless "AIDS victim." While *Newsday* labeled his current retrospective at Illinois State University—his life's work—an "AIDS exhibit."

David feels compelled to tell the Real Deal because he grew up in a violent family, and he'll never forget the way the neighbors averted their eyes and shut their mouths. Now, at age thirty-five his memories of childhood emerge in sharp vignettes, each a little horror show, but sometimes he can't affix time or place. Practically from babyhood, David was a kid on the lam. There was no place like home. So when Father found the lame bird David was caring for and forced David to watch while he shot it dead—where was that? When? David can't remember.

Father was a sailor on passenger ships, working the boiler room. Mother was fifteen when she married him. He began abusing the family after the first child was born. The mother divorced him and got custody of the three kids when David was two—but apparently she couldn't care for them. He remembers the Dickensian quasi-orphanage in New Jersey where they ended up when he was three—the beatings and lack of food. From this place, the father kidnapped them.

The hostage family then moved all the time—first to relatives in Michigan, then to various New Jersey towns with the father's new wife. The father usually had one week a month onshore, a week of long drunks and beatings, guns fired in the house, guns held to the stepmother's head. For David, the woods became safe haven, and he loved the animal life, especially the unlovable reptile and insect realms. He remembers the day the father killed their pet rabbit and made them eat it for dinner.

David recalls his first sexual experience at age five or six with a fourteen-year-old boy, recalls asking: "Are we allowed to do this?"— and the boy telling him, "Yeah." But was that before or after the first year in Catholic school—kneeling on bags of marbles, beaten by nuns?

He traced from books and magazines, but always claimed the pictures were his. When other kids confronted him and made him draw while they watched, he discovered he could actually do it.

David's older sister found their mother in the Manhattan phone book when he was eight. On their first secret visit with her, she took them to the Museum of Modern Art. David remembers a painting of a tree with babies in its branches (probably Pavel Tchilechev's surrealist *Leaf Children*). Back in New Jersey, he tried to recreate it with oil paints, but it all turned to mud because he didn't know to let the canvas dry between colors. He decided to give up oil painting.

A month later, the father suddenly announced that they were going back to their mother. David remembers the surrender in a restaurant near Port Authority, the father telling the mother what little shits these kids were, what a waste of money. After a few days with them in her one-bedroom Hells' Kitchen apartment, the mother seemed to realize she'd made a mistake. But she encouraged them to express themselves, where the father had beaten them for showing any sort of emotion. So they fought. They were trying to kill each other, David remembers, after years of pent-up rage.

One day, as David stood at a joke store window admiring the fake noses and exploding cigars, a man came up and fondled him, asking him if he'd like to make ten dollars. He snatched the ten and scooted off on his skateboard. He'd learned he could get money here for certain things.

He turned his first trick when he was nine—a man he met in Central Park. He'd been told: Never get into a stranger's car. So David took a bus to the guy's apartment. He remembers the weight of the man's body on top of him, the Polaroid shot, the man's cum. David asked for two dollars so he could get an ice cream sundae. And when he got home he looked in the mirror to see if anything was written on his face.

When he was nine or ten, he began an affair with a mildly retarded twenty-year-old. Their two mothers were friends, and they had sex on the roof that first night. David remembers the guy's penis against his face, remembers that for the first time he connected to someone emotionally through sex. This frightened him so badly he thought he might have to kill the guy; do something drastic, so no one would know he was a homo.

David began a double life. In the movie theaters along 42nd Street, he soon tapped into the man/boy underground, and sold himself once a week or so. But he was still living at home, still in school, still more interested in lonely-kid things: wandering through the Museum of Natural History, walking over the George Washington Bridge to play on the cliffs, riding the motorized scaffolds at construction sites. A few times, he narrowly escaped the father, skulking in the lobby when he came home from school. The mother, who supported herself as a model, apparently began to have trouble finding work. She obsessed about marriage to a rich man, and would introduce the children as her little friends.

He remembers thinking about suicide. He threw himself into sex. From eleven or twelve on, he left home for weeks at a time, or spent nights in hotel rooms some trick had rented. He remembers a guy who almost murdered him. Another man who picked him up gave him the first emotional warmth of his life, even kept in touch when they stopped having sex. David loved him and could have lived with him forever, if the guy hadn't been married with kids of his own. David began to steal lizards, snakes, and turtles from pet stores, letting some of them go in Central Park. He began the practice of taking a bus out into Jersey, begging his way off when he spotted a good lake or pond and wading out into it fully dressed, but otherwise never bathing.

He entered the High School of Music and Art with a portfolio he'd thrown together overnight and a shoebox full of painted rocks. He began making very violent images—three-dimensional riot scenes with pig policemen and Black Panthers firing scope rifles from windows. He'd been going to antiwar and Black Panther demos, and these were among the few things that made sense to him. He wore a black leather glove on his right fist. At Music and Art, teachers destroyed his work or begged him not to pull it out when the principal came around. He tried to set the school on fire with some anarchist-cookbook device, but failed. He disappeared from school for weeks at a time, but one of his hustling lines became, "I need money for art supplies." At sixteen, he dropped out and began living on the streets. He can't remember the last day at home.

He does remember sexy encounters with sailors, sleeping in doorways, jumping naked from an ex-con's apartment during a raid. He remembers being drugged, then raped and beaten. Twice more, he was nearly murdered on the stroll. He drew pictures on shirt cardboard and pizza boxes. He crashed in an abandoned apartment, where he was robbed in his sleep. He moved in with one of the men he'd had sex with, began shoplifting animals and building terrariums. The man, who counseled at a halfway house for ex-cons, got David admitted there as a potential jail risk. David soon left for the streets again with a young ex-con who'd done time for trying to kill his foster parents.

That year, he hit bottom. He'd go for days without sleep. He was skeletal. His head was exploding. He couldn't sell himself except to the worst creeps. He went to his mother to ask for her Medicaid card. She told him to just slip it under the door when he was done. The

Salvation Army said, "We don't help people like you." Finally, David begged the halfway house to take him back, and they did. He was seventeen or eighteen—certain that if he ended up on the streets again, he would die.

As David tells me all this and more, he worries about his mother. His father had been a monster who died long ago, a suicide. But his feelings about her are complicated. What if she sees this article? He doesn't want to cause pain.

On an overcast day, David's scorpion emerges and leaves its little snowmobile tracks in the sand of the terrarium. David says he rescued it from a pet shop. They'd kept it under a bright light, but scorpions like the dark. He'd made a cave for it. He wonders how poisonous it is; it ran at his hand one day when he was cleaning the cage—the ungrateful unpet. He says someone asked him why he wanted such a thing, and he'd told them he wanted to own death. In an adjacent terrarium live the crickets: scorpion food. They're always singing. It's part of the natural history ambience in his small East Village loft, with its baboon and baby elephant skeletons, globes and plastic lizards, framed picture of some frog or toad. David has a bed and a kitchen table with chairs. That's it. Near the front door is a framed self-portrait of Peter Hujar, the person he was closest to in the world. Hujar died of AIDS in 1987.

David says he's been thinking about our previous interview—that painful chronology of childhood. Once he'd sworn he'd never discuss it again. He regrets all the mythmaking that came of it a few years ago, that "ex-hustler makes art" stuff.

The peculiar energy, the rejection you carry when you've been living on the streets—what is that? He remembers going out in nice clothes from the halfway house and getting rejected from loading dock jobs, janitorial jobs. He'd walk in for an interview and see shock on the foreman's face. What was that?

Working in downtown clubs in the late seventies, David was the guy who collected the empties and wiped out the toilets, and he felt the groovier-than-thou looking down on him. He couldn't talk to those people. That's why he started writing as well as drawing—he couldn't communicate any other way.

In those days he walked some precarious edge, just one step away from the streets, doing everything with the idea that, in another year, he wouldn't be alive. He was playing in a postpunk band called 3 Teens Kill 4—No Motive (taken from a *Post* headline). He began stenciling the streets with burning houses, soldiers, a man with a target on his face. And he was haunting the West Side piers, for sex and to record what he witnessed. He'd write in the yellow streetlamp glow that came through the side of the abandoned structure, filling journal after journal with what he calls "coded descriptions of sexuality" and evocations of the covered piers. Dying structures, he thought; symbols of what is essentially a dying country.

In 1980 at a bar in the East Village, David met Peter Hujar, a noted downtown photographer. David didn't know who the guy was, but when they went to Peter's house, he handed David a book, saying: "This is the kind of work I do." David was stunned to see a volume he'd been drawn to years before—*Portraits in Life and Death*. Hujar's photographs of artists, drag queens, and others who intrigued him were utterly straightforward and empathetic. Along with his friends, Peter included photographs of mummies in the catacombs at Palermo.

Though their sexual connection was brief, they began what David calls "a very complicated friendship/relationship that took time to find a track to run along." With Peter, who was twenty years older, David started to feel easier with himself. "He was like the parent I never had, like the brother I never had. He helped me drop a lot of the shit I carried from the streets—the pain, the fear, the guilt. Stuff I could barely speak to people about. I remember revealing to him that I'd been a hustler our second night together. We were having dinner, and I fully expected him to reject me. And I remember he just said, 'So?' And we got into this long conversation where I just revealed all my fears."

They developed a way to signal each other—I'm here—at crowded gatherings: two fingers up like rabbit ears behind the head. Peter encouraged him to show his work, even when David thought it raw and rudimentary. He'd been spraying war imagery on gallery doors—an art guerrilla leaving a trail of El Salvador for those wafting toward the Schnabels. But he never thought he'd get his work *past* the door.

In 1979, he and Julie Hair, another member of 3 Teens Kill 4, dragged a couple hundred pounds of bloody cow bones up the steps outside Castelli Gallery and stenciled the walls. In 1982, he dropped some

Portrait of David Wojnarowicz
by Peter Hujar, 1981. (The
Estate of Peter Hujar.)

thirty "cock-a-bunnies" into the star-studded Beast Show at P.S. 1. He
hadn't been invited, and he was pissed. With dots of rubber cement,
he set some tiny ears and tails onto cockroaches from his infested
apartment. He loved how they looked—like microscopic rabbits. And
they fit right in.

He was never, till recently, his idea of what an artist should be—
not even when he emerged as a quote/unquote star of quote/unquote
East Village art. That scene made outsiders insiders, as long as their
style fell within the parameters of a certain postsuburban Neo-
Expressionism. David's apocalyptic subtext—sometimes it wasn't so
sub—fit right in.

He had his first success at Civilian Warfare Gallery, a shoebox of a
storefront on East 11th Street. Often at his openings, the artgoing
hordes had to stand outside while David stood inside finishing the
work. He liked the rudeness of that, the way it broke art-world rules.
You couldn't go to Soho or 57th Street and find the artist standing there
with a bucket of paint. In Soho, where he'd had a show in 1982, the
dealer had wondered: "Why can't you be like Keith Haring—full of
fun?" David's work was full of sex and violence—politics expressed at
the level of the body. An early painting with boys, falling buildings,
guns, and erect penises he called *The Wild Boys Busting Up Western
Civilization*.

Along with the soldiers and bombers, he painted junkies, men fuck-ing. His images had the tension of some niceness opened up to its ruined heart. In the montage style he developed, David exposed the Real Deal under the artifacts—wars and rumors of war, industrial wastelands, mythological beasts, and the evolutionary spectrum from dinosaur to humanity's rough beast. Especially in the early days, he would paint or print on found materials like maps or logs or trash can lids or supermarket posters—a way of responding to official reality. Even his image of two men kissing bears the weight of the Real Deal in its title: *Fuck You You Faggot Fucker.*

In 1984, the height of East Village hype, he had work in thirty-three different exhibitions. Fame and money arrived suddenly, relieving all that pressure to survive—the pressure that had kept him from facing his past. "I hit a really dark period. I think I became somewhat self-destructive. I was hitting against that whole childhood." He began collecting articles about children who'd killed their families, and he wondered—why hadn't he, or somebody, picked up his father's gun and shot him? Why hadn't he fought back?

Like many others in this *faux* bohemia, David tried shooting up. His arm was turning green, and he showed it to Peter one day. "We were sitting in a restaurant, and Peter just said, 'I don't ever want to see you again,' and I went: 'What?' You know, the heaviest friendship of my life, and he said: 'If that's what you want to do, don't come to my house again.' I burst into tears, and I never did it again."

To this day, David almost never looks at art—"to protect where things come from for me." And he still feels out of place in the art world. After appearing in the Whitney Biennial in '85, he found that collectors would buy anything with his name attached to it. He found he could terrorize them by announcing that he wasn't painting at the moment—just *writing.*

In 1983, he began to paint in a covered pier off Canal Street. He chose it because it wasn't a sex pier; he could be alone. And one day he'd watched a huge dog run the football-field length of the main room, toward New Jersey, and he'd followed the animal but never found it, so he began to think the place magical. Upstairs, in a rabbit warren of crumbling rooms, he painted a gagging cow across a whole wall. In another room, he did cartoon heroes—generic courage and catastrophe—with the word-balloon: "Every day my mind grows keener, my good arm stronger, my silly government more futile."

Art had found its way into other rough and tumble spaces: the Real Estate Show in an abandoned building on Delancey, the Times Square Show in an old massage parlor. But David's "pier project" was the first to develop by word of mouth. Once he told other artists what he was doing, they came in to paint too, and the media followed. Soon, artists were having fistfights over which walls they were going to get. They actually held an opening there, and someone spilled champagne down a shaft into the Holland Tunnel, setting off alarms at the Port Authority. David, meanwhile, had moved on to another pier further downtown, where he planned to work secretly. But the city tore both structures down.

David began dipping back into his waterfront journals, adding bits to the ongoing record of real life he now calls *Self Portrait in 23 Rounds*. This was age fifteen: *The sound of carwheels sluicing through puddles on the highway Ah man he says lowering himself onto my back one of his arms muscled and furry wrapping itself under my jaw and against the side of my face yer my babe ohh yer my babe. . . .* It was raw teenage street memory, charged sex in piers, five queer-bashers beating one friend. It was Peter and AIDS—the endless waiting in hospitals. It was the story of Being Queer in America, in neo-beat prosody. I mean built on the long breath that leaves one body to engulf the endless world and, returning, sees the universe in a single action. Call it a Howl: . . . *the people waking up with the diseases of small birds or mammals; those whose faces are entirely black with cancer eating health salads in the lonely seats of restaurants; those images hurling themselves from the corners of a fast paced city and you can't even imagine death properly enough to tell this guy you understand what he's railing against I mean hell he bent down the first day that he found out he had this certain virus to pick up a letter addressed to him that'd fallen from the mailbox and he turned and said: even something so simple as getting a letter in the mail has an entirely different meaning.*

David was writing—yeah, to bear witness. But also to deal with what these moments brought up inside him. He got sick writing the chapter about Peter's illness. He came down with shingles. It had been so wrenching to admit to his anger. This wasn't the easier anger he could aim at "creeps" and "fat cannibals." This was his anger at Peter.

Peter had raged, raged. David was there every day, bearing the brunt of that dark mood. His account is harrowing and desperate.

There's a trip to Long Island with a woman friend, a month or so before Peter's death, to visit a doctor who claimed his typhoid shots would spark the immune system. Peter, who's lost all feeling in his legs, can't cross a room without falling, insists he'll take the train out, then relents. They spend an hour and a half getting him dressed and into the car. Peter complains angrily that there's a faster way than the one they're driving. He insists he has to piss at a gas station where there's no bathroom, staggers off to piss in a flower bed in what David sees as "unfriendly territory." Refuses to wear a seat belt. "Don't touch me, it hurts." And when they arrive at the doctor's house, David goes off to park the car, and *in the distance I could see Peter staggering on the front lawn flailing about in rage. He staggered towards Anita then turned and teetered to the roadside. . . . By the time I reached Anita he was in the distance, a tiny speck of agitation with windmill arms. I asked her what happened. "I don't know, one minute he was complaining how long the ride took and when I said that maybe you did the best you could he went into a rage—he threatened to throw himself in front of the traffic. The saddest thing is that he's too weak to throw a proper fit. He wanted to hit me but he didn't have the strength."*

They calm Peter down, get him into the doctor's office, which "looked like it had been decorated by Elvis," and Peter stumbles through a disjointed medical history, angrily refusing help from Anita. While Peter's in another room getting his typhoid shot, David asks the doctor to explain the theory behind this treatment. The doctor admits he's really a research scientist and talks about the thymus gland, "wherever it is," and draws a diagram of circles divided by a line: "Say ya got a hundred army men over here; that's the T-cells . . ."

On the way back to Manhattan, they stop at a diner, and tell Peter about this unsettling encounter with the scientist. *He looked sad and tired. He barely touched his food, staring out the window and saying, "America is such a beautiful country—don't you think so?" I was completely exhausted, emotionally and physically from the day and looking out the window at the enormous collage of high-tension wires, blinking stop lights, shredded used-car lot banners, industrial tanks and masses of humanity zipping about in automobiles just depressed me. The food we had in front of us looked like it had been fried in an electric chair. And watching my best friend dying while eating a dead hamburger left me speechless. I couldn't answer.*

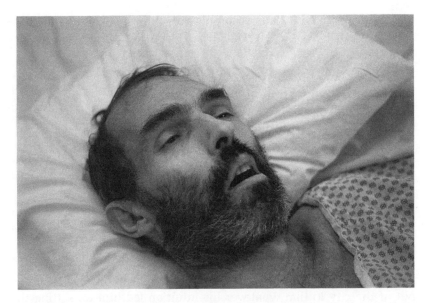

. . . this body of my brother, my father, my emotional link to the world: Peter Hujar shortly after his death from AIDS, as photographed by David Wojnarowicz, 1987. (The Estate of David Wojnarowicz.)

David had always thought he would die before Peter did.

He knew he was at risk, and if he got depressed about it, he took comfort from imagining Peter still there in some room, talking about him, explaining him, not letting him vanish.

Then, late in 1986, Peter began to complain that he felt like he was underwater. He couldn't get a full breath. The day Peter called from the hospital—to say he had pneumocystis, therefore AIDS—David picked up a television, intending to throw it through a window, but stopped himself. He went to Peter's house, in shock, not knowing what to say. It was funny—he felt this about his own diagnosis, too— how the buildings didn't collapse and the traffic kept moving and you still had to make yourself breakfast.

During Peter's illness, David did paintings of the four elements, dedicating *Wind* to his friend. It was all about portals (an open window) and extinction (a dinosaur) and destruction (a tornado), and it also had a Dürer wing. Peter kept a postcard of the Dürer, along with a mummified seagull wing, in his loft when David first met him. Peter had always wanted it tattooed on his arm—in sepia, so it would disappear when he got a tan. David had the wing carved into Peter's tombstone.

And his death is now like it's printed on celluloid on the backs of my eyes. . . . when I looked towards his face and his eyes moved slightly and I put two fingers up like rabbit ears behind the back of my head . . . and I flashed him the sign and then turned away embarrassed and moments later Ethyl [Eichelberger] *said: "David . . . look at Peter." And we were all turned to the bed and his body was completely still and then there was a very strong and slow intake of breath and then stillness and then one more intake of breath and he was gone.*

David asked the others to leave the hospital room, and then, with a Super-8 camera, he made a sweep of Peter's body, *this body of my friend on the bed this body of my brother my father my emotional link to the world.* He photographed his face, his hands, his feet. Later, using old photos, he recorded Peter's image from childhood on. Then, one day, he drove out of the city to film whatever his intuition led him to, setting the camera on a tripod at the side of a stream, taking his clothes off and stepping in to bathe, though it was winter. He wishes now he could have gotten the snowstorm that suddenly engulfed the car on the interstate and the pack of dogs on the road all standing around the one dog who'd been hit by a car, who lay there not moving.

After Peter's death; after his own diagnosis; after long depression; after an old friend, Marion Scemama, got him out of bed again; David began *Sex Series (for Marion Scemama)* to address his sense of loss. "And I wanted some sexy images on the wall—to keep me company." Working in Peter's darkroom, David made photo-montages of military/industrial/urban scenes, layered with blocks of prose about sex, about AIDS. Into each, he set small circular images of sex acts. These David took from Peter's porn collection.

David's always tried to connect his work to the world, make it about the world, paint it on the world. One death folds into the giant picture of world grief. It's true of his painting hung at the Artists Space show. One critic called *Untitled (Hujar Dead)* a picture with "the power to change lives." At the center, David silkscreened the deathbed photographs of Peter. At the edges are U.S. currency and sperm shapes made from maps, and, layered over everything is one of David's texts:

. . . and I'm carrying this rage like a blood filled egg and there's a thin line between the inside and the outside a thin line between thought and action and that line is simply made up of blood and muscle and bone and I'm waking up more and more from daydreams of tipping amazonian blowdarts in "infected blood" and spitting them at the exposed necklines of certain politicians . . . and at the moment I'm a thirty seven foot tall one thousand one hundred and seventy-two pound man inside this six foot frame and all I can feel is the pressure and the need for release.

David read this passage on *The Eleventh Hour,* while the camera focused on the clenching, unclenching fists at his sides. David told me that he thought there were painful questions to be asked about making art in a time like this. But Peter had helped him to understand that no one person can create the gesture that changes everything for everybody. And, unfortunately, the only life art can save is your own.

February 1990

■ ■ ■ "I Am Glass, Clear Empty Glass. . . ."

David Wojnarowicz died of AIDS on July 22, 1992.

He was his own best chronicler and the epidemic's visionary witness. Seeing the larger meaning of each life, each death, came so naturally to him. His paintings found the universe in a grain of sand. His writing traced the epidemic unfolding in a single body, now *the repository of so many voices and memories and gestures of those who didn't make it.*

David was someone who recreated himself with his art; who never went to art school; who barely finished high school; who would never own a suit, a couch, a credit card, but came to believe the truth of his own experience and desire.

David told me after his first East Village success that if he were straight he'd move to a small town now and get a job in a gas station because the art world was so appallingly hypocritical. But instead he began painting his world across the walls and windows of an abandoned covered pier along the Hudson, where his friend Keith Davis took me one afternoon to stumble through the rotten rooms looking for art. And this was just a few years—but they were light years— before David witnessed Keith's death from AIDS and *how quietly he dies how beautiful everything is with us holding him down on the bed on the floor fourteen stories above the earth. . . .*

During David's last stay in the hospital, he had one room with a view of the downtown we all dreamed of before we came here from out there and he would point out the roof of the building where he lived. David had ascended the steps of that building for the first time in 1980, with the man who then lived there, Peter Hujar. He hadn't of course known then that Peter would change his life, that he would love and care for Peter through his illness and death from AIDS or that he would live in this loft someday, and die in Peter's bed.

David would be changed utterly by Peter's death, becoming the one who sensed behind him those who'd left the world already; the one who began to consider love and death in the same breath. And in approaching each task as though it might be his last, he took a photo of skeletons exposed in a burial ground, then silkscreened over it these words of impending and constant loss: *When I put my hands on your body on your flesh I feel the history of that body. Not just the beginning of its forming in that distant lake but all the way beyond its ending. . . . If I could attach our blood vessels in order to anchor you to the earth to this present time to me I would. If I could open your body and slip up inside your skin and look out your eyes and forever have my lips fused with yours I would. . . .* He could say those sorts of things because he meant them. And he could lay his heart bare yet remain enigmatic.

And then he couldn't be alone anymore, though he'd always been so private, even keeping his boyfriend Tom Rauffenbart a secret from many of us. Now Tom's presence reassured him more than anything in the world, and one night in the wee hours during some post-op, drug-induced paranoia, he called Tom from the hospital and cried, "They're trying to kill me." So Tom got dressed and went up there and slept in the empty bed next to David's. In a calmer state, David said of Tom, "I worry he's going to spend his best years taking care of me."

He had a last Christmas on the iv-drug user's ward at Cabrini, saying of the junkies, "They accepted me right away." But he hated the chaos and noise, the televisions blaring and people shouting and carolers bumming everybody out. It was like trying to get better in a subway car, he complained. He was going to write about this—he said that on his good days. On Christmas Eve, each patient received a bottle of Elizabeth Taylor's Passion for Men and the ward began to reek, and he was definitely going to start making some notes.

But now he became the one who really couldn't work for the first time in his life; who would endure days, even weeks, of nonstop nausea; who had night sweats; who had headaches; who had pain in every part of his body; who one day found his feet swollen up to twice their normal size; who thought they were going to explode; who had both arms infected from iv needles; who had his gallbladder and spleen removed two months before his death; who began to lose his memory so that he'd finger the scar down his stomach and ask Tom, "What were they looking for?" Who walked down the steps he'd first ascended with Peter, walked down them for one last try at getting better in the hospital, pulling his iv out by accident so that now he was bleeding on those steps and he was puking into a bag and the ambulette driver would not help him and the blood was spurting everywhere.

He would talk now and then about suicide, but as death came closer, he didn't talk about it anymore. He'd always understood we each have to figure out what to do with the darkness. So he came home from the hospital for the last time and he put on a silver bracelet, a silver necklace with an antique cross and kachina doll charm, and on his last trip out of the apartment, he went to a jeweler with his day nurse and bought a necklace. A thick one, solid gold. He'd hung a dozen other necklaces on the wall. In this new guise he became the one who suddenly seemed to accept what was happening to him; who no longer asked questions like, "Why can't I stand up?"; who began to "travel" as his soul worked its way free; who said he'd just returned from Argentina or Illinois or Queens; who lay sleeping with his fists clenched, making faces, as friends came by to wonder what he felt and thought and dreamed.

Whose work was so prescient that, in his last published piece, he'd described it for us so we could all understand that *I am getting so weary. I am growing tired. I am waving to you from here. I am crawling and looking for the aperture of complete and final emptiness. I am vibrating in isolation among you. I am screaming but it comes out like pieces of clear ice. I am signalling that the volume of all this is too high. I am waving. I am waving my hands. I am disappearing. I am disappearing but not fast enough.*

July 1992

■ ■ ■ Afterimage

The hospital room has two walls, and they're painted a bilious green. A mustard-yellow curtain surrounds the bed, and in the window, black-white negatives flicker like heat lightning. An ugly set—but the septic ambience seems right for The David Movie. Because when he was told he'd contracted this virus, he knew he'd contracted a diseased society as well.

David Wojnarowicz made that observation in his most infamous essay, the one from which the film-in-progress takes its title, *Postcards from America: X-rays from Hell*. At the time of David's death from AIDS last summer, *Postcards* had been in development for about nine months. He'd met with British writer-director Steve McLean several times, first rejecting the project outright because McLean wanted to make a documentary—but he liked the scripted sequences reconstructing his abusive childhood, teen hustler years, and scenes from the epidemic. So McLean rewrote, developing a narrative based on David's two books, *Close to the Knives* and *Memories That Smell Like Gasoline*. David saw a second and then a third draft. (There were six by the time production began last November.) And McLean remembers David telling him: "This isn't me, but I like it."

It isn't him. But . . . I watch the crew rigging lights and dolly tracks along the toxic hospital set, for a scene in which "David" will visit a dying "older man," based on Peter Hujar. By chance, we're about three minutes away from the East Village loft where Peter lived until his death from AIDS in 1987, and where David then lived until his death from AIDS in 1992.

Several of us who knew one or both of them hover at the edges of the production, where such coincidences resonate sharply. The loft still hasn't been emptied. He seems so recently dead. But there is certainly no one better to make this film. McLean hooked up with Christine Vachon, who produced both Todd Haynes's *Poison* and Tom Kalin's *Swoon* for Apparatus Productions. Vachon hired *Swoon*'s award-winning cinematographer, Ellen Kuras, and others who worked on one or both of those landmarks in so-called queer cinema, while McLean cast Jim Lyons from *Poison* as "adult David." Lyons knew Peter and met David through him maybe ten years ago. "I never could think that I'm David," says Lyons. "All I can do is get some kind of feeling for his spirit." Though more conventionally handsome than David was, Lyons has the same lanky body and long face, the same mouth and smile, the same posture. Sometimes I see a ghost. But *Postcards* is no bio-pic. And his friends have no X-pectations. It's just that—we all have a David Movie playing in our heads.

Photographer Nan Goldin, a friend of both David's and Peter's who came all the way from Berlin to shoot stills for a week, jokes in passing that she's "policing this film." But when we sit down to talk, she reflects, "Like everybody in New York, I thought Peter was my best friend. And the loss of David is really hitting me hard. That's why I wanted to work on this. An enormous amount of my moral take on the world came from him. He set the standard for me." It was Goldin who asked David, back in 1989, to write a catalogue essay for a show about AIDS she was curating—"Witnesses: Against Our Vanishing." David then wrote the "Postcards" essay.

Like so much of his writing and painting and photography and installation, "Postcards" describes the larger meaning of a single struggle—this time, that of an anxious friend with disappearing T cells who sits at his kitchen table saying, "There are no more people in their thirties. We're all dying out." While David's work always had a layer of moral outrage, this essay burned with apocalyptic visions of real enemies ("fat cannibal" Cardinal O'Connor) and fantastical retribution (dousing Jessie Helms with gasoline), and concluded with the furious directive to "throw my body on the steps of the White House." Had it appeared at any other time, however, the essay would have probably reached the usual audience of like minds. But as it happened, "Witnesses" opened post-Mapplethorpe in a chilly and timorous climate—with funding from the National Endowment for the Arts. David's words soon hit the tabloids. And he became an iconic Angry Gay Man.

Postcards, the movie, includes very little about the epidemic and

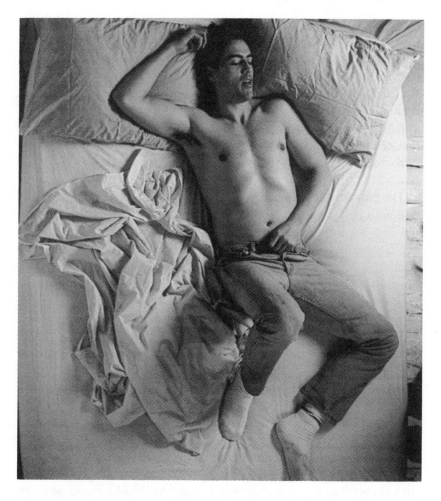

Jim Lyons as "adult David" in *Postcards from America*. (Photo by Joyce George.)

none of David's politics. Instead, it concentrates on what I think of as the "Genet material" in his work—tragic boys, violent tricks, sexy outcasts, landscapes of danger and desire that can lead one to a singular self-definition. Or perhaps to a singular doom. It isn't exactly the material I would have chosen, but I realize that if David were alive, I wouldn't really give a damn. Since he isn't alive, though, I've become protective—and not even of him but of me. My memory. My David Story.

The day they shot the hospital scene, I discussed this briefly with

Nan Goldin. We were sitting in the prop shop at Theater for the New City—with "adult David" visiting "the older man" in the next room. The encounter as scripted conflates two or three incidents in *Close to the Knives.* "It didn't happen that way," I found myself fretting, while Nan said she was upset that the actor playing the "older man" looked nothing like Peter Hujar. "But I think it's important to get David's work out," she said. "His whole thing about teenagers finding some reflection of their own experience in his work. . . ." I agreed. That would have mattered so much to him during his street kid days. He'd often said so.

The passion and defiance in David's work made him seem like someone who held nothing back. In fact, he was the proverbial "private person" who only went public with personal information—like his hustling stories—for calculated reasons. In 1990, tired of his "ex-hustler" image, he told me in an interview that he thought it was time to stop talking about those things. Besides, there was another story he now wanted out in the public domain—for political reasons. His Peter Story.

Only after Peter died did David begin to write about him, though he'd always used his image in paintings. "They were both more than and less than lovers. Peter was the one who saved him, the one who changed David's life in a major positive way. They were kindred souls. A part of David was missing after Peter went." These are the observations of Tom Rauffenbart, David's boyfriend since 1986, and part of that private life he was so good at separating from the public person.

Rauffenbert said McLean listened to his criticisms of the script, and that given who's making the film, he's optimistic. But given that he also knows the difference between David and David's work, he's nervous. McLean had been amazingly patient with all of us and the various personal David Narratives we wished to impose upon his film. He'd had to find a line to walk between them and David's own wishes: that it not be a docudrama; that it not show his art in any conventional art world way; that it have plenty of sex. McLean noted, "One thing that remains from an earlier draft is guys having sex in a gallery with his paintings in the background. He laughed at that. It's the kind of thing that really appealed to him." Then there's the Peter material. "I don't want to call the character Peter because there's a lot that I can't put in the film and I think there's a danger of misrepresenting that relationship."

A soft-spoken thirty-one-year-old with startlingly blue eyes, McLean directed the Jimmy Somerville video deleted from *Red Hot and Blue* (the television version) for its "homoerotic" content. He discovered David's writing through *Red Hot and Blue* producers John Carlin and Leigh Blake. *Close to the Knives* has now appeared in England—to disappointing reviews. "It really made me angry," said McLean. "Maybe there's a certain amount of denial going on in England. We're way behind you in terms of the progress of the epidemic, so maybe we're just not waking up. We're going to need voices like David's and we just don't seem to have them."

Inspired by seeing *Poison* at London's gay and lesbian film festival, McLean teamed with two other Brit directors, Isaac Julien and Mark Nash, to found an English counterpart to Apparatus—Normal Films. Jimmy Somerville gave McLean enough money to begin work on *Postcards,* their first feature, but they've had to stop with a third to a half in the can until Vachon can raise more money. She did not want to discuss the budget, but the results so far look like a million dollars and were achieved most certainly with a fraction of that.

I got hooked on the low-budget adventure and the dedication of the people involved, many working for peanuts or for nothing. They made a cramped Ludlow Street apartment into two different sets. Did a tracking shot of "teen David" (Michael Tighe) outside a peep show by strapping the camera to the roof of a car, Ellen Kuras perched precariously next to it while they circled the block. At an all-night shoot in an SRO with hideous tiny rooms and linoleum halls, they found the residents snappish because Woody Allen had just finished there and "you've been keeping us awake every night." They traveled with a skeleton crew to the Arizona desert because David loved the desert and they've set some key scenes there. It's David's afterlife—his work getting used.

Sometimes when I walk the East Village now, I remember how it felt before everybody died. And I know it isn't everyone who died, but so many have that grief seems a permanent ambience now. "For everyone who's still alive," Nan remarked, "it's like meeting after a shipwreck." And I wonder how many of us have made that movie in our minds—one that unfolds like the conclusion of *Longtime Compan-*

ion, a film I didn't much like, but you know the part I mean. Where everyone who's died suddenly reappears on the beach to greet the survivors. It's the ultimate fantasy and the only panacea we have at the moment. So fade in.

Fade in.

January 1993

▪ ▪ ▪ Epilogue

■ ■ ■ The Bohemian Diaspora

worn gray tepee sits at the edge of the city's oldest shantytown, just yards from where Manhattan Bridge traffic hits Canal Street. But it also sits in terra incognita. The two artists who've lived in the tepee since Thanksgiving 1990 admit to feeling "muddled" at times about what they're even doing there.

Seated in the dim interior on foam pads, Nick Fracaro and Gabriele Schafer began to explain. For years, they've collaborated at Thieves' Theatre, trying to "embody and articulate" the voice of the disenfranchised. Doing Genet's *Deathwatch* with prisoners in Illinois. Doing *Marat/Sade* with punks and ex-mental patients in Toronto. Trying to work with the homeless in the city's shelters, but rejecting it as an "us/them" experience. That propelled them into the shantytown, where they decided to stage Heiner Müller's *Despoiled Shore Medeamaterial Landscape with Argonauts* in the tepee.

As the artists struggled to explain their mission, I got the impression that they'd spent hours, days, months, trying to unravel the koans presented by their new life. How to do theater in the shantytown without being elitist. How to go public without being consumed. How to determine who the audience would be, could be, should be. Such questions become inevitable to artists without a community. I mean—apart from one's own circle of friends, is there such a thing anymore as an artist *with* a community?

Schafer and Fracaro had settled in among the alienated, but homeless people aren't necessarily bohemians. Most of them share the values of the larger world, and other residents of the Hill (as those who live there call it) saw the artists as the outsiders they really are.

Several times someone called in through the tent flap, "Hey, Chief," and Fracaro would ease himself out to talk to a neighbor. The Hill is clearly a man's world; Schafer is known there as "Mrs. Chief." She made the tepee last fall out of seventy-eight U.S. mailbags while Fracaro spent weeks getting acquainted. The artists did not want to move in without the other residents' permission. (And after much discussion, they decided not to give up their Brooklyn apartment.) They share a job at a movie production warehouse and live sparely. A few tools. A few books. They dubbed the tepee the Living Museum of the Nomad Monad. They've kept it drug-and-alcohol-free, providing coffee to their neighbors in the morning. Fracaro and Schafer say the others accept them now, but still regard them as odd.

The artists call the shantytown a "Temporary Autonomous Zone." They had come across this phrase in an obscure text called *T.A.Z. [The Temporary Autonomous Zone, Ontological Anarchy, Poetic Terrorism]* by an arcane anarchist who calls himself Hakim Bey. I'd read the book myself, since I'm interested in what's passing for autonomy these days, when a New World Order seems to permeate even our attempts at disorder or dissent. "Realism demands not only that we give up *waiting* for 'the Revolution' but also that we give up *wanting* it," writes Bey. "In most cases the best and most radical tactic will be to refuse to engage in spectacular violence, to *withdraw* from the area of simulation, to disappear." The artists in the tepee had managed to disappear by refusing to speak to reporters. ("As soon as the TAZ is named [represented, mediated] it must vanish, it *will* vanish. . . .") Only now, as they intuit that their days on the Hill are numbered, are they willing to talk to me.

I was reminded of other art satellites I've encountered over the last few years—the Neoist rituals in Tompkins Square, the Sideshows by the Seashore on Coney Island's boardwalk, the Festival of the Swamps beneath the Williamsburg Bridge—all of it unfolding far from the grant-getting vortex, part of no movement, isolated from any larger context.

Certainly I've found it harder to track the art margins lately. The climate for things experimental, for things adversarial, has not only worsened; the damage to those "autonomous zones" seems irreparable. That historic institution once called "bohemia" has been so intensively exploited that it's had to become invisible. For the first time in 150 years, bohemia can't be pinpointed on a map. The dematerialization of the artist's milieu has had a devastating impact on the entire culture—more intangible, and therefore more insidious, than the problems posed by shrinking corporate and government funding, the march of the real estate developers, and the debilitating war over free expression.

Dissent cannot happen in a vacuum. Nor can social or aesthetic movements grow in one. Community is the fabric that sustains experiment, stimulating that leap into the void and maybe even cushioning a fall.

Back when subterraneans still had a terrain, the bourgie types might go slumming through a Left Bank or Greenwich Village, but the colonizing process took much longer. No instant condos. No developer-spawned neighborhood acronyms. Now—relentless in its hunt for the Next Big Thing—the media cut such a swath through the demimonde that colonizers follow instantly, destabilizing and destroying. So, the energy that moved from Paris to New York, from West Village to East Village, from Old Bohemia (1830–1930) to New Bohemia (the sixties) to Faux Bohemia (the eighties) has atomized now into trails that can't be followed: the 'zine/cassette network, the living-room performance spaces, the modem-accessed cybersalons, the flight into neighborhoods that will never be Soho.

They're all part of the bohemian diaspora.

One winter night in 1916, Marcel Duchamp, John Sloan, and several other artists made their way to the top of the Washington Square arch, where they built a bonfire, ate a picnic, shot off some cap guns, and declared Greenwich Village an independent republic. And why not? Home to the wild advocates of socialism and anarchism, free love and free verse, the Village was a place out of sync with puritan America. Here, a left-wing monthly called *The Masses* actually opposed the Great War (for which the federal government effectively censored it). Here in 1918, Margaret Anderson and Jane Heap began serializing the banned *Ulysses* in their magazine, *The Little Review* (for which they were charged with pandering obscenity). Here, at a time when women in America did not even have the right to vote, some were joining together to form the Heterodoxy Club "for unorthodox women"—which included feminists, several "out" lesbians, and one black woman.

They were bohemians in the classic sense—people alienated from middle-class values (artistic, sexual, political) who knew where to find a community of like minds. The word came from *bohèmien*, the common French term for gypsy, a people defined in the popular mind as social outcasts. By now, "bohemian" has been recycled so endlessly it has no precise meaning—though it continues to evoke an image: the Rebel With an Aesthetic. "The bohemian spirit. Not too hard to spot," says a current ad for Bohemia beer, beneath a photo of a man in leather jacket repairing a motorcycle in his perfect white-walled loft, while a draped and available woman sits on his bed.

Even though it originated in 1830s Paris, the whole notion of a bohemia seems so American (Dream) to me, so much about "lightin' out" for the frontier. Bohemia still plays a role in bourgeois fantasy as the road not taken, where you could've would've done your own thing, free from the yoke of work and family. This quest for breathing space was always less about art than about capitalism, an escape from the rat race and the cultural cookie cutter. In this fluid zone, someone from the lower class could slip in and someone from the upper class could opt out. Certainly, a revolt against capitalism is something few people—and few artists—are interested in these days.

Today it's becoming something of a cliché to describe Western culture as a flattened landscape where the boundary between margin and mainstream has eroded. As critic Hal Foster put it, in his book *Recodings*: "the center has invaded the periphery and vice versa." It's the media spotlight that erases the line between them.

The demimonde, for example, revolved around its "third spaces" (not home, not work), the now-legendary cafés and clubs: Toulouse-Lautrec at the Chat Noir, Pollock at the Cedar Tavern, every East Village artist at 8BC. Expatriate Paris flocked to Gertrude Stein's salon, while the Harlem Renaissance had A'Lelia Walker's. But there are no equivalent hangouts now, because once they're discovered by the media, they disappear. (The night I spotted Jerzy Kosinski and David Lee Roth at 8BC, I knew the end was near.) Compound that with the problem of finding any affordable downtown space at all, and it's no accident that most of the boho energy I've encountered in Manhattan in the last couple years radiated out of a squat (Bullet Space) or someone's living room (Gargoyle Mechanique, Gusto House). An exception like the Nuyorican Poets Cafe—holdout from an older era—simply proves the rule.

Of course, bohemia was something of a media invention right from the start. The first stories about it, written by Henry Mürger and based on himself and his friends, appeared in a small Paris newspaper in 1845–46. They were adapted for the musical stage in 1849, collected in *Scenes of Bohemian Life* in 1851, and immortalized in Puccini's *La Bohème* in 1896, romanticizing what some still romanticize: the garret, the *bonhomie*, the "sacrifice for art."

But the lore of the starving artist changed with *mass* media, till image was everything. The artist became the emblematic chic figure of the eighties—the rebel fit for a beer ad. The media feeding frenzy around "East Village art" developed in part because those promoting this scene used its marginality as a marketing ploy. The ensuing spotlight quickly corrupted the playful impulses behind the original galleries and inflated the relatively modest accomplishments of many of the artists. Such inflation of reputations, of expectations, of the very idea of what it means to succeed as an artist—distorted the eighties art world. Made it a bottomless pit of neo-celebs. And of course, it inflated rents as well. Now, even the faux bohemia once known as the East Village Scene is gone, replaced by the usual Manhattan real estate protectorate where the extremes of capitalist life coexist like two sides of a knife.

By the late eighties, more and more artists had decided to leave what some of them now called the Beast Village. For the most part, they were moving directly across the river to Greenpoint and Williamsburg, just one subway stop into another space-time continuum. This is the newest artists' neighborhood, and a quiet one, barely visible in the working-class nabe around the L train or the barrio-near-the-bridge fed by the J and M. A few "spaces" are open, like Minor Injury and Brand Name Damages. (What could such names portend?)

But in contrast to the publicity-mad East Villagers, many artists in Greenpoint don't seem to want their neighborhood publicized. As a friend who's lived there for years put it, "We don't care about getting validated by people from Manhattan." There's nothing for the hype to stick to, anyway. No trendy new ism. No glamor. No "No Wave." Just cheap rent. But the artists find one another. There's a knot of community. For example, Mike Ballou and Adam Simon run a symposium called Four Walls out of Ballou's home. ("Don't print my address.") Simon started Four Walls in Hoboken a few years ago, so its move to Brooklyn follows the trail of cheap loft space. Once a month now, guest curators hang a show in Ballou's studio for a day; it ends with a discussion of the work among the exhibitors and artists from the neigh-borhood. It's always crowded.

But there are crowds and then there's the Crowd. Last June, in-trigued by flyers wheat-pasted all over the East Village, I made my way to an abandoned warehouse on the Williamsburg waterfront for a one-night-only art extravaganza called the Fly Trap. I'd heard good things about an earlier event called the Cat's Head, and so had everyone else, apparently. By midnight, the line waiting in the rutted dirt road to the warehouse was two blocks long, complete with the old buzz surround-ing *the* place-to-be. Inside, I found 20,000 square feet of huge and un-inspired installations, live bands, and beer—club fun, a contrived atmosphere of outlaw revelry. Hanging art in some decrepit quasi-forbidden old building? A veritable tradition—and we did it better in the seventies (Times Square Show). Then we did it better in the eighties (Real Estate Show, Warren Street Pier).

Artists who fled to Williamsburg precisely to escape trendification are horrified to find it following them. Painter Amy Sillman, a longtime resident of the area, said of the Fly Trap: "Don't assume that this is a summary of the neighborhood. It's just the bad old East Village come to haunt me."

Allen Ginsberg gave his first public reading on October 13, 1955, at the Six Gallery in San Francisco. Kenneth Rexroth played MC for the five young poets who would all go on to achieve some measure of poetry-fame—Ginsberg, Gary Snyder, Philip Lamantia, Michael McClure, Philip Whalen—while an unpublished and unknown Jack Kerouac, too shy to read, passed jugs of wine through the packed gallery. But this became a legendary evening on the strength of the one poem, still unfinished, read by Ginsberg: "I saw the best minds of my generation destroyed by madness/starving hysterical naked . . ."

As his biographer Barry Miles reports it, Ginsberg was "transported . . . arms outstretched, eyes gleaming, swaying from one foot to the other with the rhythm of the words" while Rexroth listened with tears in his eyes and the audience yelled "Go!" at the end of each line. "Howl" was an explosion in consciousness heard round the world, the collective howl reverberating through every outsider enduring the lonely-crowd fifties. This was poetry that changed people's lives.

In *Memoirs of a Beatnik,* Diane di Prima describes the electrifying moment when she first encountered the poem and sensed that, for better or for worse, her isolation was over. Someone had brought Ginsberg's now-familiar little square book to a dinner party at her "pad." Scanning the first lines, she immediately left her own party to read the whole thing, then returned to read it out loud to everyone. "Allen was only, could only be, the vanguard of a much larger thing. All the people who, like me, had hidden and skulked, writing down what they knew for a small handful of friends—and even those friends claiming it 'couldn't be published' . . . all these would now step forward and say their piece . . . I was about to meet my brothers and sisters."

It's hard to imagine anything with "Howl"'s impact emanating from "high culture" now. The breakthroughs, such as they are, seem to come from the "low"—the first Sex Pistols record, for example, which rewrote every rule about what music could be or say or spit on. It was during the fifties that the site of "danger" and "rebellion" began to shift from the art world to mass culture. The Beats were the first bohemian movement born under the eye of mass media. Ginsberg's biography notes that "he took pains to show the difference between the Beat Generation . . . and the beatniks." But the media didn't observe the distinction, "and the public perception was that Allen was the progenitor of all the bearded young men who wandered around Greenwich Village in handmade leather sandals." The Beats thought they could inject their vision into mass culture, but what the "bearded young men" really signaled was the beginning of the community as artifact.

In the fifties, the media image of the beatnik became a corollary to masscult images of rebellious teens. James Dean, that icon of Misunderstood Youth—wasn't he also the Tortured Artist? As for Elvis Presley—wasn't the emblematic scene in each movie the one where he dropped the dumb ballad and learned to rock, blow, go-man-go? Today it's easy to forget how two people as different from each other as Presley and Ginsberg would have grated against the status quo in the Eisenhower years.

If this didn't quite make for a mass bohemia—yet—Kerouac could still complain that the Beats were nothing but "a fad.' His own overnight transition from vision-seeking subterranean to flavor-of-the-month celebrity was a painful one. When *On the Road* appeared in 1957, he'd been trying to get the book published for six years. Suddenly *The*

New York Times declared it the testament of a new generation, and one day later, the interviewers began to arrive. What was it really like to be Beat? they wanted to know. Soon Kerouac was appearing on talk shows spouting metaphysics to the likes of Mike Wallace ("we are great empty space . . . an empty vision in one mind"). He never seemed to understand that the press wanted hot copy, not enlightenment. It was a San Francisco journalist who invented the word *beatnik* (after Sputnik), and soon the media had the movement boiled down to jive talk and a set of bongo drums. By 1959, the most famous beatnik in America was Maynard G. Krebs.

Back in 1957, while the brand-new *Village Voice* covered a few Beat moments like Kerouac's appearance at the Village Vanguard, it featured much longer pieces on old bohemians—infamous Village characters like Joe Gould and Maxwell Bodenheim, who were virtually unknown outside the neighborhood. Fierce rivals, these two impoverished writers were reportedly fed and given drinks at one Village bar for a while "so customers would come to watch the hostilities."

Bohemia itself was moving from West Village to East at the end of the fifties, and would house a very different sort of "freak." There would be no more Goulds. The *Voice* piece on his funeral speculates on the whereabouts of Gould's lifework, *The Oral History of Our Time*— eleven million words written in dime-store notebooks as he sat in Goody's Bar or the Minetta Tavern. (*Oral History* remains a lost work.) Today, Gould's portrait hangs in the Minetta Tavern, but surely someone so unkempt, ornery, and wild-eyed would no longer, uh, suit the decor. This was the boho as hobo: the rebel who could not be televised.

What the full flowering of electronic media made possible was alienation as a growth industry rather than an emblem of community. Malcolm Cowley, part of the so-called Lost Generation, describes in *Exile's Return* how the First World War and a new set of values set his generation irrevocably apart from the one before it. In the sixties, of course, this feeling infected mass culture, creating the infamous "generation gap"—for it took no more than loving the Beatles, the world's most popular group, to set one apart from one's parents. While "do your own thing" was the notion at the heart of the old bohemia, during the sixties it found a place in the heart of every teen consumer. Nonconformity, transgression, risk—adjectives once associated with bohemian values and avant-garde art—suddenly described superstars whose hits played in Peoria. And Jimi Hendrix became a Fluxus artist when he burned his guitar.

On February 9, 1967, sixteen patrol cars pulled up around the Filmmaker's Cinematheque on West 41st Street. Helmeted police converged on the stage inside and arrested artist Charlotte Moorman during a performance of Nam June Paik's *Opera Sextronique*. Moorman had been playing the cello topless. The Brahms Lullaby. A "lewd act."

Three months later, a Manhattan criminal court judge convicted her of indecent exposure. Moorman faced one to three years in prison. Judge Milton Shalleck suspended the sentence, however, calling the cellist "weak and immature." His twenty-nine-page opinion is a classic artifact of official contempt for the avant-garde, with its references to "bearded, bathless Beats" and "those 'happeners' whose belief it is that art is 'supposed to change life' as most of us know it." There the judge had a glimmer of art's true potential for transgression. It *could* change life.

And that never seemed more possible than it did in the sixties, when every art form broke apart into something rich and strange. Remember cynaesthetic cinema? Cybernetic sculpture? Intermedia? Destruction art? Underground film? The death of painting? The death of the novel? The death of the theater? One could make a case for the sixties as "the end of the avant-garde." But the media gravitated to Warhol and Ginsberg and the other supernovas of an official demimonde, ignoring the aesthetic ferment behind the personalities. It was up to critic/advocates like Jill Johnston (performance) and Jonas Mekas (film) to witness the revolution. Certainly Charlotte Moorman, an emblematic figure in the sixties avant-garde, could not expect a *Times* review. Nor a grant from the National Endowment for the Arts.

To be part of the art netherworld then was to be part of something suspect, outré, and perhaps even illegal. Moorman's arrest was no anomaly. In 1961, postal inspectors busted LeRoi Jones and Diane di Prima for sending obscenity through the mail—their literary magazine, *Floating Bear*. (A grand jury failed to return indictments.) In 1964, Lenny Bruce got a one-year sentence for using words like *fuck* and *cocksucker* onstage at the Cafe Au Go Go. (It was overturned on appeal after Bruce's death.) That same year, two detectives broke up an East Village screening of Jack Smith's *Flaming Creatures*, arresting Jonas

Charlotte Moorman
under arrest at
Filmmaker's
Cinematheque in 1967
for playing the cello
topless during a
performance of Nam
June Paik's *Opera
Sextronique*. (Fred W.
McDarrah.)

Mekas, who had programmed the film. (Mekas got a six-month suspended sentence, and Smith's film was banned in the state of New
York until 1970.) These were people who'd chosen a life in art that
would keep them impoverished, marginal, embattled. They were
"don't-wannabes." Bohemians.

The difference between censored artists in the sixties and the
nineties goes to the heart of how things have changed in the bohemian
margin. Artists like the so-called Defunded Four—Holly Hughes,
Karen Finley, John Fleck, Tim Miller—have now been catapulted out
of their contexts on the backs of the media. All the publicity did was

expose them to an audience guaranteed to find them intolerable, while artists of the "any-ink-is-good-ink" school looked on with envy. But none of the four has ever done work for a mass audience, nor have they wanted to. These days, however, transgression is just one more sluiceway into the undifferentiating whirlpool of media attention.

Censorship used to mean arrest; now it means publicity. That's the superficial observation. Imagine Jack Smith's fate if *Flaming Creatures* had been targeted by the religious right, discussed on *Good Morning America*, and televised across the country on CNN. As it was, Smith found the exploitation of his movie so unbearable he withdrew it from circulation, at one point declaring it "lost." He never completely finished another film.

As Smith once said of his own work in *Semiotext(e)*, "Nobody wants to open a can of worms, but that's the thing that has been handed for me to do." His was never work intended for mass audiences, but for kindred souls. And such work is valued less and less. Such work was the demimonde's raison d'être.

Bohemia has always been an *official* margin, the dominant culture's test site for new isms, its holding pen for "different drummers." And from its funky confines, certain artists have always been able to launch themselves into the mainstream. Such outsiders-turned-insiders fill the pages of twentieth-century cultural history. But from Rimbaud to Kerouac, they've been mostly of the whiteboy persuasion.

While there have always been significant Others in bohemia, they've rarely articulated their own cultural realities—in part because their audience, though unconventional, has always been, for the most part, straight, white, and male. If key figures in the Beat movement were bi- or homosexual, they didn't consider that an identity with its own potential for radicalism; like their straight buddies, they worshiped masculinity, despised effeminacy, and shafted women. And gay men were the most likely Others to cross over. As for women, writer Joyce Johnson, one of Kerouac's girlfriends, would write years later of being a "minor character" in the Beat scene. And as for people of color, bohemia American-style has always included folks like LeRoi Jones (Amiri Baraka), Ralph (Rafael Montanez) Ortiz, and Yoko Ono—to name just a few. But people of color and women in general remained outside the canon long after Ginsberg and Burroughs had become the stuff of Hollywood films and Nova conventions and papers presented to the Modern Language Association.

There has always been a single bohemian tradition—and it didn't include something like the Harlem Renaissance, still the demimonde most bohemians know least about. (It's barely mentioned in most boho histories.) Of course, Harlem in the twenties *was* different from the Village. Reacting to life in a racist nation, writers like Langston Hughes and Zora Neale Hurston struggled to give voice to the voiceless African American, and so were less alienated from a larger community. They sought their roots, while white artists fled from theirs. But like any other demimonde, the Harlem Renaissance had its salons and soirees, little magazines, quarrels, cranks, and utopian political ideals. Its artists and writers occasionally crossed paths with their Village counterparts at, say, Mabel Dodge's salon on Lower Fifth Avenue. But Harlem's so-called Talented Tenth made few inroads into white America. Their particular margin—being unofficial, thus invisible—couldn't launch them into the big time.

These days the whole concept of marginality is in flux, thanks to the advent of multiculturalism. No, that's not a code word for "minority representation," but a movement that would have recognized both Harlem and the Village; a movement in which every margin is visible; a movement that would redraw the map of the art world to make it more like the real world.

Much more is at stake in the margins now than there was during, say, some style war leading to the triumph of Abstract Expressionism. Throughout modernism, the demimonde had a worthy but narrow function as an official periphery. In that milieu, artists defied the official center, some crossed over, and the art world got a steady flow of new product—but never a challenge to its basic assumptions. Now, however, multiculturalism is exposing art history as exclusionary, art theory as incomplete, and bohemia as one margin among many.

Performance artist Giullermo Gómez-Peña, who has played a major role in shaping multicultural debate in the art world, invoked the image of Columbus when he spoke of the Latino Boom and the margin from which he emerged: "The model of discovery is in place. Going into the territory of the Other, discovering the Other, bringing the Other back into the mainstream. The big question of the nineties for the Chicano movement is, can we be in control of our context? Will we be able to keep our negotiating powers, or will we just die on display like the Arawak [the native people Columbus sent back to the Spanish court]?"

Now the shifts and schisms in the margins reflect the tug-of-war going on throughout the world: the trend towards globalization versus the trend towards community. The pressure to assimilate versus the urge to segregate.

Traditionally, an artist like Gómez-Peña would be seen as culturally specific, not universal. In fact, he is both, though his universalism is lost on those who see only Otherness. "Our generation belongs to the world's biggest floating population," he once wrote in one of his manifestos. And he's not just referring to an ethnic group. He means all of us—"the weary travelers, the dislocated, those who left because we didn't fit anymore, those who still haven't arrived because we don't know where to arrive at, or because we can't go back anymore. Our deepest generational emotion is that of loss." This perfectly describes the bohemian diaspora: an autonomous zone of the mind.

We've come full circle, back to the original meaning of the word *bohémien*: "gypsy." Of course, bohemia was always part of the exile tradition, the place where the lost ones went to find each other. But it was exile from one tangible place to another. Now that there *is* no place, the exiles have become nomads, and there's a whole culture of the disappeared.

February 1992

■ ■ ■ Index